The Growth of Nationalism

Germany & Italy 1815 – 1939

Ronald Cameron

(Principal Teacher of History, Tain Royal Academy)

Christine Henderson

(Teacher of History, Kelso High School)

Charles Robertson

(Assistant Head Teacher, Berwickshire High School)

Pulse Publications

Acknowledgements

We would like to express sincere thanks to Mr David Cooney for many helpful suggestions, to Mr Ernest Jacobs of Tain for translating lengthy documents from German, to Mr Tom Walker and Mr Nick Brennan of Tain Royal Academy for transferring material between word processor systems, to Herr Hans-Ulrich Reiffen, Head of History at the Rheingymnasium, Sinzig for reading and commenting on the German section of this book, to Mrs Ellen MacKenzie and Miss Elaine MacKenzie for typing half of it and to Mrs Elaine Wright for her patience in proof reading.

Thanks is due to the following for permission to quote from their publications:
Edward Arnold Ltd. *Years of Change* Robert Wolfson, *A History of Germany* W Carr, *Bismarck and the Unification of Germany* Hewison and *The Unification of Germany* Andrena Stiles. **Cassells Ltd.** *The Kaisers* T Aronson. **Mr Peter Clough** *A History of Modern Italy* Shepard B Clough and Salvatore Saladino. **Corgi Books** *The Past is Myself* Christabel Bielenberg.**Droste Verlag** *Third Reich to Kaiser Reich* Fritz Fischer. Mr Peter M Grosz pictures by George Grosz. **Robert Hale Ltd.** *History of the SS* GS Graber. **Harper Collins** *Hitler and Stalin:Parallel Lives* Alan Bullock, *The Europe I Saw* Elizabeth Wiskemann and *Bismarck and the Development of Germany* Mitchell, *The Anatomy of the SS State* Krausnick, Buchheim, Broszat & Jacobson. **Hamish Hamilton** *Bismarck* and *The Course of German History* AJP Taylor. **Paul Hamlyn Publishing** *Hitler: A Study in Tyranny* Alan Bullock. **Heinemann Ltd.** *The Last Kaiser* Whittle. **Hodder and Stoughton** *Hitler. A Study of Personality in Politics* William Carr, *Metternich* A Milne, *The Unification of Italy* Andrena Stiles and *Hitler* Norman Stone. **Hutchinson Ltd.** Hitler's *Mein Kampf* translated by Ralph Mannheim. **Nelson Blackie** *Fascism in Western Europe* HR Kedward. **The Longman Group** *Bismarck the Kaiser and Germany* BJ Elliot, *Europe in the 19th and 20th Centuries* Grant and Temperley, *Bismarck and Germany 1862-1890* Williamson, *Europe 1815-1945* Anthony Wood, *Bismarck to Hitler* JCG Rohl and *Nazi Voter* Jeremy Noakes in the August 1980 edition of *History Today*. **The Macmillan Press Ltd.** *The Mind of Germany* Hans Koln. Odhams Press *Mussolini, Study of a Demagogue* Sir Ivone Kirkpatrick. **Oxford University Press** *Germany 1866-1945* Gordon Craig. **The Royal Institute of International Affairs** *The Speeches of Adolf Hitler 1922-39, Vols.1 and 2* edited by Norman Baynes. **Unwin Hyman** *Germany in the Age of Bismarck* WM Simon, *The Third Reich* Klaus Hildebrand, *The Weimar Republic* E Kolb and *Economic Survey 1919-1939* W Arthur Lewis. **The University of Chicago Press** *Mussolini* Laura Fermi. **The University of Exeter Press** *Nazism 1919-1945* edited by J Noakes and G Pridham. **The University of Michigan Press** *Italy. A Modern History* Denis Mack Smith. **Wayland Publishers** *Italy under Mussolini* C Leeds. **George Weidenfield and Nicholson** *A Social History of the Third Reich* Richard Grunberger, *Mussolini* Denis Mack Smith and *Hitler's Table Talk*, foreword by H Trevor Roper. **Oswald Wolff Books** *The German Opposition to Hitler* Hans Rothfels.

Permission to use photographs and cartoons was kindly given by The Weimar Archive (pages 7, 13, 17, 22, 30, 45, 47, 54, 69, 101, 104, 106, 109, 118, 119 & 123), by Punch (pages 21, 35, 71, 73, 85, 89, 93, 95 & 97) , by Hergestellt im Bundesarchiv (pages 114, 116 & 121)

Every attempt has been made to contact copyright holders, but we apologise if any have been overlooked.

Published and Typeset by **Pulse Publications**
45 Raith Road, Fenwick, Ayrshire KA3 6DB

Printed by **Ritchie of** Edinburgh

British Library Cataloguing-in-Publication Data
A Catalogue record for this book is
available from the British Library

ISBN 0 948766 15 8

Contents

1 Europe Before 1815

If you compare the map of Europe in 1789 with a map of modern Europe you will see that things have changed greatly in the last 200 years. While most of the countries of Western Europe had taken more or less their modern form, in Central and Eastern Europe the picture was very different.

During the Middle Ages the idea of a nation state uniting people of the same race under one government had become pretty well established in countries like Spain, France, England and Scotland. However, in Germany and Italy political unity had never been achieved. For differing reasons, both had split up into a patchwork of small states.

Further east the scene was dominated by three large empires. The Empire of the Russian Tsars had expanded steadily in the previous 200 years: westwards into central Europe, southwards to the Black Sea and eastwards across Asia.

The ruler of the Austro-Hungarian Empire also had the ancient title of Holy Roman Emperor and had, theoretically, overlordship of Germany. In practice the Hapsburg Emperors ruled a Central European Empire including

Austria and the ancient kingdoms of Bohemia and Hungary.

Southeast Europe was ruled by the Ottoman Turks who were Moslems. Three hundred years previously, their powerful armies had threatened Central Europe and even reached the gates of Vienna. By the late eighteenth century the Turkish Empire was showing signs of decay.

In 1789 many European people were ruled by foreigners. This was not something that ordinary people worried about very much. Nationalism - the idea that people sharing the same language and culture should be ruled by their own government - is largely a concept which developed in the nineteenth and twentieth centuries.

Most people in the eighteenth century would not have understood the strong desires and passions aroused by nationalism. To understand the reasons for this, we must take a look at the way countries were run and the structure of society.

The usual form of government in most of Europe at this time was *autocracy* - the rule of one man. Kings and Princes

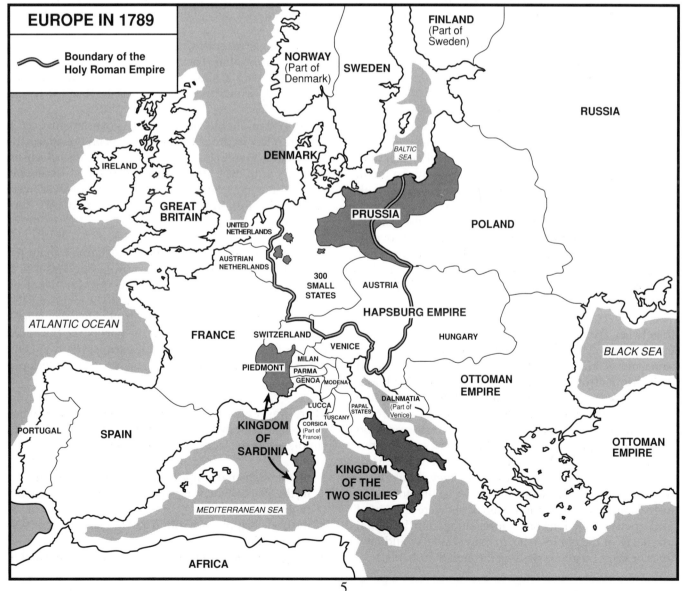

EUROPE IN 1789

— Boundary of the Holy Roman Empire

were absolute monarchs, with complete control over their subjects. They chose whoever they wanted from among their courtiers and servants to be their ministers. They did not normally have to answer to any sort of assembly or parliament, let alone hold elections.

In Great Britain the government was a *constitutional monarchy*. This meant that the power of the King was limited by an elected parliament which controlled taxation and law-making. However this was not a modern democracy - a nation where the government represents and is chosen by the whole population. Only the wealthier classes were allowed to vote. Nevertheless, people in other countries looked enviously to Britain as an example of an enlightened and liberal form of government.

In most of Europe, society was rigidly divided in clearly defined social classes. At the top of the social tree was the aristocracy, ie. the landowners. In most countries they enjoyed many privileges. They owned most of the land, the chief source of wealth at the time. They were often exempt from major taxation and enjoyed a special status in the law courts. It was normally from the ranks of the aristocracy that the Kings and emperors chose their ministers and the commanders of their armed forces.

In Eastern Europe the aristocracy enjoyed even greater privileges, for in Russia and the eastern areas of Germany and Austria-Hungary *feudalism* still flourished. The peasants were normally serfs - not merely the tenants of the landlords but also their property. A Russian Boyar or Prussian Junker had complete control over the peasants on his estates. He directed their work, supervised their private lives and punished their misdeeds.

The peasants formed the vast majority of Europe's population, because farming was still the main economic activity. For most peasants their world was limited to their local community. Few peasants would travel further than to the nearest market town a few miles away. To them, foreigners were people from the next valley. Their loyalties were to the community or village in which they lived. The landlord who controlled their land was also usually the local representative of law and order. Central government was a remote organisation, liable to make tiresome demands for taxes or for soldiers in time of war, but having little other impact on daily life. Nationalism, in other words, meant nothing to a peasant.

In between the aristocracy and the peasants was a small but growing class of craftsmen, merchants and professional men. Unlike the rest of the population they derived their income from trade rather than from the land, and their lives were centred on the towns. It was this middle class which was the leading force for change in Europe. Generally well educated, they resented their exclusion from political power, especially in countries like France where the aristocracy had become totally inefficient. Middle class businessmen did not see why they should have no say in government when they were having to pay an increasing share of taxation. Merchants were frustrated by the petty restrictions on trade resulting from the feudal privileges of the nobles who, in many cases, would levy dues or taxes on goods passing through their lands.

In Western Europe, as industry began to develop, the middle class became more significant and there was increasing pressure for political reform. This was usually along the lines of what had happened in Britain. In Eastern Europe, however, the middle class was as yet too small in number to have any real influence.

The European aristocracy of the eighteenth century tended to have an internationalist outlook. This was largely due to a shared system of education, based on the language and literature of Ancient Rome. This classical education tended to give the aristocracy a common view of the world, a tendency increased by the gentlemen from Northern Europe travelling through France to Italy on the 'Grand Tour' to complete their education. Thus a nobleman often had more in common with an aristocrat from another country than with the ordinary people of his own land. Small wonder, then, that nationalism had no appeal to the aristocracy.

THE INFLUENCE ON EUROPE OF THE FRENCH REVOLUTION AND NAPOLEON

The French Revolution began in 1789. It started as a series of spontaneous demonstrations protesting about bad government, poverty and excessive taxation. The demonstrations soon grew to a full-scale uprising. The monarchy was overthrown and the King executed. The slogan of the revolutionaries was 'Liberty, Equality, Fraternity'. These sentiments were almost unheard of in Europe before this.

The new governments which replaced the monarchy were weak and unstable. They were frequently overthrown. There followed a slide into virtual anarchy and then dictatorship which became known as the Reign of Terror.

From 1795 a slightly more stable government was in power. A key figure in this was Napoleon Bonaparte. By 1799 he was in sole charge of France and he was to remain in power until 1814. He could be described as an autocrat, a dictator, even a monarch. The French, however, were happy with this 'King' since he ran the country very efficiently.

The other European powers became alarmed about the events in France and in 1792 a war broke out. This was to last for the next twenty years. During this war Napoleon came to dominate virtually the whole of mainland Europe. Only Britain was never controlled by him. It took enormous, concerted action on the part of the European powers to defeat Napoleon and his armies firstly at Leipzig in 1813 and finally, after a last breakout, at Waterloo in 1815.

There was a good side to the Napoleonic period which affected developments in Europe for the next 100 years. In simple terms the legacy of Napoleon was:-

- that feudalism disappeared in many areas of Europe. In the places where it was reimposed it was greatly resented.
- the Code Napoleon, a sound and fair legal system, was widely adopted.
- the governments which Napoleon had established in

Metternich

the territories that he captured may not have been democratic, but they were fair and efficient.

- European nations developed and maintained large armies as a result of the Napoleonic Wars.
- national consciousness was aroused throughout Europe as people struggled to free themselves from French domination.
- the French Revolution had encouraged the rise of liberalism, the desire for governments which were representative of the people and respected rights such as freedom of speech and religion.

The French Revolution was one of the great watersheds of history and we can trace the roots of many of the developments that have occurred in Europe over the last 200 years to it.

At the end of the war representatives of the European powers who had been most deeply involved in the fighting met in Vienna to discuss the future of Europe. The main participants were Britain, Russia, Prussia and Austria. Strangely enough the defeated power, France, was also invited to attend. The conference was known as the Congress of Vienna.

Those at the conference were very keen to ensure that war on such a scale should never be allowed to break out again and to make certain that the dangerous sentiments which had sparked off the French Revolution in the first place should be suppressed.

For these reasons they made very few changes to the map of Europe or to the ways in which countries were governed. In general, they tried to restore Europe to the way it had been before 1789. The main exception to this was that the states closest to France were made stronger.

The sentiments which had been aroused during the war demanding more representative governments or for unified national states in countries like Germany, Austria and Poland were ignored.

It was also agreed that the great nations of Europe should meet together whenever the need should arise to discuss any problems which might threaten the peace of Europe. In fact they met at four other Congresses between 1816 and 1822. These became less and less effective, however, as the self-interest of states was put before the desire for concerted action. In addition to this, some great powers found that they were being dragged into conflicts to support governments which they could see were unfair and corrupt.

The central figure in the congress system was the Austrian Chancellor, Metternich. He was the President of the Congress of Vienna and had a big influence over its decisions. He dominated the history of Europe from then until 1848. What were his policies and motives?

The Austrian Empire was a mixture of many differing peoples. She had suffered badly during the Napoleonic Wars when she had lost a great deal of territory and influence. It was therefore in Metternich's interests to see a return to the pre-1789 situation. The Austrians also held considerable territory in Italy and Germany and so would not welcome any nationalist movements in those countries. There was also the added threat that these nationalist demands might erupt elsewhere in the Empire if encouraged in Italy and Germany.

Metternich was also an extreme conservative. He had been appointed by the Austrian Emperor and was responsible only to him. He had no time at all for any of the liberal demands for a parliament or any other democratic ideas. He was therefore against any liberal reforms anywhere else in Europe. He was happy to support the central policy of the Congress system which was that governments restored by the Congress of Vienna should be kept in power - by force if necessary.

ITALY BEFORE 1815

"'Italy' is just a geographical expression." So said Count Metternich, chief minister of Austria, when asked to comment on the problems of Italy. Italy did not exist as a country in 1815; it had not been united under one government since the collapse of the Roman Empire in the 5th century.

Reasons for Italian Disunity

A major reason for the disunity of Italy was the part played by the Papacy. After the collapse of the Roman Empire, the Popes had laid claim to the legacy of the Emperors. Rome became their base and the centre of a Papal State stretching across central Italy. Moreover, during the Middle Ages there was a long power struggle between the Popes and the German Emperors for control of Italy. This had allowed the towns of northern Italy to play one off against the other and emerge as independent city states. Florence, Milan, Genoa and Venice were the most important among them. Only in southern Italy had a proper kingdom - Naples and Sicily - developed. However, its fortunes were bedevilled by the struggle between two rival families for the throne, one backed by France, the other by Aragon in Spain.

By the end of the 15th century, while the Italian states feuded among themselves, the neighbouring countries of France, Spain and the Austrian Empire were developing into large, well-organised powers. Italy became their battleground. In 1494, the French were invited by the ruler of Milan to help him in a dispute with Naples, an event which ushered in a period of foreign invasions and interference when the French and Spanish and later the Austrians fought to control Italy.

This foreign domination continued until the French Revolution in 1789. By then the Austrians were in control of most of Northern Italy except Venice and Piedmont. In the south an off-shoot of the Spanish Bourbon family ruled as kings of Naples and Sicily. Between them lay the Papal States and several small duchies. In most states, autocracy was the normal form of government. The rule of the Popes was perhaps the most backward and repressive. It was propped up by the Inquisition, an organisation whose task was to hunt down enemies of the Church.

The Impact of the French Revolution

It was hardly surprising that when the armies of Revolutionary France drove the Austrians out of Italy in 1796, many Italians saw them as liberators. The revolutionary slogan of 'Liberty, Equality and Brotherhood' had a great appeal for the oppressed people of Italy. Also, the commander of the French armies was himself more Italian than French. Napoleon Bonaparte, soon to be Emperor of France, was a native of Corsica which had been taken by France from Genoa in 1768.

Under Bonaparte, the Italians experienced good government for the first time. Among the reforms he carried out were the ending of the privileges of the nobility; severe restrictions on the power of the Catholic Church; the building of roads to improve communications; and the creation of a standard law code for all areas under French control. The French also set up elected assemblies which gave Italians their first taste of political activity. Italy's economic development was stimulated by its inclusion in the Napoleonic Empire. Most important of all, the French brought unity, reducing the numerous small states to two large, semi-independent states and one area directly under French rule. Although it was a unity imposed from outside, by force of arms, it was welcome to many Italians, especially the growing middle class.

However, the defeat of Napoleon in 1815 heralded the return of the forces of reaction. The peacemakers at the Congress of Vienna were anxious to restore 'legitimate' governments and to crush all the dangerous ideas stirred up by the French Revolution. So the kings of Piedmont/Sardinia and Naples and Sicily were restored to their kingdoms. The Pope recovered his states in central Italy. The duchies of Parma, Tuscany and Modena were handed over to off-shoots of the Austrian royal family and the ancient republic of Venice was swallowed up by Austria and added to her possessions in Lombardy, as her reward

for being on the winning side in the war. Everywhere, autocratic governments were back in power and the reforms of the Napoleonic era were undone. The reactionary King Victor Emmanuel I of Sardinia showed his disapproval of reform by rejecting everything done by the French, even ripping out the street lighting which they had installed in his capital Turin!

Nevertheless, the legacy of the Napoleonic period could not be stamped out completely. Having tasted good government and unity under one ruler, Italians were not content to return to the old days. There was an increasing awareness of their national identity coupled with a growing hope that Italy would some day control her own destiny.

GERMANY BEFORE 1815

"The history of the Germans is the history of extremes. It contains everything except moderation, and in the course of a thousand years the Germans have experienced everything except normality."
(AJP Taylor *The Course of German History* Methuen p1)

In this way a famous historian, AJP Taylor, begins a book on Germany. The book was written at the end of the Second World War so the quote may be a little overstated. Nevertheless, the history of Germany is complex, fascinating and well worth studying.

Germany had never existed as a nation in the centuries before 1815. In the eighteenth century there were more than three hundred independent nation states within the area which we now call Germany.

Only two of these states were of any size and importance namely Prussia and Austria. The states within 'Germany' were all part of the Holy Roman Empire. This organisation was traditionally ruled by the Emperor of Austria. The Austrian Empire contained many non-Germans as well. The Holy Roman Empire had declined steadily in power since the wars of the seventeenth century and by 1789 it was little more than a title.

There were certain factors in addition to the Holy Roman Empire which tended to make Germany a unit. They shared a common feeling of race as distinct from the Latins or Slavs, they shared a common language and to some extent they also held in common their culture and heritage.

On the other hand, there were factors which tended to keep Germany disunited. She was surrounded by large and powerful states - particularly France and Austria - and it was very much in their interests to keep Germany weak and divided. In this way they could easily dominate her and need not fear an attack from her. During the Reformation the northern German states had adopted Lutheran Protestantism while most states in the south remained Roman Catholic. The rulers of the German states - some Emperors, some Kings, some Grand Dukes, some Princes, some Electors, some Earls, some Barons and some Bishops - were jealous of each other and keen to preserve their own independence. They were not willing

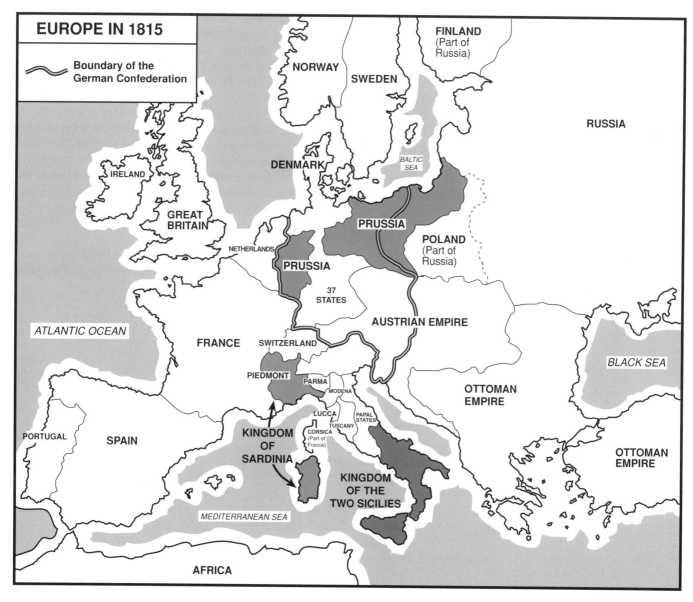

EUROPE IN 1815

〜 Boundary of the German Confederation

NORWAY

SWEDEN

FINLAND (Part of Russia)

RUSSIA

DENMARK

BALTIC SEA

IRELAND

GREAT BRITAIN

NETHERLANDS

PRUSSIA

PRUSSIA

POLAND (Part of Russia)

37 STATES

AUSTRIAN EMPIRE

ATLANTIC OCEAN

FRANCE

SWITZERLAND

PIEDMONT

PARMA

MODENA

LUCCA

TUSCANY

PAPAL STATES

CORSICA (Part of France)

KINGDOM OF SARDINIA

BLACK SEA

OTTOMAN EMPIRE

PORTUGAL

SPAIN

KINGDOM OF THE TWO SICILIES

OTTOMAN EMPIRE

MEDITERRANEAN SEA

AFRICA

to cooperate with each other. This was particularly true in terms of trade. Even though most of the states were tiny they all had large tarriff barriers and customs duties. This discouraged trade among them and seriously hampered economic development.

The style of government in all the states was autocratic. They were not all brutal, backward tyrannies but there was little room for representative government. Of the two large states, Austria was the more powerful and influential. She had a large Empire outside the German area and her Emperor was also the Holy Roman Emperor. The small states in Southern Germany which were Roman Catholic naturally looked to her as their protector. However, Austria had problems. The large Empire was difficult to control and was developing so slowly that it was beginning to stagnate. The system of government was autocratic in the extreme and there was little economic development.

Prussia was slightly different. She had been growing in size since the sixteenth century. The Prussian rulers, the Hohenzollerns, had been as autocratic as the Austrian Hapsburgs, but they were keen to see their country grow and develop. Perhaps because Prussia started from a relatively weak position being surrounded by big, powerful neighbours and having no decent natural frontiers like

rivers or mountains to protect her, she had a tradition of military strength. This was important to the Prussians and they spent a large proportion of their national income on it.

"Germany stagnated under the rule of her petty Princes, and the two real powers in Germany maintained against each other an uneasy balance."
(AJP Taylor *The Course of German History* Methuen p24)

During the eighteenth century there were gradual changes in Germany. The period, which was known throughout Europe as the enlightenment, stimulated developments in the arts which generated a feeling of German culture. At the same time there were reforms in Prussia which enabled her to modernise her government system and to stimulate economic growth.

The French Revolutionary War had a devastating effect on Germany. The small, weak states were easy prey for Napoleon's armies. Even Austria and Prussia were, at various times, forced to recognise French supremacy.

Napoleon reorganised Germany into a total of forty states. States which had supported him were enlarged and on the French border a new organisation, the Confederation of the Rhine, was established. This consisted of sixteen states which were to retain some independence under the overall control of the French. The Holy Roman Empire was finally dissolved.

"In the twenty years between 1794 and 1814, the years of French victory, most of western Germany received the benefits of the French Revolution - freedom of enterprise, equality before the law, security of property and of the individual, cheap efficient administration ... The great reforms were liberal, but they were French. A startling consequence followed. French intervention in Germany stirred into patriotism the natural resentment against the interference of foreigners."
(AJP Taylor *The Course of German History* Methuen p25)

The Battle of Leipzig marked the final defeat of Napoleon in Germany and the beginning of the restructuring of the German area. The Congress of Vienna made quite signifi-cant changes to the map of Germany. Only 39 independent states were re-established with their original rulers. These were enlarged. Large states were created along the French border in line with the policy of ensuring that France would not be able to expand again so rapidly.

Although several states gained in size and importance, the changes in Prussia were, perhaps, the most significant. She gained substantial territory in the west of Germany. These lands were not only rich economically but were also centres of culture and intellect. On the other hand, the Austrian gains in territory were in areas outside Germany and much of the Austrian's attention was focused in that direction from then on.

It is true to say that, in German terms, Prussia emerged from the Napoleonic Wars with her power and prestige enhanced while Austria had slipped backwards.

2 The Stirring of National Consciousness in Italy 1815-1848

Italian States in the Early Nineteenth Century

Piedmont-Sardinia

The official title of this kingdom was Sardinia but it is often referred to as Piedmont since this was the most important and populous part of the lands ruled by the Sardinian King. We shall hereafter refer to it simply as Sardinia.

This kingdom was relatively poor and backward since much of the land was mountainous and barren. The capital was Turin but the most wealthy city was the port of Genoa which had been acquired in 1815. The King was a reactionary autocrat but he had one virtue in the eyes of nationalists: his family, the House of Savoy, was the only truly Italian royal family in Italy.

Lombardy and Venetia

This area was part of the Austrian Empire. It was the wealthiest area of Italy, particularly the rich farmlands of the Po valley. Venice was Italy's richest port and in Lombardy the silk industry was developing. The government was efficient and in some matters quite progressive. However, political dissent was strictly suppressed by the secret police; books were censored and political prisoners filled the gaols. Taxation was heavy and Austrian rule was bitterly resented.

The Duchies

Parma, Modena and Tuscany were generally quite well run by rulers who, although they were basically autocrats,

were concerned for the well-being of their subjects. However, for Italian nationalists they all had one major fault - they were foreigners related to and kept in power by the Hapsburg rulers of Austria.

The Papal States

This area was very badly ruled. Freedom of thought was strangled by the Church. The Inquisition, an organisation originally set up to deal with Protestants and other heretics, used torture and imprisonment against those with liberal ideas. Books were rigidly censored. The people were mostly illiterate peasants and economic progress was not helped by the fact that the Pope disapproved of railways and the telegraph as dangerous modern innovations.

Naples and Sicily

The ruler, King Ferdinand I of the Spanish Bourbon family, was an autocrat whose government was brutal and inefficient. The country was very poor and backward and many peasants had turned to banditry as a result. Surprisingly, Naples did build Italy's first railway line in 1839, but no tunnels were allowed in case this encouraged immorality! The King hoped to use it to move his troops more quickly to deal with trouble.

Overall, Italy in the first half of the 19th century was backward compared with most of the other countries of western Europe. Industry was slow to develop because of a lack of capital and the necessary raw materials such as coal. The biggest obstacle to economic progress was the division into different states which seriously hampered internal trade. However, unity was out of the question as long as the Austrians dominated Italy. As the Sardinian ambassador said to the Russian Tsar in 1818, "Austria, possessing the richest and most fertile regions of the peninsula, besides nearly a quarter of the total Italian population, and also holding sway over Tuscany, Parma and Modena through princes of her ruling house, cuts Italy in half and is its actual mistress." (Michael Morrogh *The Unification of Italy: Documents and Debates* Macmillan Education Ltd 1991 p 5 from D Mack Smith *The Making of Italy 1796-1866* London 1988 p 25)

THE 'RISORGIMENTO'

Between 1815 and 1848 the Nationalist movement developed steadily. 'Risorgimento' means 'resurgence' or 're-birth' and is the name the Italians gave to the struggle for a united Italy.

By the time of the French invasions, secret societies, dedicated to freeing Italy from foreign rule, were already in existence. After 1815 their chief enemy was Austria. The most important of these societies was the *Carbonari* - the Charcoal Burners, whose name allegedly came from their habit of meeting in the woods. They had supporters throughout Italy. These were mostly drawn from the middle classes - doctors, teachers, lawyers, etc. along with a few army officers and nobles. They were patriotic ideal-

ITALY BEFORE UNIFICATION

KEY
- Austrian Occupied
- Ruled by Austrian backed Dukes
- Papal States

ists rather than practical politicians: men prepared to risk their lives for their cause but too often lacking in organisation and clearly defined aims. Some wanted an Italian Republic while others would have settled for constitutional reforms within the existing states which would be linked in some sort of federation.

In 1820 the resentment felt about the Vienna settlement boiled over into rebellion. The trouble started in Naples where some Carbonari led a revolt against the government of King Ferdinand. The royal troops were half-hearted in their efforts to put down the rising, and some of them joined the revolt which was also widely supported by the peasants. In Sicily too, the people rose in rebellion. In this crisis, Ferdinand saved his throne by promising to grant a constitution which gave all adult males the vote.

However, Ferdinand had no intention of sticking to his promises. He won the permission of his new government to attend a meeting of the major powers at the Congress of Laibach to have the changes in Naples approved, but as soon as he felt safe he changed his tune. He told the Congress he had been forced to grant the constitution under duress and he asked for Austrian help to restore his authority. Naturally Metternich, the Austrian chief minister, was very willing to oblige and the Austrian army marched south to crush the revolution. The savagery of the reprisals which followed shocked even conservative European opinion.

In Sardinia also there was revolutionary activity in 1821. Turin was taken over by the rebels and Victor Emmanuel was forced to abdicate. The liberals pinned their hopes on the King's nephew, Charles Albert, who was persuaded to grant a constitution, but when Victor Emmanuel's brother and heir Charles Felix denounced the changes and appealed to Metternich for help, Charles Albert fled and the revolution was crushed.

In 1831 further revolutions broke out, inspired by the events in France. In Parma, Modena and the Papal States Carbonari rebels tried to take over, but again, with Austrian assistance, the rebellions were put down. There was a further disappointment for the liberals when Charles Albert became King of Sardinia. His behaviour in 1821 had raised hopes that he might lead a nationalist movement but he was too scared to challenge Austrian power and the liberals' hopes were dashed.

NEW LEADERS - NEW IDEAS

So far the revolutionaries had failed, partly because of their poor organisation and muddled aims and partly because they lacked broad popular support. If the Risorgimento was to succeed, a more decisive leadership was needed. The first man to fill this gap was Giuseppe Mazzini.

Mazzini was born in Genoa in 1805. Like most revolutionaries he came from a middle-class background. As a teenager he had witnessed the crushing of the 1821 revolution and was inspired by the courage of the rebels to devote his life to the cause of a united Italy. He always wore black as a symbol of mourning for the misfortunes of his country. During a spell in prison in 1830, he developed the ideas which were to inspire the next generation of nationalists. His new movement was called *Young Italy*. Unlike the Carbonari, it was given clearly defined aims to which all its members had to swear loyalty. Young Italy was to recruit members from all social classes and to spread its ideas by education and propaganda. It was dedicated to creating a united Italy, free from outside domination and ruled by a fully democratic republican government.

> *"Young Italy* is a brotherhood of Italians who believe in a law of *progress* and *duty* and are convinced that Italy is destined to become one nation ... They join this Association with the firm intention of consecrating both thought and action to the great aim of reconstituting Italy as one independent sovereign nation of free men and equals ...
> *Young Italy* is republican and unitarian - republican because theoretically every nation is destined, by the law of God and humanity, to form a free and equal community of brothers; and the republican form of government is the only form of government which ensures this future.
> *Young Italy* is unitarian, because without unity there is no true nation. Because without unity there is no real strength; and Italy surrounded as she is by powerful, united and jealous nations, has need of strength above all things ... "
> [N Gangulee (Ed.) *Mazzini's Selected Writings*]

In 1831 Mazzini appealed to Charles Albert to put himself at the head of the nationalist movement. The King's failure to take up the challenge confirmed Mazzini in his republican beliefs. This was later to cause a dilemma for the nationalist movement when, in 1849, a Sardinian King appeared who was willing to fight for unity. After another unsuccessful revolt in 1834, Mazzini fled into exile from where he continued to direct Young Italy.

There were other theories growing up about the possible leadership of a united Italy. In spite of Charles Albert's weakness, many moderate nationalists were of the opinion that it was to the kings of Sardinia, the only native Italian royal family, that they must look. "The history of the last thirty years .. will prove that military or democratic revolutions can have little success in Italy. All true friends of the country must therefore reject such means as useless. They must recognise that they cannot truly help their fatherland except by gathering in support of legitimate monarchs who have their roots deep in the national soil." (C Cavour 1846) (Michael Morrogh op cit p15 - from a book review by Cavour in 1846 in D Mack Smith *The Making of Italy 1796-1866* London 1988 p108)

Another proposal was put forward by a liberal churchman, Gioberti. In 1843 he published a book suggesting that "The principal of Italian union is the Pope who can unify the peninsula by means of a confederation of its princes." (Michael Morrogh op cit p11 from V Gioberti *Of the Moral and Civil Primacy of the Italians 1843* in D Beales *The Risorgimento and the Unification of Italy* London 1981 p132-3) This idea, which obviously had a great appeal for Italian Catholics, was given a major stimulus when in 1846 a new Pope was elected. Pius IX hated the cruelty and repression which previous papal governments had used. He was not really a liberal, but a well-meaning man who was prepared to make some concessions. His first acts as Pope were to release two thousand political prisoners and to introduce some reforms in the administration. This led many people to take the ideas of Gioberti more seriously.

Thus by the 1840s, several different sets of nationalist ideas were fermenting in Italy. The agitation for change was spreading and in several other states rulers followed the Pope's example and introduced reforms. To add to the unrest, this was a period of economic depression throughout Western Europe. In Italy in 1846 and 1847 there were disastrous harvest failures, a serious matter in a country where 90% of the population were still peasants.

1848 EUROPE IN REVOLT

The events of 1848 in Europe seem almost incredible in retrospect. Historians still argue about the causes and significance of the revolutions which swept through Europe during that one year.

European governments had not changed significantly since the Congress of Vienna. Under the Metternich system, any attempt at nationalist or liberal reform was suppressed.

"One must not dream of reformation while agitated by passion. Wisdom dictates that at such moments we should limit ourselves to maintaining."
(Milne *Metternich* ULP p32)

Yet in the space of one year this was to change dramatically in virtually the whole of Europe.

The reasons for this happening are still unclear. It is easier to state the reasons which did not help it happen. It was not caused by a centrally planned revolutionary group nor was it anything to do with the publication that year of the Communist manifesto by Karl Marx. That was a coincidence.

What we can say is that a succession of bad harvests coupled with an economic depression in the 1840s led to a great deal of hunger and distress throughout Europe. This hit particularly hard in the cities where industrialisation led to the emergence of a new class - the industrial workers.

MAZZINI'S INFLUENCE

Mazzini

Mazzini's influence on the nationalist movement was huge. Many men who were later to play a leading part in events were in their early days Mazzinians - men like the guerrilla leader Garibaldi and the future Prime Minister Crispi. However, many of Mazzini's contemporaries such as Cavour regarded him as a dangerous nuisance and some historians share this view. It is said that Mazzini was too idealistic and impractical, too ready to encourage popular uprisings and acts of terrorism which ended in failure, loss of life and discredit for the nationalist movement. Mazzini never changed his view that Italy should be united by a great popular uprising. He never accepted the eventual union of Italy under the kings of Sardinia and ended his days in disappointed exile.

The Anglo-Italian historian, M Salvadori, has highlighted Mazzini's role as an inspirer!

"The greatness of Mazzini lies chiefly in his character, in the deeply felt passion which moved him and which was his entire life from 1831 until his death. Nothing mattered except the cause: Italy united and republican. He laboured day and night meeting people, keeping in touch with the revolutionaries in Italy and with exiles outside, collecting money, sending instructions, strengthening the weak and doubting, aiding the needy. He was an inspirer. In total devotion to the cause, in ability to stand bitterness, humiliation and defeat, few can compare with Mazzini. His writings are clear and contain nothing hysterical, but the reader can feel the extreme passion moving the writer, his power of concentration, his firm conviction, his absolute honesty, the generosity of a great soul and the universality of a great mind."
(Massimo Salvadori *Cavour and the Unification of Italy* p41 D van Nostrand Company 1961)

While Andrina Stiles would agree that Mazzini's 'great contribution' was as an inspirer, she nevertheless has played down his influence:

"How great was his influence in the 1830s and 1840s? His writings, most of which read like vague mysticism, had only a limited circulation in his lifetime. Well received, if not well understood by intellectual revolutionaries, his books and pamphlets did not contain much of general interest. Most of his earlier writings only sold a few hundred copies each. Mazzini has been blamed by Marxist historians for failure to realise the needs of the peasants and for not working for agrarian reform. This, they argue, would have won him widespread support and turned his movement into a popular one. He himself estimated the membership of *Young Italy* at about 50,000, but most historians probably think this is an overestimate."
(Andrina Stiles *The Unification of Italy 1815-70* p18 Edward Arnold 1986)

There was dissatisfaction too among the middle class because their demands for a more representative government continued to be denied. The fact that these demands had been suppressed since 1815 and had, in fact, become stronger could be the main underlying cause of the 1848 revolutions.

Incredibly, the whole thing started in January 1848 when the people of Milan gave up smoking. This protest was very effective since their Austrian rulers made a lot of money from taxes on tobacco sales. This culminated in rioting and a number of Italians were killed by Austrian troops. Disorder spread to southern Italy where a constitution and representative government was promised. In France, the King, Louis Philippe, was forced to abdicate and a republic was established. The right of every Frenchman to vote in elections was promised.

Revolutionary feeling spread to Belgium where liberal reform was granted. In Holland the King granted reforms before a revolution could break out.
In the German Confederation the rulers made similar reforms. At the same time, proposals were put forward for uniting the whole of Germany.

In March the single most important event took place. This was when revolution spread to the Austrian Empire. Reform demands throughout the Empire coupled with rioting in Vienna convinced the Royal Family that the Empire itself was under threat. In an attempt to save it and his own skin the Emperor sacked his Chancellor, Metternich - the man who had dominated Europe for the previous forty years. He also granted liberal reforms.

The pace of reform accelerated in almost every country in Europe. By the end of the year it seemed possible that Germany might be united, that the Austrian Empire might have broken down into its various parts and that every country would have a constitution, a representative government, elections with all men voting and individual freedom guaranteed.

Just as quickly as they had started, the revolutions began to fail. In most countries the monarchs had retained their thrones even though they had made reforms. Even more significantly, they had retained the loyalty and support of their armed services. The revolutionaries themselves soon became divided. The main split was between the middle-class liberals - who wanted sufficient reform to give themselves a share in the government - and the republicans who wanted a full-scale democracy. There were also disputes among the nationalists. Some were happy to campaign for their own nationalist aspirations but were not in the least sympathetic to the equally valid demands of the smaller national groups within the state that they intended to run. For example, the Hungarians wanted to be independent of the Austrian Empire, but they were quite prepared to ignore the demands of the many other peoples who lived in the area which they claimed to be Hungary.

A further complication was that the new reformed governments were often unstable and unclear as to what they wanted to do. The revolutionaries were inexperienced in

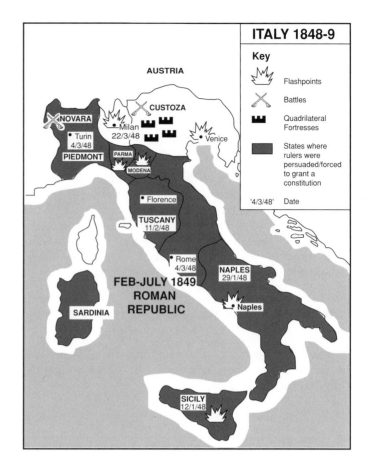

the art of government and were badly prepared. The revolutions had taken them by surprise. Quite quickly they lost popular support. They were no more able to solve the economic and social problems facing Europe than were the old monarchies. Even though they were not a serious threat, some of the extremists made more moderate reformers afraid of supporting revolutionary ideas.

The monarchs acted swiftly to crush the revolutionaries and reassert their authority and by 1849 it was alomst as if there had never been any revolutions at all. There were however some lasting results of the 1848 revolutions.

The Metternich system was smashed forever. Some states, eg. Belgium and Prussia, retained the constitutions which had been granted. The reformers learned some valuable lessons about the art of government.

The revolutions demonstrated the issues which would dominate European politics for the next sixty years. By the end of that time most of the demands of 1848 would be achieved.

Bakunin, a Russian revolutionary orator, writing in *La Reforme* in March 1848 claimed that,

"Soon, perhaps in less than a year, the monstrous Austrian Empire will be destroyed. The liberated Italians will proclaim an Italian Republic. The Germans, united into a single great nation, will proclaim a German Republic. The Polish democrats after seventy years in exile will return to their homes. The revolutionary movement will stop only when Europe, the whole of Europe, not excluding Russia, is turned into a federal democratic republic."
(Quoted in Wood *Europe 1815 to 1945* Longmans p140)

ITALY AND THE YEAR OF REVOLUTIONS 1848-49

Even before the revolution in France in February, which is regarded as the starting point of the 'Year of Revolutions' of 1848, trouble had broken out in Italy.

In January, in Sicily, protests began against the oppressive rule of King Ferdinand II of Naples. This was largely a separatist revolt, seeking greater freedom from Naples, rather than Italian unity. However, within a few days the revolt had spread to the mainland and the king was forced to agree to an elected parliament for Naples.

Meanwhile in Milan, capital of Lombardy, the people gave up smoking as an effective way of protesting against Austrian rule. (see page 14)

When the news of the stirring events in France reached Italy, this was the signal for a general upheaval. In Tuscany, Sardinia and the Papal States, the rulers were persuaded to grant constitutions, while the Dukes of Parma and Modena had to flee from their states altogether. In Milan a full-scale revolution was now under way. After five days of bitter street fighting on the 17 - 22 March the Austrian troops were forced to retreat from the city.

The events in Milan encouraged Charles Albert of Sardinia to take a hand. After some days of typical hesitation, Charles Albert, who had already granted his own subjects a constitution, decided to put himself at the head of the nationalist movement. He declared war on Austria and sent his army to help the revolutionaries in Lombardy. Meanwhile, there had also been a revolution in Venice on 22 March. The Austrians were driven out and a republic was declared led by Daniele Manin. With the government in Vienna near to collapse in the face of revolutions in both Austria and Hungary, there was little General Radetzky the Austrian commander in Italy could do. He retreated into the 'Quadrilateral' - the four fortress towns of Mantua, Peschiera, Verona and Legnano to await events.

The Failure of the Revolutionary Cause in Italy

At first all went well for the Italians, with the armies of Charles Albert winning several minor successes. However before long divisions appeared between him and the Lombards and Venetians who were not sure that they wanted to exchange Austrian rule for that of Sardinia.

> "Today the King told me about the meeting with his generals: they are extremely annoyed with the state of opinion in Lombardy, and national feeling in Piedmont is becoming really alarmed ... The only talk at Milan apparently is of a republic; and they even want Genoa to go republican too. If after so much heroic effort, if after proclaiming ourselves a nation to the whole of Europe, we then divide into as many tiny states and republics as there are cities and municipal rivalries, and if we are then swallowed up or beaten by the foreigner, we shall have left a fine page of history!"
> (Count di Castagnetto to the Mayor of Milan)
> (Michael Morrogh op cit p 28 *Count of Castagnetto to Mayor of Milan 16-4-1848* in D Mack Smith op cit p149-50)

Also, the Pope now came out against the nationalist movement. Under pressure to send troops to support Charles Albert, Pius IX instead denounced the war against Austria:-

> "Seeing that some at present desire that We too, along with the other Princes of Italy and their subjects, should engage in war against the Austrians, We have thought it convenient to proclaim clearly and openly in this our solemn Assembly, that such a measure is altogether alien from our counsels ... We cannot refrain from repudiating, before the face of all nations, the treacherous advice. of those who would have the Roman Pontiff to be the head and to preside over the formation of some sort of novel Republic of the whole Italian people."
> (Michael Morrogh op cit p 31 *The Allocation of Pope Pius IX The Roman State 1815-50* LC Farini London 1851 p106-11)

Pius IX was naturally unwilling to fight against a leading Catholic power; but his decision to oppose Italian unity was a bitter blow and cost much heart-searching for devout Catholic nationalists.

Meanwhile the Austrian Empire was recovering its strength and reinforcements were sent to its army in Italy. In July Radetzky emerged from the Quadrilateral and defeated Charles Albert's army at Custoza. An armistice was signed by which the Sardinians withdrew leaving the Austrians to reoccupy Lombardy. By August, Radetzky was back in Milan. (Later Strauss, the famous Viennese composer, wrote a march in honour of Radetzky's triumph.) This was not quite the end for in March 1849, believing he might get French help, Charles Albert renewed the war. However he suffered another crushing defeat at Novara and, in despair, he abdicated.

Failure in the South

In Naples too the tide had turned. First King Ferdinand exploited a wave of peasant unrest as an excuse to appoint a more right-wing government. Then, as soon as he felt strong enough to defy his opponents, the Neapolitan troops who had been sent to help in the war against Austria were withdrawn. Finally Ferdinand went back on his promises, abolished the new parliament and restored autocratic rule. In September government troops were ready to begin the taming of Sicily. Their ruthless methods of bombarding towns with artillery were to earn Ferdinand the nickname King 'Bomba'. By May 1849, all resistance to his rule had been crushed.

THE ROMAN REPUBLIC

The hopes of the nationalists were now centred on Rome. Here, a series of riots and the murder of his chief minister Rossi persuaded the Pope to flee to Naples for safety. In February 1849, the power of the Pope was declared to be ended and a Roman Republic was set up.

> "1 Papacy has fallen de facto and de jure (in fact and in law) from the temporal throne of the Roman State.
>
> 2 The Roman Pontiff (Pope) shall enjoy all the guarantees necessary for the exercise of his spiritual power.
>
> 3 The government of the Roman State is to be a pure

democracy, and to assume the glorious name of the Roman Republic.

4 The Roman Republic shall maintain with the rest of Italy relations required by a common nationality. (Decree of the Roman Constituent Assembly 8.2.49)"
(Michael Morrogh op cit p38 *Decree of Roman Constituent Assembly 8-2-1849* in F Eyck *The Revolutions of 1848-9* Edinburgh 1972 p137)

Shortly after, Mazzini arrived to become one of the leaders of the new state. However, the Pope begged the Catholic powers of Europe to free Rome from his enemies and his appeal did not fall on deaf ears. Louis Napoleon Bonaparte, the newly elected President of France, wanted to win the support of the Catholic Party in France, so he despatched a force of 20,000 men to help the Pope. The Austrians and Neapolitans too were ready to assist.

Led by Giuseppe Garibaldi, the guerrilla commander, the nationalists put up a fierce resistance lasting three months. Mazzini said later:-

"It was essential to redeem Rome; to place her once again at the summit so that the Italians might again learn to regard her as the temple of their common country ... The defence of the city was therefore decided upon; by the assembly and people of Rome from a noble impulse and from reverence for the honour of Italy; by me as the logical consequence of a long-matured design."
(Andrina Stiles - op cit p 25)

Nevertheless, the odds were too great and in July 1849 Rome fell to the French.

The remnants of Garibaldi's forces tried to reach Venice, the last outpost of revolution; but in August Venice too surrendered to the Austrians, after enduring a long siege with all the miseries of shellfire, starvation and disease. Thus by the end of 1849, the revolutions had collapsed everywhere and the forces of reaction had triumphed. It looked as though nothing had been achieved. However, there were a few positive results. Sardinia now had a constitutional government and a new, more forceful king Victor Emmanuel II; and Italy had a new hero, Garibaldi the defender of Rome. Above all the path towards eventual unification seemed clearer.

"The failure of the Roman Republic to command wider support in Italy revived faith in constitutional monarchy as the only generally acceptable solution. Papal federalism was killed by Pius IX's reversion to absolutism and by his reliance on foreign force. Only Piedmont could now command support, and the last desperate attempt at Novara had restored Piedmont's prestige. It was henceforth plain that only force kept Italy politically disunited; and it was equally plain that only a national army, under the House of Savoy, was likely to expel that intrusive foreign force of disruption."
(D Thomson *Europe Since Napoleon* p223-224 Pelican 1975)

Why did the 1848 Revolutions fail in Italy?
A number of important reasons can be suggested

- The initial hesitation of Charles Albert to put himself forward as the head of the nationalist movement.
- The superior military skill of Radetsky and the Austrian armies, especially after the failure of the revolutions in Austria itself allowed more troops to be used against the Italians.
- The sudden abandonment of the revolutionary cause by the Pope and the dispiriting effect of this on many Catholic supporters was a further blow.
- Lack of coordination on various fronts was an important factor also: eg. there was in the main a lack of cooperation between revolutionary groups such as between Sicily and Naples; there was a difference of opinion on what form of government should emerge - should there be a constitutional monarchy in every state or a republican form of government?; no single national leader had emerged to coordinate overall policy. The three likely candidates with their differing ideologies - Mazzini, Pius IX and Charles Albert - only added to the confusion.
- The political inexperience and military weaknesses of the provisional governments ensured that their stay in office would be short-lived, especially since they did not have popular support from the masses for long.
- Finally, the intervention of the French King, Louis Napoleon, against Mazzini and Garibaldi in the Roman Republic led to its collapse.

3 The Unification of Italy

VICTOR EMMANUEL II, CAVOUR & SARDINIA

Victor Emmanuel II, who replaced his father Charles Albert as King of Sardinia in 1849, was not a very attractive figure. He was physically small and ugly and his manners were coarse and unrefined. However he was, unlike his predecessors, totally committed to the idea of a united Italy, led by Sardinia. A man of his word, he stood by his promise to keep the constitutional government set up in 1848, in spite of strong pressure from the Austrians to scrap it. According to the French ambassador he was not a real liberal:

> "Victor Emmanuel ... does not like the existing constitution, nor does he like parliamentary liberties nor a free press. He just accepts them temporarily as a kind of weapon of war. He keeps the tricolour flag instead of restoring that of Savoy; but he looks on it not as a revolutionary standard, only as a banner of conquest."
>
> (Michael Morrogh *The Unification of Italy:Documents and Debates* Pub. Macmillan p5 quoted in D Mack Smith *The Making of Italy 1796 - 1866* p170-1)

Nevertheless, his kingdom was the one corner of Italy where, after the collapse of 1849, reaction and repression were not triumphant. Sardinia became the hope and refuge of Italian nationalists.

Cavour

(Nationalists in other states took to enthusing over the operas of Verdi not just because he wrote some cracking good tunes but also because they could conceal their nationalist fervour under cries of "Viva Verdi!" VERDI=Vittore Emmanuele Rei D' Italia.)

Count Camillo Cavour was a member of an aristocratic Piedmontese family. In his youth he travelled round Europe studying the parliamentary systems of Britain and France, and the social and economic changes which were taking place in these countries as a result of the Industrial Revolution. He supported the idea of a parliamentary system of government for his homeland. Speaking in 1850 he said, "... I tell you frankly that, until our liberal institutions are animated by real political life in the smallest villages as well as in the large cities, we shall never have a genuinely liberal system, but shall be driven to and fro from anarchy to despotism ..." (D Mack Smith *Italy: A Modern History* University of Michigan p206)

On returning to Sardinia he became involved in politics. In 1847 he started a newspaper, the *Risorgimento*, and in 1848 he was elected to Sardinia's new parliament. By 1850 his expertise in economic matters had won him the post of Minister of Commerce and Agriculture and in 1852 he became Prime Minister. While holding both offices, he promoted the economic expansion of Sardinia through the liberalisation of its economic institutions:

> "Not less important than the political struggle, was the effort made by Count Cavour to transform Piedmont economically. In this he took the initiative; often he was quite alone; but only thanks to his effort ... was that country able to become the effective champion of Italian aspirations.
> Difficulties were great. It became necessary to demolish to its foundations a building strengthened by the work of centuries: to attack ideas which had become a common heritage; to upset the vested interests of regions, communities, individuals; all this had to be done in a country where interest in economic studies was scant, and where even those who had fought for political liberty and stood for progress, bowed to economic and social prejudices and opposed the application of healthy economic concepts.
> Cavour's basic economic ideas can be summarised as follows: Sound public finances are necessary to strengthen the country - Sound finances require an expanding economic prosperity - The freeing of productive activities from obstacles of all kinds accumulated through the centuries, and the establishment of complete liberty, are the foundation of economic progress; liberty must extend from the summit to the base of the social structure, in all its component elements - The most effective stimulus to production is the diffusion of credit, in all forms - A country desiring to achieve a high level of economic prosperity and to employ to the utmost its means of production, needs a large central bank capable of regulating the circulation of currency, and of lending

money to the government, whenever this is required - a nation is truly free and civilised when it has reached the level at which free education at all levels can be given without the threat to liberty, morality and religion - Technical knowledge needs to be diffused through schools, but practical ability in production must be acquired in farms and factories - The fiscal burden needs to be distributed as much as possible in relation to the wealth of the citizens ... - The aim of the government is to keep the cost of living down as much as possible; the greater the financial sacrifice asked of the citizens - for instance in view of the war - the lower must be the cost of living."

(A Plebano quoted in *Cavour and the Unification of Italy* p 150-151 M Salvadori D Van Nostrand Company Inc 1961)

Under Cavour's guidance, Sardinia was modernised. Duties were reduced to encourage trade and free trade treaties were signed with Britain, France and Belgium. The railways were expanded rapidly and merchant shipping was developed using the latest ideas in steamship building. Reforms in banking and commercial law encouraged the growth of industry. The powers of the Catholic Church were reduced: it lost its special courts; its property rights were limited; religious orders which did no practical work were banned; and church control over marriages was ended. The army and navy were overhauled. Sardinia was thus made ready for the role she was shortly to undertake. The historian, G Procacci, has succinctly described the outcome of his economic policy:

"The fruits of this economic policy soon appeared: at the beginning of 1859 Piedmont had 859 kilometres of railways, privately and publicly owned, as against 986 kilometres in all the rest of Italy. Its foreign trade was markedly better than that of the neighbouring Lombard -Venetian Kingdom; whereas in the rest of Italy economic development marked time after its rise between 1830 and 1846, Piedmont was the one state able to keep up, to some extent, with the dizzy rise of Europe's capitalist economy."

(G Procacci *History of the Italian People* p254 Wiedenfield and Nicholson 1970)

The Need for Allies
Victor Emmanuel and Cavour had learned a lesson from 1848, namely that there was no chance of Austrian power being overthrown by the Italians on their own. Change in Italy could only come with the help of a major foreign power. The chance to win the sympathy of Britain and France came during the Crimean War of 1854-6 when Sardinia sent troops to help the allies against Russia. This earned Cavour a place at the Peace Conference in Paris and he used the occasion to raise the Italian question and try to gain the support of France and Britain. Commenting on Sardinia's apparent lack of gains from the war he said,

"What benefit then has Italy gained from the Congress? We have gained two things, first, that the anomalous and unhappy condition of Italy has been declared to Europe, not by demagogues, or revolutionaries .. but by representatives of the greatest nations in Europe; by statesmen at the head of their countries' Governments ... The second is that these same powers

have declared that, not only in the interests of Italy herself, but in the interests of Europe, a remedy must be found for the evils from which Italy is suffering. I cannot believe that the sentiments expressed and the advice given by such nations as France and England can remain for long sterile of results."

(Michael Morrogh *The Unification of Italy:Documents and Debates* Pub. Macmillan p57 quoted in AJ Whyte *The Political Life and Letters of Cavour* Oxford 1930 p222-3)

Napoleon III of France seemed the best choice for an ally against Austria. He was very ambitious and wanted to make his mark on the European scene like his famous uncle Napoleon I. Moreover, in his youth he had been involved with the Carbonari and he had often expressed his sympathy with the Italian cause. Cavour worked hard to improve relations between Napoleon and Sardinia.

Then in 1858 there was what at first sight seemed like a disaster. A Mazzinian extremist, Orsini, tried to assassinate the French Emperor at the Opera in Paris and, although he missed his target, many others were killed. However, this incident had a surprising effect on Napoleon. At his trial, Orsini made a noble speech justifying his action and pleading the case for freedom for Italy. Napoleon seems to have been greatly impressed; presumably he was reminded of his own early ideals. Certainly, events now began to move fast.

The Deal with Napoleon III
In July 1858, Cavour and Napoleon met in great secrecy at Plombieres, a French spa town near the Swiss border. They drew up a pact by which the French agreed to help the Sardinians to drive the Austrians out of Lombardy and Venetia, and set up a new North Italian state.

"...The valley of the Po, the Romagna and the Legations (part of the Papal States) would form a kingdom of Upper Italy under the House of Savoy. Rome and its immediate surroundings would be left to the Pope. The rest of the Papal States together with Tuscany, would form a kingdom of central Italy. The Neapolitan frontier would be left unchanged. These four Italian States would form a confederation on the pattern of the German Bund the presidency of which would be given to the Pope to console him ... After we had settled the fate of Italy, the Emperor asked me what France would get and whether Your Majesty would cede Savoy and the county of Nice. I answered that Your Majesty believed in the principle of nationalities and realised accordingly that Savoy ought to be reunited with France ... "

(Michael Morrogh *The Unification of Italy:Documents and Debates* Pub. Macmillan p59 quoted in D Beales *The Risorgimento and the Unification of Italy* p132-3)

Napoleon insisted that the Austrians must appear to be the aggressors, so Cavour set about provoking them into action. Anti-Austrian speeches in parliament and a series of troop movements and frontier incidents soon had the Austrians so enraged that they issued an ultimatum to Sardinia demanding that she should demobilise her armies. Naturally Cavour refused and the Austrians declared war. Within a few days Napoleon had in his turn declared war in support of his ally and the die was cast.

War with Austria

The war of 1859 was a short and bloody one. The French and Sardinian armies won two victories at Magenta and Solferino, at the cost of heavy casualties on both sides. (The Red Cross was founded by a Swiss doctor who witnessed the carnage at Magenta and was appalled at the lack of care for the wounded.) Then suddenly, without consulting his ally, Napoleon signed the Peace of Villafranca with the Austrians. His motives are not entirely clear.

A simplistic view is that he was appalled by the bloodshed his victories had cost and was fearful of the even greater casualties to be expected in an attack on the Quadrilateral, to which the Austrians had retreated. More likely he was taken aback by the results of his own policies. The outbreak of the war had been the signal for revolutions in the Duchies and parts of the Papal States. All of them were now asking to join Sardinia. Events were going much further than he had intended. He had aimed to create a small, grateful client state in North Italy, not a powerful new neighbour. The threat to the Papal States was especially embarrassing since there were still French troops there protecting the Pope. The Catholic Party in France was infuriated by his support for the Nationalists. Also he must have been worried about the intentions of the Prussians who had begun to mobilise their army. If they came to Austria's help he would face a war on two fronts.

Peace

The deal reached by Napoleon with the Austrians arranged for Lombardy to be handed over to France to give to Sardinia. Venetia, however, was to remain Austrian. An Italian Confederation was to be set up under the presidency of the Pope who was asked to consider reforms in his states. Cavour was in despair. After a furious row with Victor Emmanuel in which he tried to persuade the King to continue the war without the French, he resigned.

There remained the problem of what was to happen to Tuscany, Parma, Modena and the Romagna (the northern Papal States), all of which were still demanding union with Sardinia. Napoleon was not happy about such a large extension of Sardinian territory. Finally Cavour returned to office in 1860 and negotiated a deal which satisfied both sides. Plebiscites were held in the Duchies and Romagna on union with Sardinia; needless to say the vote in favour was overwhelming. At the same time, plebiscites in Savoy and Nice cleared the way for them to be handed over to France.

Thus Napoleon had emerged from the crisis with useful gains for France while Sardinia was now the head of a large North Italian state; and it was all legitimised by popular votes.

GARIBALDI AND THE THOUSAND

Scarcely had the North Italian question been settled when there was a fresh revolution in Sicily. This was the start of one of the most remarkable episodes in modern history, the conquest of Southern Italy by Garibaldi and a thousand volunteers.

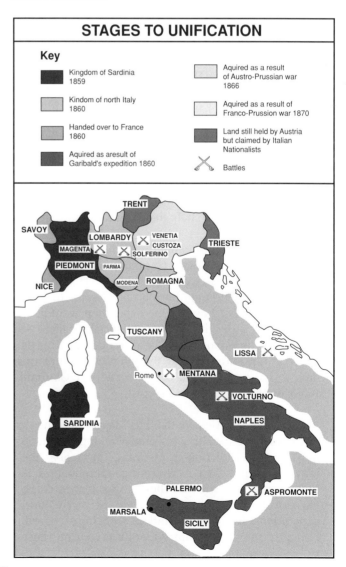

Brave, straightforward, headstrong, not very intelligent, Garibaldi was very different from Cavour the subtle, aristocratic politician. Born at Nice, he had led an adventurous youth, running away to sea when he was fifteen. He became involved with Mazzini's 'Young Italy' movement and was condemned to death for his part in the unsuccessful revolution of 1833. He escaped and spent the next twelve years in South America. Here he learned the art of soldiering, raising a guerrilla army of Italian exiles to fight for Uruguay against Brazil and Argentina. It was at this time that he adopted the famous 'Redshirt' uniform, possibly borrowed from the slaughterhouses of Buenos Aires.

It was also in South America that he met his first wife Anita, carrying her off in a whirlwind romance, though she was already pledged to another man. He is supposed to have spotted her from the deck of a ship. His first words on meeting her were, "You must be mine." She was to accompany him on all his adventures until her death in 1849, during the retreat from Rome.

In 1848 Garibaldi and his men returned to Italy and fought first against the Austrians in the north then against the French in Rome. Although they were defeated, the story of the defence of Rome and the heroic forced march of the 'Garibaldini' across the Appenine Mountains in an attempt to bring help to the last republican stronghold of Venice became an epic tale to inspire all nationalists. After the failures of 1848, Garibaldi once again fled into exile.

The Thousand and the Capture of Sicily
By 1859 he was back in Italy and took part in the war with Austria. Then in 1860 came shocking news; his home town Nice was to be handed over to France. Garibaldi was sure that the plebiscite was a fraud. He was actually preparing to raid Nice to destroy the ballot boxes when, fortunately for the history of Italy, he was diverted by the news of a rebellion in Sicily. The reports of events in the north and the death of the hated King 'Bomba' had combined to produce a rebellion among the Sicilian peasants. This was the moment Garibaldi had been waiting for. He gathered an army of a thousand volunteers at Genoa, ready to sail at a moment's notice to help the Sicilians.

Cavour and Victor Emmanuel were now faced with a serious dilemma. To prevent Garibaldi's expedition, perhaps by arresting him, would have been very unpopular - and in any case he might bring useful gains to Italian unity. On the other hand, if the expedition went ahead Austria or France might intervene, especially if there was any threat to the Papal States. The attitude of the King and Cavour is not entirely clear though Victor Emmanuel seems to have been quite keen to support Garibaldi. Cavour wrote in a letter on 24 April:

"I have reason to believe that His Majesty who has a weakness for Garibaldi ... is secretly looking to remove me from the direction of affairs ... (In Genoa) the Mazzinian agitation is regaining strength and is rallying around Garibaldi. There is a desire to force the Government to come to the aid of Sicily, and expeditions of arms and munitions are being prepared. I suspect the King of imprudently favouring these

projects. I have given orders for a close watch to be kept and to stop - if that is possible - these desperate endeavours."
(Michael Morrogh - op cit p80-1 Cavour writing to Nigra 24-4-1860 from AJ Whyte op cit p391)

This suggests that there was a major difference of opinion between the King and Cavour and that Cavour himself was totally opposed to Garibaldi's plans. Yet at the same time he seems to have given other people the impression that he wanted the expedition to go ahead but dared not risk giving it public support. Historians still argue about whether Cavour and Victor Emmanuel were in fact engaged in some sort of double game, giving covert support to Garibaldi while publicly disowning him.

Certainly, every possible obstacle was put in Garibaldi's way, short of actually stopping him. He was prevented from getting modern rifles and his recruiting efforts were blocked. It was made clear that he was acting without the backing of Sardinia. Cavour even sent orders for his arrest to the governor of Cagliari in Sardinia - after he had sailed.

"Garibaldi has embarked with 400 volunteers ... If he enters a port of Sardinia arrest the expedition. I authorise you to employ, if required, the squadron commanded by Count Persano ... Do not arrest the expedition out at sea. Only if it enters a port."
(Michael Morrogh op cit p83 from G M Trevelyan *Garibaldi and the Thousand* London 1909 p206)

Admiral Persano interpreted this to mean he was not to interfere with Garibaldi.

What happened next was little short of miraculous. Garibaldi's ill-equipped little force could easily have been stopped from landing in Sicily by the Neapolitan navy. However, their arrival at Marsala coincided with that of two British ships which were there to protect British property. The British were known to be sympathetic to the Italian cause which may help to explain what happened. The Neapolitan commander seems to have mistaken Garibaldi's Redshirts for red-coated British marines and, fearing a quarrel with Britain, allowed them to land unopposed.

Soon Garibaldi had gathered more recruits bringing his army up to about 3000 men and he was able to advance towards Palermo. Here he skilfully out-flanked an army of 20,000 government troops and captured the city. Sicily was his. His only problem now was to end the violent peasants' revolts which had started the whole crisis. He urgently wanted to get on with the next stage of his plan - the invasion of Naples. Minor concessions to the peasants did not bring peace so he used force against them, a measure which won him the support of the landowners but left the peasants bitter.

Cavour, the British and the
Crossing of the Straits of Messina
Garibaldi now prepared to cross the straits of Messina and attack Naples. Cavour was extremely worried by this. He was not entirely certain of Garibaldi's loyalty. Although Garibaldi had so far said he was operating on behalf of

Victor Emmanuel, he was not prepared to accept instructions from Sardinia and there was always the risk that he might remember his old loyalties to Mazzini and the republican movement. Cavour wrote to the Sardinian Ambassador in London:-

"Garibaldi has let himself become intoxicated by success and by the praise showered on him from all over Europe. He is planning the wildest, not to say absurdest schemes. As he remains devoted to King Victor Emmanuel, he will not help Mazzini or republicanism. But he feels it is his vocation to liberate all Italy, stage by stage, before turning her over to the King. He is thus putting off the day when Sicily will demand annexation to Piedmont, for he wants to keep the dictatorial powers that will allow him to raise an army to conquer first Naples, then Rome, and in the end Venice."

(Michael Morrogh op cit p88 *Cavour to Nigra 12-7-1860* from D Mack Smith *The Making of Italy 1796-1866* London 1988 p325-6)

It was clear that, with Naples conquered, Garibaldi would march north and attack Rome, a move that would have disastrous consequences, since it would certainly provoke outside intervention. (The French still had a garrison there defending the Pope.) On the other hand if Garibaldi's activities could be controlled then Sardinia might profit from them.

Precisely what policy Cavour and Victor Emmanuel followed is still a subject of argument. Publicly they discouraged Garibaldi from attacking Naples (though in private the King seems to have been in favour of the idea). Cavour even tried to set off a pro-Sardinian revolution there, which would forestall Garibaldi. On the other hand they seem to have used secret diplomacy to stop other powers from interfering. When the French proposed a joint Anglo-French naval force to stop Garibaldi from crossing the straits of Messina, Cavour publicly supported the idea but privately urged the British to oppose it. The British government was friendly to the Italian cause and used its influence to make sure that no outside power sent ships to the area. With little opposition from the Neapolitans, Garibaldi's army crossed the straits and marched towards Naples. The royal armies crumbled and he entered the city virtually unopposed.

Cavour now decided to take a major gamble. The only way of checking Garibaldi's advance northwards was for the Sardinian army itself to invade the Papal States and advance south to meet him. Cavour won Napoleon's backing for this move by promising that Rome itself would not be attacked. The Sardinian armies headed south, carefully by-passing Rome, and entered Neapolitan territory.

Meanwhile Garibaldi had been fighting the last battle of the campaign on the Volturno River. On 27 October the King and Garibaldi met at Teano and a few days later Garibaldi formally handed his conquests over to Victor Emmanuel. Shortly afterwards his army was disbanded and, disillusioned with politics, he retired to the island of Caprera where he had a small farm. Meanwhile the usual plebiscites confirmed the inclusion of Naples and Sicily

GARIBALDI THE LIBERATOR;
Or, The Modern Perseus.

Punch expresses its warm support for Garibaldi's liberation of Sicily

and most of the Papal States in the Italian kingdom.

"Like all mediocre men, Victor Emmanuel is jealous and quick to take offence. He will find it difficult to forget the manner of his triumphal entry into Naples, when, seated in Garibaldi's carriage - Garibaldi in a red shirt - he was presented to his people by the most powerful of all his subjects. People are mistaken in crediting Victor Emmanuel with a liking for Garibaldi... After all what sovereign, placed in the same situation, would not resent the fabulous prestige of Garibaldi's name?" (A comment by one of the French Embassy staff)

(Andrina Stiles op cit p 67)

THE LAST STAGES - ANTICLIMAX

Only Rome and Venetia now remained to be won. Unfortunately in 1861 Cavour died suddenly; his political skill was to be greatly missed in the next few years. The last chapter in Italian unification was to be an inglorious affair after the triumphs of 1859-60.

In 1862, Garibaldi tried to repeat his earlier successes. He raised an army of volunteers and headed for Rome. However, the Italian government dared not risk confrontation with the French army in Rome, so it was their troops who stopped him. Garibaldi's actions brought Italy close to civil war. He himself was injured in an undignified scuffle, trying to stop fighting between his own Garibaldini and the Sardinian army at Aspromonte.

"'We're also expecting Colonel Pallavicino, who did

King Victor Emmanuel meets with Garibaldi at Teano

so well at Aspromonte.' This phrase from the Prince of Ponteleone was not as simple as it sounded. On the surface it was a remark without political meaning, mere praise for the tact, the delicacy, the respect, the tenderness almost with which the Colonel had got a bullet fired into General Garibaldi's foot; and for the accompaniment too, the bowing, kneeling and hand-kissing of the wounded Hero ... At heart, though, Ponteleone thought that the Colonel 'did so well' by managing to stop, defeat, wound and capture Garibaldi, in doing so saving the compromise so laboriously achieved between the old state of things and the new."

(Giuseppe di Lampedusa *The Leopard* Collins and Harvell Press revised edition 1961 p175)

After this dismal episode came further humiliation. In 1866 Italy allied herself with Prussia against Austria in the Austro-Prussian War. In the subsequent fighting, the Italians suffered two crushing defeats, on land at Custoza and on sea at Lissa. However the Prussians had completely overwhelmed the Austrians at Sadowa so, when peace was made, Italy got her promised reward, Venetia. (For more details see the section on Italian Foreign Policy 1860-90 p34-36.)

In 1867 Garibaldi's obsession with Rome got the better of him again. He was convinced that the Italian Government had betrayed the national cause by making an agreement with the French about Rome. Once again his forces marched on the city; this time he was stopped by French troops at Mentana.

However, in 1870 Rome fell into the hands of the Italians after France's defeat in the Franco-Prussian War. Provoked into a disastrous war by the Prussian Chancellor Bismarck, Napoleon III was defeated and captured at Sedan. The French troops were withdrawn from Rome and so Italian soldiers were able to capture the city without any real fighting. Italian unification was complete at last even if it had not, in the end, been a very glorious achievement. The King was now able to move his administration to Rome, the natural capital of Italy.

Unfortunately, the beginning of the new state was marred by a quarrel with the Pope. He was allowed to keep a small area round his palace the Vatican. However, he refused to accept the loss of his possessions or to recognise the new Italian state and retired into self-inflicted imprisonment in the Vatican. The quarrel was not to be settled until 1929 and was to be a continuing problem for the government.

Someone else who condemned what had happened was Mazzini, for the new state bore little resemblance to his dream of a democratic, republican Italy, united by a popular revolution. He commented bitterly

"I had thought to evoke the soul of Italy, but all I find before me is a corpse ... (The country is) rotten with materialism and egoism." (D Mack Smith *Italy: A Modern History* University of Michigan 1969 p14)

A UNIFIED STATE?

The union of Italy in 1860 did not bring tranquillity. On the contrary, the new state was faced with many problems, some of which have never been fully resolved. To make matters worse Cavour died suddenly of a fever in June

1861, depriving the infant state of its greatest politician. The men who ruled Italy in the next fifteen years tried to follow his policies as far as possible, but they lacked his genius.

One major cause of strain in the new state was the way it had been brought into being - not by a great popular revolution as Mazzini and his supporters had hoped, but as a result of the military and diplomatic activities of one state, Sardinia. In a sense what had happened was not so much unification as a takeover by Sardinia of the rest of the Italian peninsula. Significantly, Victor Emmanuel II did not change his title to Victor Emmanuel I of Italy. Until 1866 when the government moved to Florence, Turin in Piedmont remained the capital, though it was dreadfully out of the way for MPs from the centre and south. During the early years after unity most of the government ministers were either Piedmontese or 'Piedmontezzani' (supporters of Piedmont/Sardinia).

Apart from educated middle-class liberals, few people had any real sense of being 'Italian'. Many of the revolts of the previous fifty years had been *against* bad governments rather than *for* unity. Regional loyalties remained very strong. There was not even a national language; the people spoke their own regional dialects - Venetian, Tuscan, Sicilian, etc. - which were virtually incomprehensible to those from other parts of Italy. 'Italian' was a fancy literary language used only by writers - and sometimes not even by them. (Cavour preferred to write in French!)

There was particular resentment against Sardinian control in the south. The rebellion in Sicily in 1860 had begun because of local grievances and had really been hijacked by Garibaldi. When he failed to satisfy the demands of the people he had come to 'liberate' they turned on him. As we have seen, Garibaldi put down the revolt with considerable force, causing much bitterness. In Calabria too there were soon risings against the new government by discontented peasants who felt that it was even less willing to deal with their grievances than the old Neapolitan government had been. These rebellions, officially labelled as 'brigandage' by the government, took four years to suppress and cost the Sardinian army more casualties than the Wars of Independence had done.

On their side, the Sardinians found it hard to understand the very different society of southern Italy which Cavour described as " ... the weakest and most corrupt part of Italy." They were appalled by the backwardness, ignorance and superstition of the southern peasantry and a sort of racism developed between North and South which still lingers on today. For the authorities the obvious answer was strong government to restore law and order; in practice this meant summary arrests and executions. To some people the 'liberation' of southern Italy seemed more like a colonial conquest of the South by the North.

The problems were made worse by the form of the new government. Some politicians had suggested that the new state should be a *federal* one allowing each region to keep considerable control over local affairs. However, this was rejected in favour of a *unitary* state with a highly centralised government. Prefects were appointed by central government with wide powers to run the cities and districts. If the government had represented the mass of the people, this centralisation might not have been too serious, but the constitution was a very narrow one which restricted the right to vote to a small minority.

The constitution of Italy was simply an extension to the whole peninsula of the constitution or Statuto drawn up for Sardinia by Charles Albert in 1848. Although it was by the standards of the time a 'liberal' constitution, it was very far from being democratic. A great deal of power had been reserved for the King.

> "The King alone has the executive power. He is the supreme head of state, commands all the armed forces by sea and land, declares war makes treaties of peace, of alliance, of commerce, but giving notice of them to the two houses as far as security and national interest permit ..."
> (Article 3). (D Mack Smith *Italy: A Modern History* University of Michigan 1969 p28)

The wording of the Statuto had been deliberately vague on whether ministers were to be responsible to the King or to parliament. On several occasions Cavour and his successors had problems with Victor Emmanuel when he tried to follow an independent policy (eg. he encouraged Garibaldi's march on Rome). Lanza the Prime Minister 1869-73 remarked of Victor Emmanuel,

> "The King is in practice his own minister of foreign affairs, and in order to form his policy he keeps up a secret and direct correspondence of his own with our ambasssadors and with Louis Napoleon. This may not be constitutional but it is unfortunately a fact."
> (Ibid p105)

Crispi, Prime Minister in the 1890s, said about King Umberto,

> "When the King turns against a ministry he conspires in parliament with the deputies he thinks most influential and organises a hostile movement."
> (Ibid p 203)

Clearly the King's power to intervene in affairs was considerable.

Parliament consisted of two chambers. The members of the upper house, the Senate, were nominated by the King for life. The lower house was elected, but since voters had to be over twenty five, literate and meet a property qualification, only about 2% of the population of Italy actually qualified for the vote. The tiny number of voters was particularly obvious in the poor and mainly illiterate south.

The result was that for the vast majority of Italians the state appeared to be a remote organisation which had little to do with the daily concerns of ordinary people. It only touched their lives when they had to pay their taxes or their men-folk were conscripted for military service. This alienation of the majority made doubly difficult the task of unifying the different elements which made up Italy into a coherent national state.

Some Arguments about Italian Unification

The first writers about the unification of Italy saw the events as part of an inevitable process to which the four great heroes, Mazzini, Victor Emmanuel, Cavour and Garibaldi each contributed a vital share. More critical modern writers, however, have challenged this point of view. They suggest that there were profound differences of opinion dividing the four and that often they worked against each other.

"The new Italy emerged out of the basic conflict of the opposing patriotic forces and the personal hostility of the leaders, not out of what traditional historiography was long inclined to interpret as the complementary and implicitly harmonious roles of the four 'heroic' leaders - Victor Emmanuel, Cavour, Garibaldi and Mazzini - walking arm-in-arm towards a preordained unified state."
(Stuart Woolf, *History of Italy 1700-1860*, 1979 quoted in Andrina Stiles *The Unification of Italy* p88 Edward Arnold 1986)

Most writers agree on the inspirational role of Mazzini:-

"In a country where Machiavellianism in politics is often debased to a mere form of scepticism, Mazzini's asceticism, his statement that 'thought and action' must be absolutely one, demanded respect from his opponents and excited enthusiasm among his followers, raising the general level of political life to a new tension and seriousness. In this sense the influence of Mazzini in the history of the Risorgimento can hardly be overestimated, and goes well beyond the confines of the political movement he directly inspired and organized."
(G Procacci *History of the Italian People* p288 Pelican Books 1973)

But Mazzini has his critics too. His activities in the 1850s, when he continued to encourage a popular, republican revolution as opposed to the more diplomatic approach being taken by the Piedmontese moderates, have provoked this comment by W R Thayer: "If Piedmont had taken [Mazzini's] advice after 1850, there would have been neither independence nor unity." (William Roscoe Thayer as quoted in C Delzell, *The Unification of Italy 1859-61* Holt, Rinehart & Winston, 1965)

A recent text on *The Unification of Italy 1815-70* by Andrina Stiles gives a more balanced view of Mazzini's work in the complex process of unification.

"Whose is the credit for unifying Italy? The question has been discussed at length by historians since 1861. The *Risorgimento*, the Italian movement of 'resurgence' or 'national rebirth', which began in the eighteenth century, had gained ground in the early decades of the nineteenth century through the secret societies and under the leadership of Mazzini. He provided the intellectual basis for the nationalist movement, as well as the inspiration for revolution among those, like Garibaldi, with whom he came in contact, but his writings were too academic to have a wide readership or much popular influence." (Andrina Stiles, *The Unification of Italy 1815-70*, p 87 Edward Arnold, 1986)

However, the Italian historian Luigi Salvatorelli has argued that the Mazzinians can take credit for pushing Cavour and Napoleon III into action in the 1850s.

"The three most important events in bringing about unity were: the insurrections in central Italy, the expedition to Sicily, and the expedition into the Marches and Umbria. All three were Mazzinian inspired examples of 'thought and action', and popular and revolutionary enterprises."
(Charles F Delzell, *The Unification of Italy, 1859-1861*, p 32 Holt, Rinehart & Winston, 1965)

Not surprisingly the debate over the respective roles of Cavour and Garibaldi has been lengthy and long-standing. Initially the dominant role in unifying Italy was attributed to Cavour. This was mainly due to the circulation of the pro-Piedmontese version of events by Piedmontese scholars and acceptance of that particular view by late 19th and early 20th century British historians. Arthur J Whyte was one such British historian writing in the 1920s.

"Cavour is known in history as the architect of the modern Kingdom of Italy ... It was Cavour who by wise domestic policy first won the respect and confidence of Europe, and later by a bold and hazardous statesmanship sent the flower of the little Sardinian army to the aid of France and England in the Crimea, raising the prestige of Italy and earning the gratitude of the Western Powers. It was Cavour who pilloried Austria in the eyes of Europe at the Congress of Paris and knew how to utilise the defeat of Russia to wean England from her traditional alliance with Austria to become the warm supporter of Italian freedom. Finally, it was the same clear brain and firm hand which brought Napoleon III into Italy in 1859, broke the power of Austria and kept Italy free from foreign interference while Garibaldi won the Kingdom of Naples for Italy and Victor Emmanuel."
(Charles F Delzell, *The Unification if Italy, 1859-1861*, p 12 Holt, Rinehart & Winston, 1965)

Even today Cavour's role is still regarded as vital, as can be seen in a recent book by Denis Mack Smith in which he argues that, despite various errors by Cavour on the road to unification, he was ultimately most successful.

"The unification of Italy was in the end a great success story, but some incidental mishaps along the way are an essential part of the picture and throw into relief the full extent of the ultimate triumph. Sometimes Cavour appeared to be at the edge of total failure; sometimes he made what by his own admission were serious mistakes

of judgment and employed methods that he knew would be thought discreditable; often he appeared to be the plaything of circumstance as events seemed to conspire against him. Cavour's ability can be appreciated only after tracing not only his successes, but the difficulties, the uncertainties, the errors, and what he himself referred to as the less admirable side of his handiwork. His capacity to recover from mistakes and exploit adverse conditions was an essential ingredient in what was empirical statesmanship of the very highest order. No politician of the century - certainly not Bismarck - made so much out of so little. It was a thousand pities that he did not live long enough to apply his skill and intelligence to the initial problems of the kingdom that he did so much to create."
(Denis Mack Smith, *Cavour*, p xii Weidenfeld & Nicolson, 1985)

On the other hand, Garibaldi's part in the proceedings has not been overlooked by sympathetic British historians such as Denis Mack Smith and his mentor, George Macaulay Trevelyan. Both have argued that the differences, disagreements and mutual suspicion between Garibaldi and Cavour were vital for the unification of Italy. More recently Andrina Stiles has supported this viewpoint.

"Did the new Italy arise out of conflict? Certainly there was hostility between Cavour and Garibaldi. If Cavour had not distrusted Garibaldi and feared in 1860 that he might make himself ruler of an independent southern Italy, and that it might even be a republic, he would not have made the decisive move to invade the Papal States, which still divided Italy geographically ... It was Cavour's greatest contribution to unification that his invasion of the Papal States effectively prevented Garibaldi from carrying out the second part of his plan, the attack on Rome, just as it was Garibaldi's greatest contribution that he was able to carry out the first part, the conquest of Sicily and Naples, despite Cavour."

Undoubtedly too Garibaldi's vacating of the political scene in 1860 made the task of unification easier:

"Garibaldi's readiness to surrender Sicily and Naples to Victor Emmanuel avoided civil war and left the field clear for Cavour and Piedmont to take over Italy."
(Andrina Stiles, *The Unification of Italy, 1815-70*, p 89 Edward Arnold, 1986)

As for Victor Emmanuel's role, Italians consider him more important than would British historians:

"Victor Emmanuel II, King of Piedmont and first King of a united Italy, the *Re galantuomo* (the gallant King), played little active part in the *Risorgimento*. He enjoyed great personal popularity however, with his bluff and hearty manner, and perhaps because of the now largely discredited belief that he alone defied the Austrians and maintained the constitution in 1849, he is regarded by Italians as one of the heroes of the movement. Non-Italians have been less enthusiastic and are inclined to agree that his claim to fame is that he simply 'allowed Italy to create herself'. He was there at the right time and place to be the figurehead for Italian nationalism. As Garibaldi said, 'let Italy be one under the *Re galantuomo* who is the symbol of our regeneration and of the prosperity of our country'. It was who he was, not what he did, that gained Victor Emmanuel his place in *Risorgimento* history.
(Andrina Stiles, *The Unification of Italy, 1815-70*, p 89-90 Edward Arnold, 1986)

No discussion on the unification would be complete without considering the important contribution made by Napoleon III of France. Although ignored by many British historians, LCB Seaman and AJP Taylor, and more recently Andrina Stiles, have attempted to redress the balance:

"And the later observer must confess that the unification of Italy might well have been impossible, unless Napoleon III had been brought in to defeat Austria in 1859. After all, the victory of nationalism was not inevitable. Poland had to wait until the twentieth century, despite a much stronger national sentiment."
(AJP Taylor, *Europe: Grandeur and Decline*, p 83 Pelican, 1967)

"British historians have largely ignored the other important figure in the unification of Italy, a non-Italian, who has generally had a bad press, Napoleon III of France. Whatever his motives, the fact remains that without his involvement and support, the Austrians would not have been driven out of Italy and an independent and united Italy would have been impossible. Many Italians must have echoed Garibaldi's words after the Peace of Villafranca: 'Do not forget the gratitude we owe to Napoleon III and to the French army, so many of whose valiant sons have been killed or maimed for the cause of Italy.' "
(Andrina Stiles, *The Unification of Italy 1815-70*, p 90 Edward Arnold, 1986)

Perhaps the final words in this matter should be left to the Italian historian Giuliano Procacci.

"The idea of Cavour as the diplomatic and patient weaver of the slowly-achieved unity of Italy is one of the most commonly accepted. But it would be wrong to suppose that the goal of unity, which he was in fact to achieve, was clear before his eyes from the beginning, or that all his diplomatic activity was directed towards this great end. For as we shall see, up to a quite late date Cavour considered the unity of Italy under the house of Savoy to be a practically unattainable objective, and his talent was not an inflexible ability to wait for situations to mature and the days of decision to arrive, but rather the empiricism of a statesman who knew how to draw the maximum advantage from situations and circumstances as they gradually arose. He was able to do this because he was fully aware of the fact that, as events were to show, the existence of an unclearly-defined European political situation was an indispensable condition for any Italian initiative."
(Giuliano Procacci, *History of the Italian People*, p 256 Weidenfeld & Nicolson, 1970)

4 The Character of the New Nation State of Italy 1860 - 1914

ROME AND THE CATHOLIC QUESTION

Article 1 of the Statuto stated:

> "The apostolic Roman Catholic religion is the only religion of the state. Other cults now existing are tolerated, in conformity with the law."
>
> (Michael Morrogh op cit p19 Article 1 of the Statuto from D Mack Smith *The Making of Italy 1796-1866* London 1988 p136)

This seemed to guarantee the position of the Roman Catholic Church but in fact relations between Church and state were a continuing problem.

As we have seen, the uniting of Rome with Italy came about as a result of the collapse of the Pope's protector, France, in the Franco-Prussian War, rather than because of the efforts of the Italian government. Indeed the government had felt obliged to intervene to stop Garibaldi and his supporters from reaching Rome in 1862, so as to avoid a confrontation with France and the rest of Catholic Europe - a decision which infuriated the more extreme nationalists.

In 1866 the government negotiated a deal with the French by which they were to remove their troops from Rome in return for a guarantee that the Italian government itself would protect the Papal States. Garibaldi's second attack on Rome in 1867 was largely caused by the anger which many nationalists felt at this 'betrayal' by the government. His actions gave the French an excuse to send their soldiers back to Rome; the attempt to find a political solution had failed.

When in 1870 it was at last possible for the Italian army to march into Rome, much was made of the event; photos showed soldiers in action making a breach in the city wall. In fact though, resistance was nominal and Rome was captured without any heroism - a sad letdown for those nationalists who remembered the exciting days of 1860.

The capture of Rome marked the start of a quarrel with the Pope which would embitter Italian political life for many years to come. The government did try to reconcile Pius IX to the loss of his temporal power (as ruler of a state) by offering him certain rights, including an annual payment of three million lire. However, the Pope rejected any compromise; he shut himself in the Vatican and placed the Italian government under a Papal anathema (condemnation). Catholics were forbidden to take any part in politics either as voters or as candidates for parliament. Other Catholic powers were urged to deny recognition of Italy. Even before the fall of Rome, the Pope had effectively declared war on all liberal ideas in the *Syllabus of Errors* of 1864, while the doctrine of Papal Infallibility of 1869 stated that on moral and spiritual matters the Pope's word was to be final and binding on all Catholics. Thus from the start the Italian state had to face a serious challenge to its authority and legitimacy and this led to a sense of insecurity at home and abroad.

For Italian Catholics too, the Pope's attitude caused a serious crisis of conscience. Cavour, although his policies had earned him Papal condemnation, was nevertheless a sincere Catholic who sought the last rites of the Church on his deathbed. (The priest who attended him was later sacked.) His dilemma was shared by all those Italians who were forced to choose between their desire to serve their nation and their religious faith. At first, when the number of voters was very small, the nonparticipation of the Catholics was not a very obvious problem. As the vote was extended to a wider number of people, though, there was a growing desire among Catholics to get involved in their country's affairs.

In practice, at a local level Church and state often tolerated each other fairly well. After all, the Constitution recognised Catholicism as the official religion of Italy, but at the national level Church-state relations were very bitter. The consequence was a growing anti-clericalism (anti-church feeling) among Italian liberals which sometimes resulted in violence against the Church. During the funeral of Pius IX an angry mob threatened to throw his corpse into the river Tiber! Government Prefects often banned religious festivals and processions on the grounds that they were a danger to public order.

During the 1880s there were attempts to open negotiations between the Pope and the government. However the Pope refused to cooperate and the Benedictine monk who had been the government's contact man was made to 'retire' to the monastery of Monte Cassino. Hostilities resumed. In 1898 during a serious crisis, the Catholics found themselves being treated like any other dissident group, their leaders arrested and their newspapers closed down. In the years before the First World War, the government of G Giolitti did take a more conciliatory line, discouraging anti-clericalism among government officials. There was, however, no formal accord between Church and state until 1929.

ITALIAN POLITICS

A glance at the list of Prime Ministers on page 27 makes it obvious that one of the big problems for the Italian state was the chronic instability of its governments. In the fifty four years between 1860 and 1914 Italy had no fewer than thirty two prime ministers, many of whom lasted only a few months. This was because Italy did not have a strong parliamentary system like, for example, Britain.

For a start, the King retained considerable power. He could and sometimes did intervene directly in affairs, regardless of elections and parliamentary majorities. In 1898 for example, when Italy was on the brink of a revo-

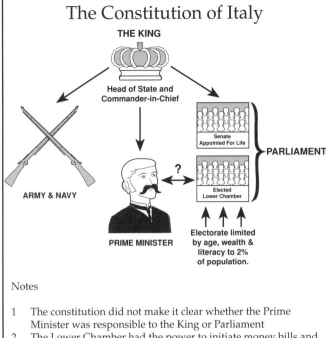

The Constitution of Italy

THE KING

Head of State and Commander-in-Chief

PARLIAMENT

Senate Appointed For Life

Elected Lower Chamber

PRIME MINISTER

?

ARMY & NAVY

Electorate limited by age, wealth & literacy to 2% of population.

Notes

1   The constitution did not make it clear whether the Prime Minister was responsible to the King or Parliament
2   The Lower Chamber had the power to initiate money bills and was the more influential of the two.
3   The king kept considerable powers to deal with foreign policy.
4   Local officials - prefects, police chiefs etc. were appointed by the central government.

Extensions to the Vote:
1882 - Vote extended to 7% of the population
1912 - Vote given to all males over 30

lution due to a wave of strikes and riots, King Umberto I appointed his own nominee, General Pelloux, as Prime Minister. The king also played a big part in shaping foreign policy. The foreign minister was often chosen by him and he might also deal directly with his ambassadors without consulting his ministers. The Triple Alliance was largely the work of King Umberto.

The most significant factor in the weakness of parliamentary government was the lack of a real party system. Apart from the extreme Socialists, there were no proper parties with clear aims and policies. A prime minister built up his parliamentary majority by winning the support of deputies from a range of political groups. Every Italian government was a coalition of deputies who shared, for the moment at least, similar interests. Most governments were either moderate right or moderate left and there were even governments which included both 'left' and 'right' ministers. This system of using coalitions became known as *Trasformismo* (transformism) after a speech by Agostino Depretis in 1876 in which he said:-

"I hope my words will help bring about the fertile transformation of parties, and the unification of all shades of liberals in parliament, in exchange for those old parliamentary labels so often abused ... Whereas it used to be said that the government represented a party, we intend to rule in the interests of everyone ... and will accept the help of all loyal and honest men of whatever group."
(D Mack Smith *Italy: A Modern History* University of Michigan 1969 p110 & 113)

Depretis supplied the name and he developed

transformism to a fine art, but the idea was not new. Since the time of Cavour, prime ministers had used this method to secure majorities. However, these broad-based coalitions were inherently unstable and rarely lasted long. A skilful prime minister like Depretis might reshuffle his government several times according to the changing loyalties of his supporters.

The chief limit on the power of a prime minister was the weakness of the coalitions on which he depended. Prime ministers often resigned without waiting for a parliamentary vote to unseat them, a practice which allowed the king to appoint the next government, unhampered by the bother of an election. The outgoing prime minister often used his influence to get his friends into power and might even serve in the next government in some lesser post. Thus a change in government might mean very little in practice.

Another big problem was corruption, votes often being bought through the use of government patronage. There were many valuable contracts to be won from government departments for railway construction, work on public buildings, military and naval contracts and so on. Crispi, commenting on this in 1886, said:-

"In parliament a kind of bilateral contract is often made; the minister gives the local population into the hands of a deputy on condition that the latter promises the ministry his vote: the prefect and chief of police are nominated in the interests of the deputy in order to keep local interests in his favour ... There is pandemonium in parliament when an important vote comes along as agents rush through rooms and down corridors collecting votes and promising subsidies, decorations, canals and bridges."
(D Mack Smith *Italy: A Modern History* University of Michigan 1969 p199)

In the south in particular, party politics played little part in the elections compared with the wheeling and dealing which went on between the deputy and the local businessmen and power groups such as the Sicilian Mafia or its mainland equivalent, the Naples Camorra. Many businessmen considered it worth their while to buy themselves a deputy who would keep an eye on their interests in parliament.

If there was any real challenge in the election, the government could use its influence to secure the return to parliament of its favoured candidates. The Italian form of government was highly centralised and many local officials were appointed by central government. Each administration could appoint new prefects to run the districts and towns of Italy; thus they were in effect agents of the government of the day. A prefect who did not show suitable support for a government candidate might find himself removed from his post. The local police chief could do his bit too, arresting opposition voters on phoney charges or releasing criminals so that they could vote. Teachers, magistrates and other state employees knew that supporting an opposition candidate could lead to them being posted to the back of beyond. Sometimes the illiteracy rules were used to remove people from the voters' roll. Even in 1900 there were still many constituencies where there were fewer than 5000 voters, so that it was easy to secure a suitable election result by bribery and corruption. Throughout the south such tactics were normal.

> "It is called the blocco when the whole contents of the voting urns are changed; or the pastetta when one changes only a part of them. There is still no word for when absent people and even the dead are made to vote, though one will appear when this usage becomes general ... Such practices have always been endemic in Southern Italy but for some little time now they have begun to infect the whole country."
>
> (D Mack Smith *Italy: A Modern History* University of Michigan 1969 p220-1)

Not surprisingly, most Italians held their politicians in low esteem. For the ordinary peasant or worker, the activities of parliament were irrelevant to his daily life. The deputies were unrepresentative of the people, consisting mainly of middle-class professionals. In 1900, over half the deputies were lawyers but under ten had any connection with farming, the occupation of most of the population. Since deputies were unpaid, it was in any case almost impossible for ordinary people to become members of parliament. The widespread corruption amongst politicians led most Italians to be cynical about parliamentary politics and as a result many did not bother to vote, or else turned their attention to extremist groups.

ITALIAN POLITICIANS

In spite of the frequent changes in government, it is possible to divide Italian politics between 1860 and 1914 into four distinct phases, three of which were dominated by outstanding politicians, Depretis, Crispi and Giolitti.

The First Fifteen Years - Cavour's Successors

The early years of the new state were dominated by followers of Cavour. These tended to be right-wing liberals such as Ricasoli and Minghetti and were mostly northerners drawn from the nobility or upper middle class. They were usually conscientious men who tried to continue Cavour's work but lacked his talent. They concentrated on building up a strong, centralised state, completing Italy's unification and establishing her as a power in Europe.

> "Cavour's former colleagues succeeded him in turn as Prime Minister - Ricasoli, Rattazzi, Farini, Minghetti, Lamarmora and Lanza ... all claimed to follow Cavour's policy. All were honourable men, and much in each was to be admired. But none of them lasted very long; none had the vision, the courage, the strength of character possessed by their predecessor, nor his financial experience and acumen. Not one of them had his ability to manage Parliament, nor his fertility of expedient in Foreign policy, nor the sheer virtuosity in every branch of the political arts which Cavour exercised."
>
> (DM Smith *Cavour* p274 Weidenfield and Nicholson 1985)

They had some success. Rome and Venice were added to the new state and under the stimulus of unity Italy's industrial revolution got under way. Nevertheless, there were problems too. The conversion of Rome into a capital city, which meant finding accommodation for 40,000 state officials, meant huge spending on public works. This led to much speculation, often dishonest, in land in the city. Also, unfortunately, much of old Rome was destroyed as the new regime tried to put its own distinctive stamp on the city of the Popes. A Roman diarist, Ferdinand Gregorovius recorded that:

> "They have demolished the porta Salaria, the ancient ... gate through which the Goths once passed ... They whitewash the houses and even the ancient and venerable palazzi ... Convents are transformed into offices ... they open the cloister windows and pierce new ones through the walls."

Rome was an unsatisfactory capital. Milan and Turin were the centres of industrial and financial activity and the concentration of political power in Rome was resented by the other regions of Italy.

Finance was another problem. Italy was the most highly taxed country in Europe, but little of the money went into developing her economy. The wars of unification had

PRIME MINISTERS OF ITALY FROM UNIFICATION TO THE FIRST WORLD WAR

1860-June 1861	Camillo di Cavour
June 1861-February 1862	Bettino Ricasoli
March 1862-November 1862	Urbano Rattazzi
December 1862-March 1863	Luigi Carlo Farini
March 1863-September 1864	Marco Minghetti
September 1864-June 1866	Alfonso La Marmora
June 1866-March 1867	Bettino Ricasoli
April 1867-November 1867	Urbano Rattazzi
November 1867-November 1869	Luigi Federico Menabrea
December 1869-July 1873	Giovanni Lanza
July 1873-March 1876	Marco Minghetti
March 1876-March 1878	Agostino Depretis
March 1878-December1878	Benedetto Cairoli
December 1878-July 1879	Agostino Depretis
July 1879-April 1881	Benedetto Cairoli
April 1881-July 1887	Agostino Depretis
August 1887-February 1891	Francesco Crispi
February 1891-May 1892	Antonio di Rudini
May 1892-November 1893	Giovanni Giolitti
December 1893-March 1896	Francesco Crispi
March 1896-June 1898	Antonio di Rudini
June 1898-June 1900	Luciano Pelloux
June 1900-February 1901	Giuseppe Saracco
February 1901-October 1903	Giuseppe Zanardelli
November 1903-March 1905	Giovanni Giolitti
March 1905-February 1906	Alessandro Fortis
February 1906-May 1906	Sidney Sonnino
May 1906-December 1909	Giovanni Giolitti
December 1909-March 1910	Sidney Sonnino
April 1910-March 1911	Luigi Luzzatti
March 1911-March 1914	Giovanni Giolitti
March 1914-June 1916	Antonio Salandra

built up a huge national debt, which the sale of church lands had done little to reduce. The new public buildings and large army considered necessary to Italy's dignity as a European power consumed most of the money. The revenue was tripled by heavy taxes such as the intensely unpopular Grist Tax - a tax on ground corn which forced up food prices. However, a balanced budget was not achieved until 1876.

Depretis and the New Left

Opposition to the government at first meant the extreme republicanism of Mazzini and his followers. However, by the mid-1870s a 'New Left' had appeared, made up of radical liberals who were less idealistic, more moderate and more willing to work within the existing political system. They were drawn largely from new social groups, the expanding middle classes of the north and new land-owners and professional men in the south. They wanted to see the burden of taxation reduced and the state less dominated by the north and more aware of the needs and desires of ordinary people.

The Left first won a substantial number of seats in 1874. The following year their policies were set out in a major speech by their leader Agostino Depretis. It was clear that they provided a credible alternative to the right-wing liberals and in 1876 they were elected to power. Depretis became Prime Minister, a post he was to hold, with a few brief intervals, until his death in 1887.

A series of important reforms followed. In 1876 free primary education was provided for all six- to nine-year olds. This was a big step forward in a country where more than three-quarters of the people were illiterate. However, although it was supposed to be compulsory, in practice many children still did not attend school. In 1879 the hated Grist Tax was abolished. Reforms in the law codes included a recognition of the workers' right to strike. Most important of all, in 1882 a major electoral reform was pushed through after much debate. The age qualification was reduced from 25 to 21 and the tax qualification from 40 to 19 Lire. This extended the vote to most middle-class men and even some of the upper working class, a move which increased the electorate from 500,000 to 2,000,000 voters (still less than 10% of the population).

"... But it must be noted that this reform was designed in such a way as to benefit the towns more than the countryside. So those who gained most from the extension of suffrage were the lower middle class and the upper levels of the working and artisan classes ... The class limitation of the 1882 electoral reform was of course more apparent in southern Italy, where the absolute increase in the number of voters was smaller ... than in the north."

(G Procacci *History of the Italian People* p278 Weidenfield and Nicholson 1970)

The monarchy accepted this gradual move towards greater democracy. It really had no alternative, having thrown in its lot with the 'revolutionaries' who had united Italy. Thus Victor Emmanuel II and his successor Umberto I came to accept that normally their ministers should be responsible to parliament, rather than to the king, a point which the constitution had left unclear.

Depretis was far less radical than had been expected. He recognised the need for change but he was not a keen reformer and his chief concern was to keep the government stable. As we have seen he did this by developing 'transformism' - ruling through a series of broad-based coalitions. In foreign affairs too, Depretis was a moderate. He was cautious about the Triple Alliance which was largely the work of King Umberto who was an admirer of Germany. He also showed little enthusiasm for involving Italy in the race for colonies.

Under Depretis some social reform was achieved, without arousing too much opposition from right-wing conservatives. However, for some left-wing politicians this was not enough. The growing working classes in the cities, poorly represented in parliament, were increasingly restive and turned to Socialism as the answer to their problems. In 1882 Andrea Costa, Italy's first Socialist deputy, was elected to parliament.

Francesco Crispi

The last decade of the 19th century was a time of increasing violence in Italian politics. The ideas of militant Socialists such as the Russian anarchist Bakunin had become popular among poor workers in the developing industrial cities of the north where strikes and violent protests were a regular feature of life. The depression in agriculture which hit all of Europe at this time affected Italy particularly badly, especially the backward and mainly rural south where peasant unrest led to growing violence.

In this situation, many Italians felt that what was needed was a strong leader and Francesco Crispi seemed to fill that role. Crispi was a somewhat contradictory figure. He was a Sicilian who in his youth had been a supporter of Mazzini and had fought with Garibaldi's 1,000. However, his intense nationalism had converted him to a supporter of the monarchy which had united Italy. In theory a supporter of the power of the people, Crispi was in practice a dictatorial man who was quite ready to ignore parliament and rule by royal decree if he felt this served the national interest. In 1895, for example, he dismissed parliament and ruled without it for six months. He despised the deputies as corrupt time-servers, but he was himself quite happy to use bribes to win elections. He regularly bought the support of newspapers and in the 1895 election was accused of using money from the Calabrian Earthquake Relief Fund for his own purposes.

Crispi's first term as Prime Minister from 1887-91 saw a number of useful social reforms - public health legislation, prison reform, the setting up of local government elections, laws to control church charities and the reform of the civil and criminal law codes. He was chiefly interested in foreign policy, being a great admirer of the German Chancellor Bismarck and a firm supporter of the Triple Alliance which he felt gave Italy the status of a major power. Encouraged by Bismarck, Crispi was very hostile to France and the two countries came close to war in 1889 as a result of his aggressive policies.

The quarrel stemmed from a trade war. Under pressure from Italian industrialists Depretis had increased tariffs on some French manufactured goods. The French of course retaliated in kind. Crispi, determined to show that Italy was not dependent on France, now scrapped the trade treaty between the two countries. He said in 1888:

"France must now forget the history of the supremacy and influence which she once possessed on this side of the Alps; she should recognise that the Italian nation is as good as herself and must now be allowed to enjoy its independence and profit from it." (D Mack Smith *Italy: A Modern History* p160 University of Michigan 1969)

The results were devastating for Italy. Her exports to France were cut by over 70% in ten years and the withdrawal of French capital led to the collapse of several banks. New trade treaties with her Triple Alliance partners did little to ease the economic crisis which added greatly to the hardship already suffered by the poor.

In 1891 Crispi fell from power, but in 1893 he was back again, following the resignation of Giolitti as a result of a banking scandal. The scandal had been simmering since 1889 but Crispi had managed to cover it up. It concerned profiteering in land and building contracts and many politicians were shown to have been involved, receiving payments from the banks in return for their services.

Although Crispi's own role in the affair was questionable he was recalled to power, since to many Italians he was the strong man who could restore national unity, since by that time Italy was in the grip of a major crisis. Apart from the bank scandal, there was serious industrial unrest in the north with widespread strikes and riots, while in the south the Sicilian peasants were in open revolt. Crispi's answer to both situations was to use repression. Martial law was declared in Sicily and over 1,000 prisoners were shipped off to penal islands. In the north too, martial law was used. Strikes were put down by force; the Socialist Party was banned and its leaders arrested; laws were passed to restrict the press; and 100,000 people were removed from the voters' roll on the grounds that they did not have the correct qualifications. When parliament tried to look into Crispi's part in the bank scandal he simply closed it down.

Many people admired Crispi's strength but others, both conservatives and left-wingers, were alarmed at his dictatorial behaviour. In spite of Crispi's repressive measures, the Socialist Party increased their support, winning 20 seats in the 1895 election compared with 5 in 1892. However, it was events abroad that finally brought him down.

An ardent nationalist, Crispi decided that the answer to Italy's problems was the creation of an Italian Empire which would make her rich and powerful and provide an outlet for Italian emigrants trying to find a better life abroad. As we will see, the result of this was the crushing defeat at Adowa in 1896 which ended Italy's dreams of an Ethiopian empire. (See page 36) After this disaster Crispi was forced to resign.

For the next few years Italy stood on the edge of revolu-

Giolitti

tion. Rising bread prices sparked off a wave of riots and a state of emergency was declared in Milan after 80 people were killed and 450 wounded in street fighting. The King resorted to a military man, General Pelloux, as Prime Minister, but he was soon forced to resign. Then in 1900 King Umberto was assassinated by an anarchist. Fortunately, this did not unleash a right-wing backlash. The new King Victor Emmanuel III was a more moderate man than his father and the middle classes were beginning to understand that repression simply did not work. Helped by an upturn in the economy, Italian politics entered a more moderate phase which was reflected in the policies of the man who was to dominate the early 1900s - Giovanni Giolitti.

Giolitti - The Return to Moderation
Giolitti served as Prime Minister three times between 1901 and 1914 and was involved in most of the other ministries of the period. He was a moderate liberal who had reached the top by a skilful use of political patronage. His success in politics depended, as one commentator remarked, on his "happy art of leaving a sinking ship" - resigning before he was openly defeated so that he could then influence the choosing of the next ministry. His cautious and undramatic style was in contrast to the fiery nationalism of Crispi.

Although he opposed Socialism, Giolitti realised the importance of attacking Italy's social problems to achieve political stabilty. He carried through a programme of reforms which met many of the Socialists' demands. His social welfare reforms included the introduction of Old Age Pensions, a Health Insurance scheme, laws to limit the exploitation of female and child labour in factories and improved laws on safety and health at work. In 1912 the vote was given to virtually all adult males. Even illiterates were allowed to vote if they were over 30. (The electorate was tripled in size to over 9 million.) Women, however, were denied the right to vote in spite of a campaign for them to be included in the reform. (Italian women would remain disenfranchised until 1945.) He also tried to shift the burden of taxation onto the rich through income tax, though this ran into severe opposition.

Giolitti was not very interested in colonial or foreign affairs but increasingly he was forced to attend to them. A new brand of aggressive Italian nationalism was becoming a powerful political force amongst young idealists who believed in Italy's destiny as ruler of the Mediterranean. It was largely to satisfy this national feeling that Giolitti launched the conquest of Libya in 1912. (See page 37)

In foreign affairs, there was a gradual shift away from the Triple Alliance and towards France, although Giolitti was quite prepared to flirt with both sides. The Triple Alliance was renewed in 1902, 1907 and 1912, but at the same time relations with France were steadily improved. Already in 1896 France's claim to Tunisia had been accepted and in 1898 the Tariff War had ended. In 1900 discussions were held to sort out French and Italian colonial claims in Africa and soon after this the Italian fleet visited Toulon. In 1902 Prinetti, the foreign minister, promised the French ambassador:

"If France is directly or indirectly attacked, Italy will maintain a strict neutrality and it will be the same if France, as a result of direct provocation, is compelled to declare war in defence of her honour and security."
(D Mack Smith *Italy: A Modern History* p264 University of Michigan 1969)

At the Algeciras Conference in 1906 and again during the Moroccan Crisis in 1911 the Italians leant towards supporting France, rather than their ally Germany.

This policy was supported by King Victor Emmanuel III who disliked the German Alliance (all the more after a state visit by the Kaiser when he was overheard making disparaging remarks about his Italian hosts!) The Queen Elena, a Montenegran princess, was hostile to Austria and bound to Russia by family ties. Public opinion too was against the Triple Alliance. Irredentism, the demand for Trent and Trieste to be returned to Italy, was once again growing powerful as the tide of nationalism ran stronger. Hostility towards Austria increased even more when she seized Bosnia in 1908. This was seen as a dangerous extension of Austrian power in an area where Italy herself had interests. In 1909 the Tsar of Russia visited Italy and agreements were reached on the need to control Austrian expansion.

It was becoming clear that, in the event of war, the Italians were unlikely to stick by the Triple Alliance. Italy had little to gain by supporting her allies. On the other hand by supporting the French and Russians against the Austrians and Germans, or at least following a policy of friendly neutrality, she ran the chance of gaining Trent, Trieste and perhaps other land in the Balkans. Moreover any war against France would almost certainly involve fighting

France's entente partner Britain with whom Italy had long ties of friendship and valuable trading connections.

In any case Giolitti had already given up power when the crisis broke. In February 1914, faced with a possible railroad strike, he had resigned. No doubt he expected to be back in power soon but in fact his career was virtually over, although he had a brief spell in power after the war.

THE ITALIAN ECONOMY 1860-1914

Italy in the early 19th century was economically backward, her farming primitive, her communications poor and her industry almost nonexistent. Italian nationalists were optimistic that unification would bring prosperity. Trade and industry would flourish once the separate states and their customs barriers were swept away and the whole peninsula became one economic area with a single currency. These hopes were ill-founded as Italy had several problems which inevitably made her development slow.

Industry
Italy was poorly supplied with the natural resources needed as a basis for the industrial revolution which, it was hoped, would establish her as a fully fledged 'power'. There was a certain amount of iron in the Northeast, Elba and Sardinia, but there was little coal with which to process it and this basic fuel had to be imported. (One factor in Italy's reluctance to be drawn into war on the side of Germany in 1914 was that most of her coal imports came from Britain.)

ITALIAN COAL IMPORTS	
1879	1.5 million tons
1885	3 million tons
1914	12 million tons

Apart from iron, Italy's chief mineral resources were the sulphur mines of Sicily which employed 10,000 in 1861, and the marble quarries of Massa and Carrara. However, the methods of extraction tended to be backward compared with Italy's competitors. Textiles were produced in the north - wool in Piedmont and silk in Lombardy - but without adequate resources of coal for steam power factories were slow to develop. Even in the 1880s, much 'industry' was still organised on a craft or rural basis with many workers also working part-time on the land.

Another difficulty was the lack of a strong internal market. This was partly due to the poverty of the peasants whose subsistence wages did not allow them to spend on manufactured goods. Poor transport also hampered internal trade. Over much of the country, roads were virtually nonexistent (only 227 out of 1,848 villages in Naples had roads in 1860) and there were few navigable rivers. Only after railways began to expand in the 1870s did a national market for industrial products begin to grow.

During the 1870s and 80s Italian industry began to take off with several major enterprises getting under way. In 1872 in Milan, the first Pirelli rubber factory was founded by a veteran of Garibaldi's red-shirts. In 1881, two large ship-building companies combined to form the Navigatione Generale which flourished on government contracts as Italy tried to build up her naval power. The Terni steel-works, founded in 1886, also did well with large government contracts for arms.

The free trade policy which had helped the economic growth of Sardinia in the 1850s did not bring similar benefits to a united Italy. Much southern craft industry was put out of business by northern and foreign competition once protection ended. In 1878, to recover the revenue lost by the abolition of the Grist Tax (an unpopular tax on ground corn), the government abandoned its free trade policy and put tariffs on some imports. Industrialists were quick to realise the advantages of this as industries such as silk flourished thanks to protection from foreign competition. Increasingly, Italian economists favoured the German protectionist model rather than British-style free trade. By 1886, Prime Minister Depretis had been persuaded to increase tariffs and his successor Crispi carried this much further.

Italy's major trading partner France, angered by this policy, raised her tariffs in retaliation, so in 1888 the nationalistic Crispi, keen to show that Italy could stand on her own feet, scrapped the trade treaty with France. The resulting trade war was disastrous for Italy, as these figures show.

VALUE OF ITALIAN EXPORTS TO FRANCE	
1887	405 million lire
1888	170 million lire
1897	116 million lire

Many businesses failed in the depression brought on by the trade war, while the withdrawal of French capital caused the collapse of several banks. German and Austrian investment in Italy did repair some of the damage; but the continuing depression caused great hardship, the more so since high tariffs on grain had pushed up food prices. The violence of Italian politics in the 1890s was largely caused by these economic difficulties.

However, by the turn of the century trade was again growing and the economy entered a more prosperous phase. From 1896 to 1908 the annual growth rate of Italian industry was running at the high rate of 6.7%. By now electricity was being developed. The Italian Edison company was set up in 1883 and Italians such as Volta and Marconi played a big part in pioneering electrical power. The development of cheap hydro-electric power was an obvious course for a country so heavily dependent on imported fuel. Milan was one of the first European cities to have electric lighting. Another new industry in which Italy took a lead was motor cars, first made at Turin where in 1899 Fabbricia Italiana Automobile Torino (FIAT) was set up. By 1907 there were seventy companies involved in motor car production.

Agriculture

Only in Northern Italy was there a reasonably well-developed agricultural system based on extensive irrigation in the Po valley. Farms were run on the 'mezzadrina' system whereby the landlord provided the seed and animals and the tenant farmer provided the labour and tools. This, however, tended to discourage initiative and improvement on the part of the farmer.

Further south Italian agriculture was very backward and the most primitive methods survived well into the 20th century. In Naples and Sicily the picture was particularly bleak. Hopeful nationalists had assumed that the area's poverty was due mainly to the feudalistic system which had existed under the Bourbon Kings and that, freed from this restraint, Sicily would resume the role she had had in ancient times as the bread basket of Rome.

The reality was very different. Centuries of deforestation and over-exploitation, combined with an extreme climate, had resulted in serious erosion. Treeless hillsides, baked by the summer sun, were often washed away by the sudden torrential rains of autumn. In low-lying areas were undrained swamps where malaria was rife. This, combined with the endemic lawlessness of the south, forced the peasants to live in hill-top villages, often several miles from their farmland. As well as malaria, pellagra was common among the peasants, this disease being caused by a poor diet based almost entirely on grain.

Unification brought no improvement. Indeed the Kings of Naples had had a policy of banning grain exports and when this was ended, food prices were pushed up. Northern competition destroyed many rural crafts and so the problems of the poor got worse. The sale of church lands did not benefit the peasants at all. Most land was still controlled by landlords, either nobles or members of the new middle class, who did not work it themselves but rented it out to the peasants. The plots were often too small to provide a decent living and many peasants lived in abject poverty. As the population grew there was a large surplus of labour and, with no industry to provide alternative employment, most southerners lived a miserable existence as landless farm labourers, paid below subsistence wages and often unemployed. The 1881 census showed that almost 90% of the rural population of Italy was landless.

The end of protection and the rise in taxation after unity pushed farmers into growing cash crops which put them at the mercy of market forces. Grain was the main crop but in the 1880s cheap grain from America and Russia began to flood the European markets and this forced prices down by 30% resulting in much land going out of production. The failure of the wine industry in France, when the vines were virtually wiped out by the phylloxera disease, gave Italian farmers the chance of a new outlet. Huge areas were turned over to grapes and during the 1880s Italy was, for a time, the leading European wine producer. However, the French replanted and recovered, and the poorly organised Italian wine industry could not compete, resulting in many bankruptcies. The tariff war of 1889 made matters worse. Similar problems hit the fruit and olive oil producers. Italian fruit growers working on a small scale were unable to compete with the development of the Californian fruit industry in the 1890s, while new seed-based oils undermined the olive growers' markets.

To these problems must be added the periodic problems of drought and natural disasters such as earthquakes. In the first decade of the 20th century, for example, there were eruptions of Vesuvius in 1906 and Etna in 1910, an earthquake in Calabria in 1905, and another in 1908 resulting in a tidal wave which killed 62,000 people at Messina and Reggio. For most of the population in the south, life was a constant struggle to survive in the face of squalor, disease and natural disasters, with no hope of improvement.

The government was slow to deal with the needs of the peasants. Few northern politicians visited the south and its desperate poverty was too often blamed on southern laziness and stupidity, even though a survey in the 1870s had identified the chronic lack of employment as the real difficulty. By the 1880s, some schemes had been started to drain the malarial marshes around Rome and to halt the deforestation of the Appenines. In the early 1900s measures were passed to improve the working conditions and health of the peasantry, and government investment led to schemes such as the aqueduct to bring water to Apulia from the Appenines, a project which was finally completed in 1927.

The continuing poverty of the south can be judged from the fact that in Sicily in 1900, 80% of the population was still illiterate and 90% of conscripts were found to be unfit for military service. Even in the more prosperous north the lot of the peasant had worsened; a government survey in the early 1900s showed that wages had actually fallen in real terms over the previous thirty years. Small wonder that every year thousands of Italians opted to emigrate in search of a better life.

Emigration
Poor, unskilled and illiterate, the Italian emigrant workers provided cheap labour for the countries they went to. They helped to build the harbour at Marseilles, the Suez Canal and the Forth Bridge. As often happens with immigrant minorities, they were frequently the targets of racist violence, the worst outbreaks being at Aigues-Mortes in France in 1893 and at New Orleans in the USA in 1890. As a result they tended to stick together for support, forming close-knit communities in the cities where they settled, defending their identity and culture through their church and, in the USA, the Mafia! The money they sent back to their families was a valuable source of income, while the skills they learned were sometimes brought home to Italy.

Most emigrants, however, settled permanently overseas, mainly in the USA, Brazil and Argentina. This huge loss of people, usually the young and go-ahead, worried nationalists, and provided colonialists with an argument for imperialism. Alas, Italy's colonies were unattractive compared with the opportunities which the Americas offered. Successive governments showed surprisingly little concern as the emigration figures climbed steadily higher in the years before the war.

The Role of the State
From the start the Italian government had been concerned to build up a strong modern state, able to take her place among the great powers of Europe. Thus there was heavy investment by the government in the basic public services - roads, railways, the postal system, telegraph service, etc. These services grew impressively in the years after unification.

However, a major drag on investment was Italy's huge national debt, which by 1865 was consuming 33% of the annual revenue in interest payments. Unity had been expensive, the wars fought by Sardinia between 1848 and 1866 having cost 1,300 million lire, to which had been added the debts of all the states she had taken over. This, and the continued heavy spending on the armed forces, meant that taxation in Italy was the highest in Europe and so few Italians had savings to invest. Thus Italy depended heavily on foreign investment and much of her industrial development was under foreign control.

State action was essential for large-scale schemes like railway building, the draining of the Pontine marshes and the tunnels through the Alps which linked Italy to France and central Europe (the Mont Cenis tunnel 1871, the St Gotthard tunnel 1882 and the Simplon tunnel 1906.) However, state support could also have a weakening effect where industries were propped up by subsidies because they were considered to be vital national interests. Thus shipbuilding was heavily subsidised to safeguard the needs of the Italian navy (though in fact many Italian ships were built abroad); and the Terni steelworks' success was due mainly to government contracts for arms at greatly inflated (and sometimes corruptly fixed) prices - all of which had to be paid for out of the tax-payers' pockets.

Taxation was as high as 30% for the average Italian, and since most taxes were indirect and paid on basic com-

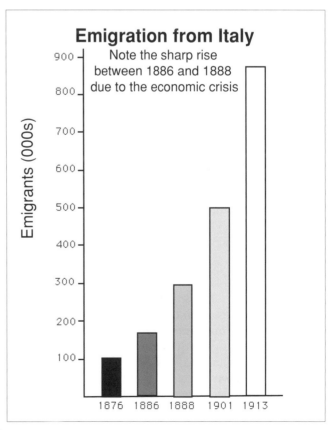

Emigration from Italy

Note the sharp rise between 1886 and 1888 due to the economic crisis

Emigrants (000s)

1876 1886 1888 1901 1913

modities such as salt, they hit the poor much harder than the rich. The cost of the government's determination to be a great power weighed heavily on a country whose national income between 1911 and 1913 was half that of France and only a third that of Great Britain.

During the period 1860-1914, Italy had moved a long way to becoming an industrial nation, as can be seen from the growth of her cities.

The Growth of Italian Cities		
	1871	1921
Milan	200,000	700,000
Turin	250,000	500,000
Rome	220,000	700,000

However, the industrial growth had been built on the backs of the poor who endured long hours, poor wages and heavy taxation. Much of what had been achieved depended heavily on state help and could not be sustained without it. In spite of the better conditions of the early 1900s, Italy was still a poor country where average wages were only one-third of those in Great Britain. Moreover, the progress was mostly concentrated in a small area around Turin, Milan and Genoa, while the south continued to be plagued by poverty, ill-health and illiteracy from which the only escape was emigration. When Zanardelli, the Prime Minister from 1901-1903 visited the south, (the first PM to do so), he was somewhat surprised to be greeted by one mayor "on behalf of the 8,000 people in this commune, 3,000 of whom are in America and the other 5,000 preparing to follow them." (D Mack Smith *Italy: A Modern History* University of Michigan 1969 p242)

ITALIAN FOREIGN AND IMPERIAL POLICIES 1860 - 1914

At first Italy had few friends in Europe. Napoleon III had deep misgivings about the new Italian state. His intention, when he signed the pact at Plombieres in 1858, had not been to create a powerful new neighbour. He would have preferred to keep Naples separate, perhaps with a Bonaparte as king, and loosely linked in a federation with the other Italian states. Austria-Hungary was, of course, openly hostile. Russia and Prussia were suspicious of any changes to the established order in Europe. Another threat came from the exiled rulers of Naples and the Duchies who still hoped to recover their thrones. They were supported by the Pope. Only Britain was whole-heartedly sympathetic to Italy. Thus the chief aim of the Italian government was to win acceptance of Italy's new position as a European power.

Their first success came in 1866 in the shape of an alliance with Prussia. The Italians undertook to support Prussia in a war with Austria, with the promise of Venetia as their reward. Victor Emmanuel and his ministers did fairly well in their dealings with the devious Prussian Chancellor Bismarck, a man who would use anyone ruthlessly in pursuit of his own aims. They avoided any long-term commitment which might be to Italy's disadvantage, insisting that the war must take place within three months

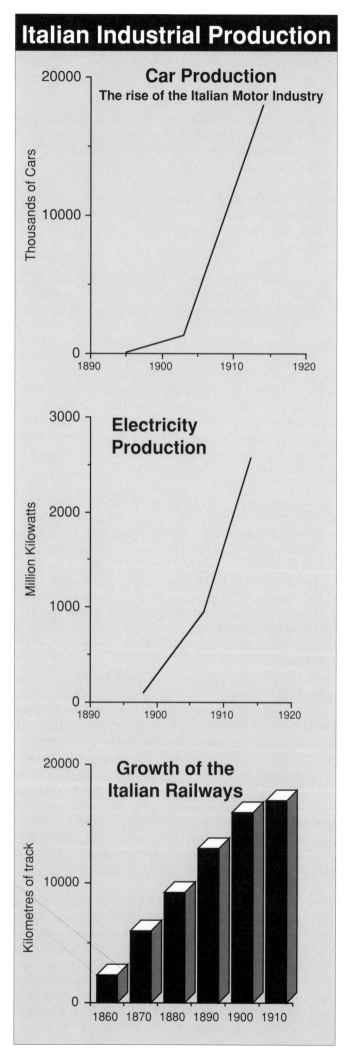

SNUBBED!

Mossoo (aside). "HA!—WITH MY HATED RIVAL! WHY WAS I SO RUDE TO HER?!"

*Italy, angered by the occupation of Tunis by France, joins her
enemy, Germany, in the Triple Alliance of 1882*

and Austria must be the aggressor. They did miss a chance to get Venice without any fighting; as war approached, the Austrians offered to do a deal but by then Italy had signed the Prussian Alliance.

Bismarck duly provoked Austria into hostilities. The Seven Weeks War which followed was brief but, for the Italians, disastrous. Defeat on land at Custoza was followed by defeat on the sea at Lissa. Nevertheless, the conflicts served their purpose, tying up 20,000 Austrian troops. Fortunately, the Prussians inflicted a crushing defeat on Austria at Sadowa and she was forced to sue for terms. In the Treaty of Prague, Italy got her reward, Venetia. (It was not handed to her directly but to Napoleon III who acted as mediator. He enjoyed this chance to pose as a great diplomat but the Italians resented this roundabout arrangement.) Thus, despite the defeats, the war could be regarded as a success. It also reduced the likelihood of further Austrian interference in Italy. In 1870, when the Italians occupied Rome, the Austrians took no action to prevent them.

Relations with France had become steadily cooler as a result of the Roman situation. The defeat of Garibaldi by French troops at Mentana in 1867 still rankled with Italian nationalists. On the other hand, during the 1870s Italy drew closer to Germany and, more surprisingly, to her old enemy Austria. This upset many nationalists who believed Italian unity would not be complete until the Austrians had been driven from Trent and Trieste, their last toe-holds in Italy. In 1873, Victor Emmanuel visited both Berlin and Vienna. The Congress of Berlin in 1878, called

to sort out a major crisis in the Turkish Empire, was another landmark for Italian foreign policy, not because Italy made any gains but, quite simply, because she had taken part in it as one of the European powers. Her status as a leading nation was now fully recognised.

However, for many Italians this was not enough. Nationalism was strong among the new middle classes. They looked back to the days when Rome had been the centre of a great Empire and dreamed of reviving it. Mazzini had argued that Italy's historic mission should be to become the political and cultural leader of the Mediterranean. Hopes centred on Tunis in North Africa which was still technically part of the Turkish Empire. There were many Italian settlers there - 30,000 by 1878 - and it seemed only a matter of time before it became a province of Italy. Bismarck of Germany encouraged these ambitions. They would distract the Italians from their claims against Austria which had become his ally in 1879. Moreover, Italy's involvement with Tunis would bring her into conflict with France which also had ambitions in the area and this suited Bismarck's policy of keeping France isolated.

It was a major shock to Italian self-esteem when, in 1881, the French occupied Tunis. The newspaper *Rassegna Settimanale*, remarked, "The subjection of the north coast of Africa to France will bring with it as a necessary consequence the destruction of Italy's future as a great power." (D Mack Smith *Italy: A Modern History* University of Michigan 1969 p131). This check to her colonial ambitions pushed Italy into the arms of the Central Powers and in 1882 she joined Germany and Austria in the Triple Alliance.

By its terms, if either Italy or Germany was attacked by France the others would come to her aid. Italy also promised to support her allies if either of them was attacked by two other powers but she was not obliged to support them in a war of aggression. A special clause said that the alliance could not be directed against Britain with which Italy had strong political and economic ties. Another clause was added in 1887 at the insistence of the Italian foreign minister Robilant. This clause said that:

> "If ... Austria-Hungary or Italy should be compelled to alter the status quo in the Balkans ... (this) shall not take place without previous agreement between the two powers, based on the principle of reciprocal compensation for every advantage, territorial or otherwise."
> (D Mack Smith *Italy: A Modern History* University of Michigan 1969 p124)

In other words if Austria expanded in the Balkans Italy would get compensation, the implication being that she might receive Trent and/or Trieste. (It should be noted that when organising the Triple Alliance, Bismarck did not tell the Italians about the existence of the Dual Alliance between Germany and Austria.) According to the Italian historian, G Procacci, many Italians believed that " ... Italy had finally come of age with the Triple Alliance , ceasing to be a second class power and winning back some of the prestige she had lost with the disastrous war of 1866."
(G Procacci *History of the Italian People* p288 Weidenfeld and Nicolson)

Not all Italians were happy with the Triple Alliance. The

radical nationalists or 'irredentists' would not be satisfied as long as Trieste and Trent remained under Austrian rule. When a Triestian extremist, Guglielmo Oberdan, was hanged for attempting to assassinate the Emperor Franz Josef in 1882, there were widespread anti-Austrian demonstrations in Italy, which caused the government considerable embarrassment.

France was now seen as the chief obstacle to Italy's colonial ambitions and this was the reason that the Mediterranean Pact was signed with Britain in 1887. By this Italy was promised support for her colonisation of Tripoli in return for backing Britain's takeover of Egypt. (The pact was later extended to include Austria with the aim of checking Russia's ambitions in the Eastern Mediterranean.) The Germans also agreed to back Italy's expansion in Tripoli, if the French tried to take over more of North Africa. By now relations with France were at rock bottom and in 1888 this led to a damaging trade war between the two countries which cut Italy's exports to France by nearly three-quarters.

Thus, the forces of nationalism had led Italy to enter the race for colonies, with France as her main rival. Paradoxically, her alliance with Austria seemed to run counter to nationalist aims. Italian foreign policy throughout this period up to 1914 was dominated by the need to satisfy national pride by playing the part of a great power. However, In the years before 1914, Italy gradually drifted away from her Triple Alliance partners, and there was some rapprochment with France.

THE ITALIAN SEARCH FOR EMPIRE

Like most European countries in the later 19th century, Italy entered the race to acquire a colonial empire. It was generally believed that colonies were of great value, both as sources of raw materials and as markets for Europe's industrial products. For Italy though, there were other more pressing motives for having an empire. It was partly a matter of national pride. Now that she was a nation, Italy must resume her role as an imperial power; a role which looked back to the great days of the Romans and to the trading empire of medieval Venice. It also seemed to offer a solution for another problem. Every year thousands of Italians left their native land, mainly for the USA, to escape from poverty at home. How much better it would be if this loss of people could be stopped by giving emigrants the chance to settle in Italy's own colonies.

Even before Italian unity in 1870, Italian missionaries, traders and explorers were active in Southeast Asia and in various parts of Africa. (An adventurer tried to claim Sumatra, on the grounds of his marriages to local princesses, with a view to presenting it to his native Italy!). As we have seen, Italy's hopes of taking over Tunis were rudely checked by the French. In Egypt too, it was clear that, in spite of Italian involvement in the building of the Suez Canal, the dominant power was Britain. Only Tripoli (Libya) remained in north Africa as a possible area for colonisation, but it was unpromising desert. The Italians began to look elsewhere.

Ethiopia and East Africa

An Italian trading post had been started at Assab on the Red Sea and in June 1882 the Italian government declared its sovereignty over the area. Soon the Italians penetrated into the interior to 'protect' their colony and in 1885 they took over Massawa. This alarmed the Emperor John of Abyssinia (Ethiopia) who was worried about losing his coastline. In 1887, after several incidents, the Italians sent in a punitive expedition. This force of 500 men was destroyed by native tribesmen at Dogali, dealing a severe blow to Italian pride. As a result, extra military spending was approved because, as Crispi remarked, "We cannot stay inactive when the name of Italy is besmirched."
(D Mack Smith *Italy: A Modern History* University of Michigan 1969 p181)

Meanwhile the Emperor John had been murdered by dervish fanatics (who also killed the British General Gordon at Khartoum in 1885). In 1889 a new emperor Menelik was installed with Italian support, backed up by generous supplies of weapons. He signed the Treaty of Ucciali which the Italians interpreted as giving them a protectorate over the whole of Ethiopia. The Emperor, however, did not see things that way, as soon became clear.

Crispi, the Prime Minister from 1888 until 1891, was an enthusiastic imperialist. He decided that a colonial success would be good for Italy's prestige so he ordered troops to occupy Asmara, and in January 1890 Eritrea was declared to be an Italian colony. Italian troops also occupied part of Somaliland. Crispi's aggressive policies were relaxed by his successors but when he returned to power in 1893 Italian expansion in east Africa was resumed.

However, he was reluctant to provide the extra men and supplies needed since this would mean heavy taxation at home. The commanders in Eritrea found that they were expected to carry out Crispi's plans for colonial expansion on a shoestring budget. When in 1895 the Emperor Menelik's forces defeated a small Italian force at Amba Alagi (using their new Italian weapons), Crispi accused the Italian commanders of incompetence and cowardice. Stung by this accusation, General Baratieri foolishly tried for a quick success before he was replaced. In 1896, with inadequate maps and poor intelligence reports of enemy movements, he marched his men to a shattering defeat at Adowa. Six thousand Italian soldiers died in one day and

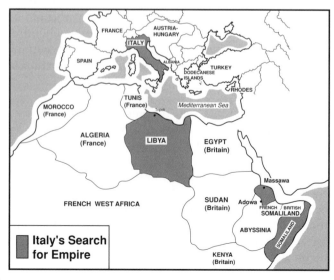

Italy's Search for Empire

many more were taken prisoner; it was a devastating blow to Italian self-esteem.

Thus Italy's attempt to seize Ethiopia ended in disaster and humiliation. Baratieri was tried for treason but it soon became clear that the worst he was guilty of was stupidity and that the government's failure to supply the colonial war adequately had contributed to his downfall. As Giolitti said,

> "Crispi's second ministry completely changed our colonial policy ... inviting the joint opposition of a united Abyssinia and the dervishes. This policy was wrong and its execution even worse. One part of the ministry wanted war, the other just allowed the drift into war while refusing the means necessary to win it. On top of this there was incredible incompetence in the organisation and military direction of the enterprise."
> (D Mack Smith *Italy: A Modern History* University of Michigan 1969 p184)

Crispi was forced to resign. Soon after, the Italians withdrew from most of Ethiopia. Eritrea was retained but its climate made it unattractive for settlers and it had few resources, so that it became a drain on Italy's already weak economy. In the long term, the psychological wound of the defeat at Adowa was never healed and this explains Mussolini's determination to conquer Ethiopia in 1935.

War in Libya
For the next decade, the Italians avoided any major colonial engagements. In 1896 relations began to improve with France, and Italy recognised the French occupation of Tunis. In 1900 there followed an agreement on the frontier in Somalia and a recognition of each side's interests in North Africa, the French in Morocco and the Italians in Libya. However, by 1910 the tide of nationalist and imperialist feeling was once again flowing strongly. New nationalist groups had emerged which saw war as an ennobling activity, and dreamed of the 'imperial destiny' of the Italian race. There was talk of conquering Albania in the Balkans, an idea which was bound to cause friction with Austria and other European powers.

Giolitti, the Prime Minister for most of the early 1900s, had followed a cautious foreign policy. Now he decided that this nationalist fervour could be most safely channelled into a colonial war in North Africa. For many years, Italian interests had been developing in Libya; the Banca di Roma, for example, was involved in land, industry and mining. However, Libya's Turkish overlords were increasingly hostile to this economic colonialism. Moreover, the Germans were developing their interests in the area in competition with the Italians. France's takeover of Morocco after the crises of 1905 and 1911 highlighted the need for Italy to assert her own colonial claims clearly. Rather than risk a repeat of the Tunisian humiliation of 1881, the Italian government decided on a military takeover, to secure an area they regarded as already theirs. Turkish measures against foreign business interests provided an excuse to pick a quarrel and in September 1911 war was declared. At first the war against Libya was popular in Italy.

> "Unlike previous colonial exploits, the Libyan war was popular among broad sectors of public opinion. Nationalists saluted it as Italy's return to the Mediterranean policy of ancient Rome; Catholics saw it as a new crusade against the Moslems, and many people, especially in the south, saw the new colony as a land that would absorb thousands upon thousands of peasants, and so put an end to emigration. Among non-socialists only a few isolated figures ... warned that Libya was not that promised land which many had imagined ... but an enormous sandpit which would cost Italy far more than it would earn her."
> (G Procacci *History of the Italian People* p327 Weidenfeld and Nicolson 1970)

Things did not go quite as expected. Italy was ill prepared for the war which developed. It was easy to bombard and take over Tripoli and other coastal towns but the interior proved to be much more difficult to control. It had been assumed that the local Arab population would welcome the Italians as liberators from Turkish oppression, but this did not happen. There was soon a vigorous resistance to the Italians by Arab guerrillas who could vanish quickly into the desert beyond the reach of the Italians' modern weaponry. Some ill-advised remarks comparing the war to a Christian crusade were enough to turn this guerrilla action into a 'jihad' - a holy war against the infidel invaders.

The war now extended to Turkey's possessions in the Dodecanese Islands and Rhodes. Finally, after a year's fighting, peace was signed at the Treaty of Lausanne by which Italy was recognised as ruler of Libya and Rhodes. However, the Turks retained the right to safeguard the religious interests of the Muslim population in Libya.

The war thus appeared to be a success for Italy but in practical terms it proved costly. The expenses of the fighting (512 million Lire)had pushed up the national debt and caused serious inflation. The war had severely damaged Italian trading interests in the Turkish Empire with thousands of Italians expelled from Turkey during the hostilities. The new colony in Libya proved to be of little value, because of the continuing cost of military operations against hostile natives; Italian rule was effective only along the coast. Also, the crops grown in Libya were similar to those of Southern Italy, resulting in unwelcome competition for the farmers there. Few emigrants were willing to exchange the prosperous cities of the USA for the deserts of North Africa.

More seriously, the war had gravely undermined the Turkish Empire. This opened the way for the Balkan Wars of 1912-13 which in turn heralded the crisis which caused the First World War.

5 The Crisis in Italian Democracy

In 1918 few countries, if any, in Europe had much cause for satisfaction. The Italians were more discontented than most and they had been on the winning side in the Great War.

When war broke out in 1914, Italy did not join her Triple Alliance partners, claiming that Austria was fighting a war of conquest and aggression while the Triple Alliance was a defensive agreement. A period of intense diplomatic activity followed in which the two sides vied with each other to offer Italy more and more territory, mainly at the expense of Austria-Hungary, if only she would fight on their side. A vigorous public debate was conducted in Italy as to whether the country should join the war and if so, on which side. Finally, Britain and France made an offer which Italy could not refuse. If Italy fought and the allies won she could have the following provinces from Austria:

1 The South Tyrol in the North, a German speaking area just south of the Alpine crest.
2 Trentino, an Italian speaking area just south of the South Tyrol.
3 A substantial parcel of land stretching from her North Eastern frontier down the eastern side of the Adriatic Sea including Gorizia, Gradisea, Trieste, Istria, bits of Dalmatia and adjacent islands in the Adriatic.
4 Extra land in Africa. Libya was to be extended as were the Italian colonies of Eritrea and Somaliland adjacent to Abyssinia (Ethiopia).
5 Italy would get a share of any reparations extracted from the defeated powers.

In a touch worthy of double glazing salesmanship, Italy

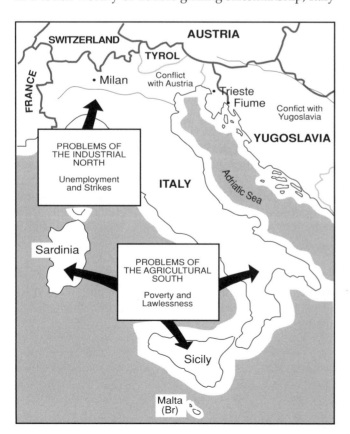

had to declare war within a month or the deal was off. The secret Treaty of London was signed on 26 April 1915. On 23 May, after a furious debate both in and out of Parliament, Italy declared war on Austria-Hungary. However, she proved to be something of a military liability to the allies. British troops had to be sent to Italy to hold back the Austrians after the Italian rout at Caporetto (October 1917). This in turn meant that the British did not have enough infantry to follow up the breakthrough secured by their tanks at Cambrai (November 1917). The war ended with the allies feeling less than generous towards Italy. In addition to this, the American President, Woodrow Wilson, had not signed the Treaty of London. He disapproved of it since it would result in many non-Italians being ruled by Italy. This violated his principle of self-determination, that each people or nation should be free to govern itself or decide how it should be governed.

The Peace Settlement and After

At the Versailles conference Italy was virtually ignored by the 'Big Three', Georges Clemenceau (France), Woodrow Wilson (USA) and David Lloyd George (Britain). Señor Orlando, Italy's Prime Minister, walked out in protest but came back in time to ensure that Italy got something.

The Treaty of St Germain with Austria gave Italy almost all the European territory she had been promised. She acquired the South Tyrol, Trentino, Istria and the useful port of Trieste, but while the British, French, Belgians, Japanese, Australians and South Africans all acquired German colonies, Italy got nothing. Nor was she to receive a share of the reparations the defeated countries had to pay. The peace settlement was therefore a cause of massive discontent in Italy and stirred up feelings of patriotic indignation. There were other reasons for discontent.

Economic Problems

The war caused havoc with strong economies like Britain's. Its effects on Italy were devastating. For a time there was a boom in war related manufacturing industry. Peace brought this to an end but the associated inflation continued while unemployment rose and was added to as soldiers were demobilised and returned to civilian life. Returning veterans noted that, while they were jobless, many had done well from the war. Industrialists had profited and some ambitious peasants had bought more land and yet food was in short supply.

Trade union membership had been rising sharply, from about 310,000 in 1918 to 3,160,000 in 1920. Outraged nationalism and economic grievances boiled over into two years of strikes and industrial chaos - 1918 to 1920 is known as Biennio Rosso (two red years).

Political Weakness

Since unification Italy had been governed by middle class Liberals who had gained an unenviable reputation for corruption. Under Liberal rule Italy had developed some industry in the North but the South had remained primitive and backward, emigration to the USA continued to be high and finally Italy had been involved in a pointless war costing 600,000 lives. In a period of relative prosperity in 1912 the electorate had been tripled so that almost all men had the right to vote. This led to the rapid growth of two new political parties – the Socialists or PSI which had been founded in 1892 and the Catholic Partito Popolare founded in January 1919. The PSI rapidly became Italy's biggest party. In 1919 it rejected the path of gradual reform and adopted Russian style revolution as its goal.

Proportional representation was introduced for elections in 1919. This system is designed to be fair to all parties and to ensure that the proportion of the vote that each party polls is reflected in its share of seats in the Parliament. It has the effect of encouraging the growth of small parties and making it almost impossible for one party to achieve an overall majority and to form a strong government on its own. Thus all governments have to be coalitions or alliances of parties. This can be difficult to achieve when a country is deeply divided and in crisis. For comparisons with the situation in Britain and in postwar Germany see page 103.

MUSSOLINI

After the First World War Italy was ripe for a major political transformation. The man who succeeded in taking advantage of the situation and seizing the leadership of the country was Benito Mussolini. Denis Mack Smith summarises his career thus:

"Mussolini was neither born great nor had greatness thrust upon him but had to fight his way out of obscurity by his own ambition and talents. So well did he succeed that he ruled Italy as a dictator for over twenty years and attracted more popular admiration than anyone else had received in the whole course of Italian history. At the peak of his success he then fell an easy victim for the flattery that he invited or ordered from his cronies, and was beguiled into playing for the yet higher status of world domination. But he lacked the necessary resources, whether the material resources of a rich country, or the requisite personal qualities of mind and character. By the time of his death in 1945 he left ... an Italy destroyed by military defeat and civil war. He was, by his own admission, the most hated person in the country ..."
(Denis Mack Smith *Mussolini* p xiii)

So huge was Mussolini's role that Mack Smith had to remind his readers that he was writing a biography of one man and not a history of Italy at that time.

Benito Mussolini was born in 1883 in the village of Predappio in the Romagna, a region of North Eastern Italy known for its left-wing republican politics. His father, Alessandro Mussolini, was a lazy, drunken, adulterous blacksmith. He did not work a lot, never went to church and beat his children. Alessandro was also heavily involved in left-wing revolutionary politics. Benito inherited most of his father's personality including his physical and political violence and an insatiable appetite for women. Alessandro's wife, Rosa, kept the family on her school teacher's pay and tried to bring them up as good Catholics.

As a baby Mussolini was slow to talk. Once he started nobody was ever able to stop him for long. He led a violent and disorderly youth. He was expelled from a church boarding school for stabbing another boy. He repeated this feat in his next school but was allowed back after suspension. As he matured he began to visit brothels and in his autobiography, *La Mia Vita*, boasted of raping a girl. Like his father he was actively interested in revolutionary socialism.

He qualified as a teacher and in 1902 got a job in a village school. He could not keep control of his class and tried to bribe the children to be quiet. He ran up debts, had an affair with a woman whose husband was in the army, drank heavily and stabbed a girlfriend. Finally, he ran away to Switzerland in 1903, got into trouble and was sent back. Faced with military service he ran away again before returning in 1905. He served his term in the army and proved to be an exemplary soldier. The wild revolutionary was trying to appear responsible. For a while he worked as editor of a small socialist newspaper in Trentino, at that time an Italian speaking province of Austria.

Mussolini's first venture into journalism was sufficiently offensive to result in his expulsion from Austria. Back in Italy he continued in his new trade. In 1910 he set up house with Rachele Guidi, the daughter of his father's mistress. He finally married her in 1915.

At this stage of his career Mussolini was well to the left in Italian politics - an international Marxist and revolutionary, a critic of the Church and the Italian Liberal Establishment and not an Italian Nationalist. He became editor of the socialist newspaper *Avanti* and moved to Milan. The paper's circulation grew throughout Italy.

The Parting of the Roads
When war broke out in 1914 Mussolini took the standard Marxist view that the Proletariat should have nothing to do with it. As the debate raged over whether Italy should join, he gradually shifted his position. He established his own paper, *Il Popolo d'Italia* (The Italian People), apparently with French financial backing. The debate continues about whether the French paid him because he supported Italian entry on their side or whether he supported Italian entry because the French paid him to do so. *Il Popolo d'Italia* claimed to be a socialist paper and came up with some lusty slogans.

'A Revolution is an idea which has found bayonets'
'Who has steel has bread'

However he was being financed not only by the French, and perhaps the other allies, but also by Italian industrialists, whose order books would benefit from war, and by the government. The young men of Italy were urged to prepare themselves for war and Mussolini was expelled from the PSI. His socialist days were effectively over. As the weeks passed Mussolini's stated war aims demanded the annexation of more and more territory. He predicted that the war would be of short duration as Italy's army would tip the balance against Germany and Austria and threatened civil war or a coup d'état if the government stayed neutral.

THE FIRST FASCISTS

Among the pressure groups trying to push Italy into war were the Fascio di Combattimento or fighting squads. (Fascio means bundle or group). The Fascisti were mainly young thugs who had left the socialist movement before Mussolini to campaign for war. He rapidly became a leading influence among them and later claimed to have started the group, the seed corn of postwar Fascism.

Finally, in April 1915 Mussolini's wish was granted. In September he was called up and saw service in the trenches, reaching the rank of lance-sergeant. In his last editorial in *Avanti* he wrote:

"We have the unique privilege of living in the most tragic hour of the world's history. Do we wish - as men and socialists - to be passive spectators of this grandiose drama? Or do we wish to be ... its protagonists? Let us not salvage the letter of the party if it means killing the spirit of socialism."
(Quoted by Ernst Nolte , a German Historian, in *Three Faces of Fascism*)

His former socialist views denied him a commission. During a training exercise in February 1917 a grenade launcher exploded killing a number of soldiers and peppering Mussolini with over forty fragments. In July he was invalided out of the army and returned to his paper. He later claimed that the war began to go badly for Italy when Sergeant Mussolini left the army.

1918
As the Great War drew to a close, Mussolini's ideas underwent quite dramatic changes in a very short time. Firstly, his socialism continued to wither. Marxism was condemned for being riddled ridden with outdated ideas like the class war. His pronouncements on capitalism became more favourable.

Secondly, when Italy joined the war Mussolini saw it as a war of liberation for the subject nations of the Austrian Empire. A year after the defeat at Caporetto, Italy's war came to an end and national self-respect was restored by victory at Vittorio Vinetto, described in *Il Popolo d'Italia* as the greatest victory in World History. Mussolini then began to demand the annexation of non-Italian land such as the German speaking South Tyrol and Serbo-Croat Dalmatia, whereas previously he had championed the rights of the Serbs to national self-determination. He had changed from an internationalist into an Italian nationalist. Denis Mack Smith explains the change simply:

"Mussolini's journalistic style prompted him to take an extreme position whenever possible. Extremism is always dramatic and eye-catching. He was far more concerned with tactics than with ideas, and his violent changeability was bound to seem confused if measured by strict logic; but he had discovered that readers liked extreme views and rarely bothered with consistency."
(D Mack Smith *Mussolini* Paladin edition p39)

This attitude to ideas, principles and beliefs followed Mussolini into power. To him, Fascism was not so much an ideology as a means to obtain personal political power.

The Formation of a Party
On 23 March 1919, a meeting took place in a Milan hall which was attended by as ill-assorted a collection of political freaks and extremists as could be expected to fit under one roof. There were anarchists, communists, republicans, Catholics and an assortment of Nationalists and Liberals. This was the origin of the Fascist Party. A programme of sorts gradually emerged. They proposed to:

1 abolish the monarchy
2 confiscate church property
3 confiscate war profits
4 give workers a say in factory management
5 increase taxes on the very wealthy
6 give land to landless peasants
7 defend free speech and freedom of the press
8 legally enforce a minimum wage
9 give votes to women

These ideas show the influence of socialist and liberal ideology and are exactly opposite to what Mussolini did once he had power.

Soon after the Milan meeting the offices and print works of *Avanti* were attacked and wrecked by a mob, many of whom wore the black shirts of the Arditi, Italy's shock troops of the Great War. From this time onwards, such action by Fascio or Fascist squads became a feature of Mussolini's quest for power. In this time of industrial trouble, the Biennio Rosso, the Fascists won the support of wealthy industrialists and rich landowners by making the squads available to break up strikes and land grabs by starving peasants.

By this time the Fascists had begun to use the fasces (an axe tied up in a bundle of rods) as an emblem. The fasces were the symbol of the consuls' power in ancient Rome and were carried by police-like officials called Lictors. They symbolised the power of the consuls to punish the citizens. It was no accident that a power symbol from ancient Rome became the badge of the Fascists.

D' Annunzio and the Occupation of Fiume
Mussolini was not the only would-be leader seeking to capitalise on nationalist feeling in 1919. Austria signed the Treaty of St Germain with the victors of the Great War in September. This apparently finalised the plan that the new state of Yugoslavia, and not Italy, was to get the Adriatic port of Fiume. Although they had received most of the European territory promised to them in the Treaty of London, the Italians still felt cheated. That same month Gabriele D'Annunzio, poet, Great War aviator, man of action and national hero seized Fiume with the help of a colourful assortment of desperados, including an ample smattering of black-shirted Arditi. He also had the support of factions of the Italian army. D'Annunzio appeared

to be continuing the Garibaldi tradition of direct action. He challenged Mussolini to join him in Fiume and accused him of cowardice when he did not.

No government moved to eject the poet, who ruled the town in anarchic fashion for a year. Supplies became hard to get, discipline cracked and stories began to emerge of what HR Kedward has described as "mass orgies, sexual abandon and endless political intrigue".

The Italian government finally ended the farce and Fiume became an independent city by agreement between the Yugoslav and Italian governments. Mussolini was probably glad that he had stayed out of Fiume while an important rival for the leadership of Nationalist Italy had discredited and eliminated himself.

Elections November 1919
Italy adopted proportional representation for the elections of November 1919. Single member constituencies in the British style were abolished and the new system was designed to ensure that each party's support in the country, as shown by the percentage of the vote it received, was reflected in its strength in parliament. While this was democratically desirable, it was likely to cause further difficulties for Italy where it was already hard to form a stable government because of the large numbers of existing parties and the factions within them. Proportional representation tends to encourage the growth of small parties and the division of existing ones.

The Fascists fought the election on their left-wing programme and failed to win even one seat in parliament. In his home village of Predappio nobody voted for Mussolini! The socialists polled forty times as many votes nationally and staged a mock funeral of Fascism in Milan, calling at Mussolini's house to invite him to attend.

At this point he appears to have decided that there was not much future for him in left-wing politics. He thought that he might have more luck on the right. Denis Mack Smith says that at this time "he took care to confuse the issue stressing that, inside his movement, there was room for all political beliefs or none at all." Later he said, "There is no right and wrong in politics, only power." To Mussolini ideology was largely unimportant. Power over others was what mattered. He began to say that Fascist foreign policy was imperialism and national expansion.

The 1921 Elections
As new elections approached, Mussolini entered an alliance with the government, led by the veteran Liberal Giolitti. The campaign was notable for the outrageous violence of the Fascio, the Fascist squads. The Fascio were essentially local phenomena, lacking any real national organisation. They were led by powerful local chiefs known as 'Ras'.

Ras was the Abyssinian title for a chieftain. The Italians had learned this from their colonial experience in Eritrea and their defeat at the hands of the Abyssinians at Adowa in 1896.

When not engaged in political violence the Ras ran protec-

tion and extortion rackets, or else broke up strikes for any factory owner who paid them enough. In 1921 Mussolini could not rely on the automatic support and loyalty of these brigands, all of whom had ambitions of their own. It was one of his greatest achievements that he convinced desperados like Roberto Farinacci, Dino Grandi and Italo Balbo that their best interests would be served by following him and that they would never achieve power without him. Balbo, a 25-year-old ex-soldier, unable to adjust to peace, wrote about this period:

> "When I came back from the war I, like so many others, hated politics and politicians, who, it seemed to me had betrayed the hopes of the fighting men and had inflicted on Italy a shameful peace and on those who worshipped heroism a series of humiliations. Struggle, fight to return the country to Giolitti who had bartered every ideal? No. Better deny everything, destroy everything in order to build everything up again from the bottom. Many at that time, even the most generous souls, turned towards nihilist Communism, which offered a ready and more radical revolutionary programme and was engaged on two fronts in a struggle against the bourgeoisie and against Socialism. It is certain, I believe, that without Mussolini three-quarters of the Italian youth coming home from the trenches would have become Bolsheviks. They wanted a revolution at any cost."
>
> (Italo Balbo *Diario 1922* Quoted by Sir Ivone Kirkpatrick in *Mussolini, Study of a Demagogue*)

As the election approached, the Ras set their black-shirted Squadristi on the opposition, especially the Socialists. The army or the police could have crushed these hooligans

A Fascist election poster showing the symbols of the black shirt and the Rod

The Growth of Fascism 1919 - 1922

KEY

▨ Chief industrial region

▨ Regions of rural conflict after 1918 and of dramatic Fascist expansion between 1920 and 1922

easily but instead they stood aside and let them get on with their task of intimidation, sometimes providing transport and weapons. Judges were generally soft on Fascists who appeared before them. Giolitti may have expected to control and manipulate the Fascists, whose ideology was as blurred to him as to everybody else. Instead he gave them an entrance to Italian politics with 35 deputies and about 7% of the votes. The results were:

Liberal Democrats	159	(in various factions)
Socialists	146	
Partito Popolare	104	
Fascists	35	
Agrarians	26	
Communists	11	
Nationalists	10	
Republicans	7	
Slavs, Germans etc.	12	

(From *Mussolini* by Sir Ivone Kirkpatrick p 103)

Of the 1921 election HR Kedward wrote:

"The revolution had not arrived. Those who wanted it were bitterly disillusioned, those who feared it began to move from the defensive to the attack. The situation was one which favoured an appeal to order and recovery. By intuition and political ruthlessness Mussolini and the local Fasci provided this appeal. Capitalising on the fears of the middle classes, utilising the nationalism of d'Annunzio without repeating his mistakes, fascism sold itself to the Italian people in 1921 as the patriotic answer to the Red Socialist danger and the political chaos of ineffective liberalism ... the original revolutionary aims of 1919 were shelved and a renewed emphasis placed on Fascist order, reliability and power."
(HR Kedward *Fascism in Western Europe 1900-45* p 42)

Giolitti could not gather enough support among the many and varied Liberal factions to form a coalition, so Mussolini promptly ditched him. The Liberals represented parliamentary government which Mussolini now characterised as weak, degenerate and primitive. An advanced civilisation called for dictatorship - the dictatorship of Mussolini. When Mussolini took his place in Parliament he sat on the extreme right of the chamber, a place previously shunned, and called for the privatisation of postal services and the railways. His transformation from leftwing internationalist revolutionary to right-wing materialist opportunist was largely complete.

Fascist contempt for parliamentary convention was dramatically illustrated when their deputies attacked a Communist member and ejected him from the chamber on the pretext that he had been a deserter during the war. In the British House of Commons, or any well-run democratic legislature, this type of behaviour would attract vigorous disciplinary action. The Fascists got away with it and their progress to power continued, since the Italian Establishment failed to recognise them as a threat and use the power at its disposal to deal with them.

THE MARCH ON ROME

In 1860, Garibaldi had dreamed of marching on the eternal city, driving away Italy's enemies and proclaiming a Republic. In the end he settled for less, but his strategy lived on in the hearts of others with different dreams of personal power and national salvation. D'Annunzio intended that his seizure of Fiume would be the start of a process which would end in Rome.

Luigi Facta, the least able of all Italy's Liberal faction leaders, became Prime Minister in February 1922. Being a political weakling he was unable to form a strong coalition. Sensing a power vacuum the Fascists began the forceful takeover of local administrations. They were feeling their way towards power rather than following a definite strategy. Italo Balbo, the 25-year-old hatchet man extraordinaire of Fascism, moved through the North East deposing socialist local governments and closing down trade union offices to the delight of local businessmen who financed his operations. A trail of death and devastation followed his Blackshirts. Everywhere the Fascists' Roman salute and the Fascist hymn, Giovinezza, Salvadore Gotta's song of youth, once popular with the Arditi, came to mean fear or awed respect. Known opponents suffered the 'Fascist baptism', being forced to drink a pint or more of castor oil, sometimes mixed with kerosene. Occasionally anti-Fascists were required to eat a live toad for the sake of variety. In his diary Balbo recorded

"We went through Rimini, Sant' Arcangelo, Savigano, Cesena, Bertinora, all the towns and centres of the provinces of Forli and Ravenna, and destroyed and burned all the red buildings, and the seats of Socialist and Communist organisations. It was a terrible night. Our passage was marked by huge columns of fire and smoke. The whole plain of the Romagna was given up to the reprisals of the outraged Fascists determined to break for ever the red terror."
(Italo Balbo *Diario 1922*. published in Milan, 1932)

Facta's Government took no action. When people dared to remonstrate with the Blackshirts over any of their outrages the invariable reply was "Me ne frego", literally "I don't give a damn!" This is more offensive in Italian than in English and characterises neatly the Fascists' cavalier attitude to law and order.

In August the Socialists called a General Strike. Posing as the defenders of law and order, the squads attacked pickets and destroyed the printing presses of Socialist newspapers. Italy was rapidly degenerating into chaos. Parliamentary government had failed, law and order had broken down and few public services functioned. The political Establishment worried more about a Bolshevik-style revolution from the left than a Fascist takeover. It was felt that a patriotic party would not harm the state. The Liberals felt that Mussolini would have to be brought into the government to help end the chaos. There was little in his ideology that upset them other than his anti-parliamentarianism which they chose to ignore.

In October, Mussolini addressed the Fascists of Naples. "Either we are allowed to govern, or we will seize power by marching on Rome" and "take by the throat the miserable political class that governs us". The army was confident that it could handle the Squadristi but Facta chose to ignore the threat and failed to declare a state of emergency. On 27 October the Fascists began to take over government buildings and telephone exchanges throughout Italy. The cabinet met in emergency session and agreed to advise the King that the rebellion had to be put down by force. Victor Emmanuel III was initially willing to sign the declaration of a state of emergency and the imposition of a state of martial law. With Fascist columns straggling towards Rome from all directions the army and police began to act, driving them out of public buildings and halting all semblance of a march. General Badoglio, head of the General Staff, told his political masters:

> "The army has no desire for conflict with the Fascists, but should the latter break the law, I will undertake to restore order in no time. Five minutes of fire will put an end to the whole thing."
> (Pietro Nenni *Ten Years of Tyranny in Italy* p 133)

Then came the unexpected news that the King had changed his mind and refused to sign the declaration. Facta resigned. Mussolini made it clear that he would not serve in the government except as Prime Minister. Again the King backed down and invited the Fascist editor to form a government.

Mussolini travelled from Milan to Rome by train on 30 October. At his insistence, the army was allowing the Fascist marchers to shamble into the city. Their leader, Il Duce, toyed with the idea of entering the city on horseback at the head of his columns, but finally rejected the idea as liable to ridicule. He went the whole way by train. He found no difficulty in getting men to serve in his cabinet. His list of ministers contained only two other Fascists, the Minister of Justice and the Minister of Finance. His coalition contained Liberals, Nationalists, Popolari and Social Democrats. Only the Socialists and Communists opposed him. He trusted few of his fellows and in any case he required the support of other parties in Parliament. He retained two vital portfolios for himself, the Ministry of the Interior and the Foreign Ministry.

Romans generally welcomed the new government. After a few days of rape, pillage and attacks on political opponents, the Squadristi were allowed to parade past the Royal Palace, many having been brought in by lorry from the provinces for the day. They were then loaded onto special trains and safely packed off to their homes.

The March on Rome : the First Fascist Myth
In later years legends grew about Mussolini's 'Revolution'. Three hundred thousand armed Blackshirts, led by Mussolini on a white horse, had forced the King's hand but only after the death of 3,000 Fascist martyrs. In reality they were a poorly armed rabble who were held at bay by 400 policemen until the King lost his nerve and handed over power to Mussolini, who was still in Milan.

Why did the King capitulate?

This has never been completely explained but there does seem to be a number of possible reasons:

1. He did not want to exceed his constitutional powers, but he felt that the Liberal leaders were unable to deal with either the collapse of law and order or deadlock in Parliament.
2. He thought Mussolini would
   - be tough and clamp down on disturbances
   - stand up for Italy in Foreign Affairs
   - expand his Empire.
3. He wanted to avoid civil war or a violent solution to the crisis. Laura Fermi, the widow of a famous scientist who fled Italy to escape Fascist persecution, said:

> "The King and the government, poorly informed, overestimated the number, strength and determination of the Blackshirts, some of whom had already been driven back to their homes by rain and want of food. With very little bloodshed, with a few tanks and planes, the army could easily have pushed back the Fascists."
> (Laura Fermi *Mussolini* University of Chicago Press 1961)

FL Carsten, a German Academic who fled Nazi Germany for Britain, has written:

> "The March on Rome succeeded largely because there was nobody to oppose it. All the forces of the state - the army, the police, the civil service, the judiciary - supported it in one form or another, exactly as they had condoned Fascist violence and lawlessness during the previous years ... Hardly anybody recognised that Fascism represented an entirely new political and revolutionary force which could not be 'tamed' or brought under control, but would continue to develop its own dynamism, and would eventually sweep away the old order."
> (Quoted in *History in Focus* BBC Publications 1974)

PRIME MINISTER TO DUCE : THE PATH TO DICTATORSHIP

The March on Rome made Mussolini the constitutional Prime Minister of Italy. He did not seize power in a revolution, as he claimed. He had it bestowed on him by the King and there were many who expected him to lose it as quickly and as easily as he had gained it.

At first he had to work as a Prime Minister, struggling to secure a majority in Parliament at every vote. His hold on power was sometimes tenuous, but by the end of 1925 he was finally established in power as a dictator, the source of law, unquestionable and irremovable.

EARLY FOREIGN POLICY: SUCCESS OR DISASTER?

Mussolini immediately pursued a foreign policy which can only be described as active and vigorous. It left experienced foreign practitioners in this field with the feeling that he was a dangerous idiot and a political lightweight. In Italy it was hailed as a great success and helped to make him popular.

The Lausanne Conference on Turkey
A week after coming to power Mussolini attended international negotiations on the new peace treaty for Turkey. He began by demanding that the meetings should take place nearer Italy and left a demand that the British and French should meet him at a town on the Swiss-Italian border. There he insisted that they promise to treat Italy as an equal. Anxious to get on with the job they agreed and the Conference moved back to Lausanne. The Italian press hailed this as a great victory. The diplomatic world wondered what kind of madman had been sent to plague them. After a few days Mussolini tired of all the talk and went home.

The Prime Minister's next venture into the world of diplomacy was at a London meeting on German reparations, a serious business which he almost reduced to farce. A huge fuss followed the discovery that the French delegates had better hotel rooms than the Italians. British journalists seeking an interview were told he was unavailable as he might be busy in bed with a woman. No British Prime Minister had ever made such an excuse, although it was

often the case with Lloyd George! Italian diplomats were relieved when he agreed not to carry his manganello (Fascist club) in public. Once again the Italian press reported that Mussolini held centre stage and was dominating proceedings. Mussolini was both suspicious and critical of the League of Nations. He alternately saw it as a conspiracy by the old established powers (Britain and France) to keep virile young Italy down, and an organisation which allowed small nations too much influence at the expense of more civilised states, like Italy. However, Mussolini was not all idle talk. He felt the need to do something spectacular. Men like this are always dangerous.

The Corfu Incident
In July 1923 he ordered preparations for the invasion of the Greek island of Corfu. The boundary between Albania and Greece had never been properly determined, so an International Commission was attempting to do this when one of its members, the Italian General, Tellini, was murdered on Greek soil. There is no evidence that the murderers were Greeks. They probably came from Albania and some suspect that they were sent by Mussolini. The Italians responded with suspicious speed. Corfu was first bombarded by the navy and then occupied in the face of international outrage. Mussolini refused to deal with the League of Nations, saying that small nations must not be allowed to criticise great ones, like Italy. The Conference of Ambassadors, a body derived from the delegates to the Versailles Conference, took over the task. Mussolini was obliged to withdraw but the Greeks had to pay compensation of 50 million lire, (£500,000). This was not a large sum, but Mussolini claimed a great victory. To many Italians he was a hero; to the leaders of Europe he seemed to be a dangerous maniac who might plunge the continent into war by a mad dog act.

In January 1924 Italy secured Fiume by negotiation with Yugoslavia. Using conventional diplomacy Mussolini had succeeded where d'Annunzio had failed. His apparent successes in foreign affairs had strengthened his position in domestic politics.

Changes in the Electoral Law
Two weeks after becoming Prime Minister Mussolini made what was considered to be a very anti-parliamentary speech.

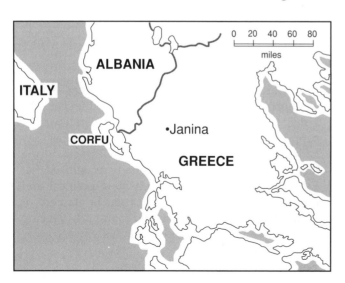

> "In the brief period of a decade it has come to pass for the second time that the Italian people has supplanted a Ministry and has given itself a government above and against the wishes of Parliament. The decade ... goes from May 1915 to October 1922 ... I am here to defend the Black Shirt revolution and bring it to its fullest realisation ... I could have abused my victory, but I refused to do so. I imposed limits on myself. I said to myself that the greatest wisdom is the one that does not abandon you after victory. With 300,000 men armed to the teeth, ready for anything and almost mythically ready to obey my orders, I could have punished all those who have defamed Fascism and have tried to besmirch it. (*approval from the right*) I could have converted this grey and dull hall into a bivouac for my squads ... (*lively applause from the right; rumblings; comments*)

(interjection from Modigliani) Long live Parliament! long live Parliament!

Mussolini : I could have bolted the Parliament and formed a government exclusively of Fascists. I could have done this but, at least for the present, I have chosen not to ..."
(Italian Parliamentary Records translated by Clough and Saladino in *A History of Modern Italy* p 411-413)

Soon after this Mussolini demanded the right to make what he considered necessary changes to the electoral system. The fact that both the Chamber of Deputies and the Senate voted to accept Mussolini's demands indicates the extent to which Liberal Italy had lost confidence in itself. He was given authority to raise taxes and run the country without seeking the consent of Parliament.

In July 1923 Parliament accepted changes to the electoral system. They agreed that the party with the most votes would automatically get two-thirds of the seats in the Chamber of Deputies, provided that they secured a minimum of 25% of the votes cast. In the elections of May 1921 the Fascists were a long way from being the most popular party or gaining the magical 25% but Mussolini had reason to be confident that the next election would be different.

Fascist Squads to National Militia

The excesses of the Fascist squads caused concern and alarm in many quarters. Mussolini conceded that such illegal actions by private gangs would have to come to an end. This was achieved by making the squads into a 'National Militia'. Its leaders were accorded the ranks of Consuls and Centurions, reminders of the glory of ancient Rome, and the state had to meet the costs. Amply encouraged by their Duce, the squads continued with their campaigns of intimidation, murder and extortion, but now these could be described as legitimate police action in defence of the state instead of unjustified private violence. A reign of terror produced the murder of three opposition parliamentarians and violent attacks on at least fifty others. The regular police were also under the Prime Minister's personal control and were not permitted to interfere with squad action.

The Elections of 1924

Fascist preparations for these elections began as soon as Mussolini came to power and included the changes in the electoral system. Leading politicians had their telephones tapped and very heavy pressure was applied to non-Fascist newspapers. The first form of censorship was simple and direct. Fascist squads visited print works and destroyed whole editions or wrecked the presses. The effect on profits was devastating. Editors were intimidated or imprisoned on phoney charges and fabricated evidence. Before long the media became subservient to the Fascist will and little criticism of the Party appeared in print. As the elections of April 1924 drew near, the harassment of opponents increased. Niti, a Liberal ex-Prime Minister, had his home pillaged, Matteotti, a Socialist deputy, was frequently attacked by Fascist gangsters. Amendola, a Liberal Conservative, found himself facing assault charges when he drove off five stalwart squadristi

Matteotti

with his umbrella. Elected local councils with a non-Fascist majority were dissolved and replaced with Fascist nominees who then had the useful duty of organising the voting arrangements in their area for the general election.

Despite these gross violations of democratic principles and procedures many Liberal leaders continued to support Mussolini as the saviour of Italy from Socialism. Orlando and Salandra campaigned with the Fascists while Giolitti supported their anti-Socialist stance. It seems remarkable now, but these experienced politicians had failed to recognise the true nature of Fascism, a mistake which they would regret for the rest of their lives.

The election was a landslide. The Fascists polled 65% of the votes and received 374 seats against the 180 secured by all the other parties. The 1923 electoral changes had proved totally superfluous. Mussolini appeared to have achieved complete control of Italy.

The Murder of Matteotti

Only one man had the desperate courage needed to stand up to the thugs. Giacomo Matteotti knew what he was doing as he had often been attacked by Fascist gangs. On 30 May 1924 he said to the Chamber of Deputies:

"[We Socialists] maintain that the government's majority list which received a nominal vote of more than 4 million ballots ...

(interruptions) *(voices from centre)* And even more!

Matteotti: In fact this list did not obtain these votes freely and it is therefore doubtful that it obtained the percentage necessary (*interruptions, protests*)

... for it to receive, even according to your law, the two-thirds of the seats assigned to it ... No voter was free in this election because everyone knew a priori that, even if the majority of voters dared to vote against the government, there was a force at the government's disposal that would annul any contrary results. (*interruptions*) This intention of the government was reinforced by the presence of an armed militia. (*lively applause and shouts from the right of 'Long live the militia'*) ... About 60 of our 100 candidates were not able to move about freely. In 90 per cent of the cases ... the supervising body at the polling places was wholly Fascist, and the representatives of the minority lists were not allowed to be present during voting ... Newspapers were destroyed, headquarters devastated and beatings were administered ... The poor peasants knew that any resistance was useless, and for the sake of their families they had to submit to the law of the strongest, the law of the master, by voting for the candidates assigned to them by the local boss of the Fascist Union ... (*interruptions*) ... In fact only a small minority was able to give its vote freely... For all these reasons and for others that I forego presenting because of your noisy importunings - you know very well what these reasons are because each one of you was at least a witness to them (*rumblings*) ... we request that the election of the majority be annulled in toto ... We request that all elections compromised by violence be deferred to the Committee on Credentials. (*Applause from the extreme left; lively rumblings*)"

(from Italian Parliamentary Records translated by Clough and Saladino in *A History of Modern Italy* p 425-426)

He also opposed Mussolini's demand that thousands of new Fascist laws should be enacted at once without any real discussion. Matteotti had denounced the fraud, violence and ballot rigging which had given the Fascists their election victory. One man had the courage to say what everybody knew. It threatened the regime and damaged its reputation in other countries. Giacomo Matteotti deserves an honoured place among those who have sacrificed themselves in the cause of democracy. He knew the risk he ran and his courage cost him his life. He ended his speech with the words

" 'and now you can prepare my funeral oration' ... He had spoken without veiling his meaning in a cloud of philosophical abstractions. He called a spade a spade and a bandit a bandit."

(Peitro Nenni *Ten Years of Tyranny in Italy* p 165)

On 10 June 1924 Matteotti was dragged into a large Lancia car as he left his home. The car drove away at speed. A witness reported the incident to the police and although the car and its owner were found no sign of Matteotti was found, other than blood stains on the seat. It became obvious that he had been murdered by Volpi and Dumini, Fascist hit men recruited by Mussolini for such missions, and that they had been acting on their master's orders. The subsequent investigation was carried out by a Fascist Police Chief and not by a magistrate, as was the regular procedure. Matteotti's body was found in a shallow grave while the investigation was in progress. Dumini was found guilty of murder and was imprisoned for two years. Mussolini's name was kept out of the case and he was not required to testify. One of Matteotti's killers later testified that his last words were:

"You may kill me; you will not kill the ideal. My children will be proud of their Father. The workers will bless my dead body."

(Oskar Pollak in the foreword to *The Fascisti Exposed* by Giacomo Matteotti. Published posthumously by the Independent Labour Party, London)

For a while the Fascist Government was in very precarious situation. Some prominent Fascists left the Party and minor protest strikes broke out in a number of cities. The Socialists, Catholic Popolari deputies and Amendola's Liberal Conservatives withdrew from the Chamber in protest, a move called the Aventine Succession. [In ancient Rome the Plebs (Roman poor) had once withdrawn onto the Avantine Hill in protest at their treatment by the Patricians (rich Romans).] If the King had decided to sack Mussolini, Fascism would have been finished but Victor Emanuel still feared civil war and did nothing. Liberals in the Senate refused to pass a vote of censure on Mussolini as they feared he might be replaced by Socialism. The Avantine deputies lost their only chance of making themselves heard by their withdrawal. Mussolini survived. There were no more Matteottis left to point out his misdeeds, publicly at any rate. In the months that followed, the last vestiges of Italian democracy were swept away and a totalitarian regime established as Mussolini's confidence recovered. (A totalitarian regime is one which seeks to control all aspects of society and to completely dominate the lives of all the people. Criticism and dissent are not tolerated. The government is a dictatorship.)

6 The Fascist Dictatorship in Italy under Mussolini

MORE CHANGES IN GOVERNMENT

By the time he had finished, Mussolini had made a complete pig's breakfast out of what had been Italy's system of government, while claiming to be a revolutionary who had created an efficient and effective new system.

Mussolini's problem was simple. He wanted complete power and authority for himself. He did not, and could not, trust anybody else including, and especially, his own Party. It is impossible for one individual to govern a large modern state on his own. Inevitably some power has to be delegated. Mussolini knew this. To enhance his own position he wanted to reduce the authority of traditional organs of state such as the cabinet or parliament. Since he could not run things entirely on his own he created his own alternative bodies to either replace or check the influence of the traditional ones. Rightly suspicious of his own followers, he would then undermine the authority of his own creation. The chaos which followed was impressive, even by Italian standards. A fine example of this is the Grand Council of Fascists, created in 1922 as a counterbalance for the Cabinet, in which Fascists were a minority. It did not have executive powers but was meant to advise on new legislation which would then be presented to Parliament for approval without discussion. Its meetings became less and less frequent and it ceased to hold discussions. Like Parliament it was required to approve, automatically, the dictator's demands. In 1928 it became an official organ of government, which was tantamount to being abolished altogether. Throughout his years in power Mussolini tinkered with and amended the system of government. Late in 1925 he took the title 'Head of Government' instead of Prime Minister. He was permitted to make laws without Parliament and to fix his own pay. Parliament was not allowed to discuss anything unless Mussolini asked it to. This sham Parliament survived until its abolition in 1939 when it was replaced by a purely nominated body. Mussolini disliked discussion. He habitually presented Parliament with collections of new laws which it was required to approve en masse and without discussion - 2,364 such proposals were passed in 1925. In all 100,000 decrees were made in the 17 years of his rule. Since there was no discussion, nobody could point out even the most glaring faults and so many idiotic laws were enacted.

More Changes to the Electoral System

In May 1928 universal suffrage, the right of all adults to vote, was abolished. The electorate was cut from 10 million to 3 million as only those over 21 who paid over 100 Lire in taxes retained the franchise. In the 1929 elections an extremely novel system of choosing Parliamentary deputies was used. Trade unions and employers submitted names of possible candidates to the Fascist Grand Council who selected 400 of them. The electorate then had to accept or reject the entire list. Ordinary Italians now had no influence on their government through the ballot box.

Press Censorship

In his early days as a Socialist editor Mussolini had condemned censorship. After the March on Rome he practised it informally by using the squadristi to intimidate journalists and wreck the presses of critical publications. In 1925 the system was formalised when local councils were given the right to close down anti-Fascist papers. Since elected councils were replaced by Fascist nominees in 1926 this worked well for Mussolini. Foreign journalists were expelled if they criticised the regime. They were also subject to intimidation and bribery. The result was a remarkably favourable image of Italy in Britain's press. This system of censorship is employed against Western newspapers by many Third World countries today. Partly because of this effective censorship of the press and partly because he could be immensely charming to foreigners when he put his mind to it, Mussolini was, for many years, highly thought of in British political circles. In 1925 the British Foreign Secretary, Austen Chamberlain wrote of Mussolini:

Mussolini speaking

"... if I ever had to choose in my own country between anarchy and dictatorship I expect I should be on the side of the dictator. In any case I thought Mussolini a strong man of singular charm and I suspect of not a little tenderness and loneliness of heart ... I believe him to be accused of crimes in which he had no share, and I suspect him to have connived unwillingly at other outrages which he would have prevented if he could. But I am confident that he is a patriot and a sincere man; I trust his word when given and I think we might easily go far before finding an Italian with whom it would be so easy for the British Government to work."
(Sir Charles Petrie *Life of Sir Austen Chamberlain*, p 295-6 Quoted in Martin Gilbert *Britain and Germany between the Wars*)

The One Party State

The level of violence and intimidation had effectively made Italy a one party state by the time of Matteotti's murder. In 1925 and 1926 there were a number of attempts on Mussolini's life. One of these, in 1925, resulted in the formal dissolution of the Socialist Unitary Party. In April 1926 Miss Violet Gibson, an Irish lady, arrived in Italy determined to shoot either Mussolini or the Pope. As she aimed her pistol at him, Mussolini threw back his head and stuck out his chin in one of his characteristic poses. The bullet hit his nose. Mussolini's superb sense of the dramatic emerged again as he seized the opportunity to cultivate his image as a superman. With blood seeping through the hastily applied dressings he called out, "If I go forward, follow me. If I go back, kill me. If I die, avenge me." How long had he waited for the right moment to say these lines? Miss Gibson was gallantly sent back to Ireland, unpunished. In November, following another attempt on his life, "the circumstances" of which

"have always remained shrouded in mystery, the government adopted a series of measures sanctioning the end of whatever autonomous political life remained in Italy. All parties and associations pursuing activities judged to be contrary to the regime were dissolved ... the Aventine deputies were expelled from the chamber."
(Alberto Aquarone *Mussolini's Italy* in *Purnell's History of the 20th Century* Chapter 39)

The measures referred to were reported in *The Times* on 8th November 1926. *The Defence of the State Act* included these clauses:

"The cancellation and revision of all passports issued to date and the taking of the severest action against those who attempt to cross the frontier without a passport."
"The suspension for an indefinite period of all newspapers opposed to the Fascist regime."
"The disbandment of all parties, associations and organisations whose acts are opposed to the regime."
(Quoted in C Leeds *Italy under Mussolini*, p 78)

Further Repression

Up until November 1926 repression had been achieved largely by the action of the squads. From that time onwards it became increasingly formalised and accorded

some sort of legal status. Alberto Aquarone records that the death penalty was brought in for serious political offences. A special tribunal of army and militia (squad) officers was set up to try even minor offences. Special courts are a common feature of authoritarian or totalitarian states. They rarely concern themselves with rules of evidence or justice and fair trials are very low on their list of priorities. No appeal was possible against decisions by Mussolini's tribunals.

In 1927 a secret police force was set up. Mussolini called it OVRA. Nobody knows what these letters stand for. Perhaps it was hoped that an air of mystery surrounding the organisation would strike fear into people's hearts. They spied on each other, on prominent members of the party and on ordinary Italians but lacked the brutal efficiency for which Nazi Germany's Gestapo or the different generations of Soviet secret police (CHEKA, OBPU, NKVD and KGB) became notorious. According to Aquarone,

"The police regime thus created was harsh but not inhuman or bloodthirsty by comparison with other totalitarian regimes ... The death sentences pronounced by the special tribunals in peacetime ... did not exceed ten. There were over 4,000 prison sentences, sometimes very heavy ones, while for (those) judged to be less dangerous there was temporary banishment ... to a remote area. ... There were never any true concentration camps ..."
(Alberto Aquarone *Mussolini's Italy* in *Purnell's History of the 20th Century*)

Hugh Dalton, a leading member of the British Labour Party, who visited both Germany and Italy at this time wrote in his memoirs:

"Italian Fascism, just because it was Italian, was much less intense, more casual, and therefore less evil than German Nazism."
(*The Fateful Years* p 41. Quoted by M Gilbert op. cit.)

While this may be true of Fascism in Italy, it should not be forgotten that Fascists murdered huge numbers of Abyssinians after the conquest of that country in 1936, and Yugoslavs during the Second World War.

These measures rapidly drove opposition underground and for a time it was fairly active until police action finally destroyed it in the early thirties. Many leading anti-Fascists fled to France. Nitti was the most prominent of these. Carlo Rosselli led a group of radical, democratic intellectuals from Paris and edited a newspaper *Giustizia e Liberta* (Justice and Liberty). He fought in the Garibaldi Brigade with anti-Fascist Italians against Mussolini's 'volunteers' in the Spanish Civil War. On his return to Paris he was assassinated by Fascist hit men. Rosselli had, all along, displayed Matteotti-like courage. In 1926 he had helped an old friend in ill health, Filippo Turati, a seventy-year-old socialist, to escape to Corsica, in France, by motor boat. For this crime he was sent into internal exile. Later he fled to Paris.

Equally brave was Lauro de Bosis, a poet, who flew from France to Rome and scattered leaflets to remind Italians of their lost freedom. He threw out a history book, *Fascism in Italy* by Bolton King to give the other side of the official version being pedalled in schools.

> "As one throws bread on a starving city, one must throw history books on Rome." "He flew very low over the streets, and, in places it seemed as if snow had fallen, so thickly were the leaflets strewn. He dropped them in the laps of spectators at an open air cinema, and among the tables of the cafes in the squares. There have been many rumours as to his fate but no trace of his plane was ever found. How he died was never known."
>
> (De Bosis *The Story of my Death* and Sforza *Contemporary Italy* Sforza quotes eyewitness accounts to de Bosis's girlfriend, Ruth Draper. Both sources quoted in C Leeds *Italy under Mussolini*)

These accounts go some way towards justifying the claim that "It was the Italians who first fought Fascism" and that they fought it when others in Europe thought that it was "a jolly good thing, bringing order to chaotic Italy". In the end most Italians learned to keep their heads down and their mouths shut.

THE DOPOLAVORO

In 1932 an article in the British magazine *The Spectator* quoted a prominent Fascist:

> "What was wrong with our people before the war was that they used to think and talk too much about politics. They were alright when they were working, but then their minds were on their work; they were alright when they were asleep, for then they didn't think at all, at least consciously. Their leisure hours were a danger spot for the whole nation."

The Fascists wanted to remove the threat of the Italians thinking about politics in their leisure hours. Fascist action against trade unions had helped to hold down workers' living standards so they wanted to defuse potential discontent by compensating the workers in some way. The Dopolavoro (National Institute for After Work Activities) was the result. Created in 1925 it took control of almost all sports, cultural and leisure organisations, and annexed their property. It took over control of football and a chief referee in Rome, equipped with a gold whistle, licensed referees. Italy's victories in the World Cup in 1934 and 1938 were hailed as Fascist triumphs as was Primo Carnera's world heavyweight boxing title in 1933. Mussolini said that boxing was "an essentially Fascist method of self-expression" and orders were issued to newspapers never to print pictures of Carnera being knocked down in a bout.

According to Christopher Leeds in *Italy under Mussolini* (p 48)

> "On the 10th anniversary of Fascism, the Dopolavoro controlled 1,350 theatres, 3,265 libraries, 2,208 dramatic societies, 3,324 brass bands, 2,139 orchestral societies and a membership of 1,667,000. By 1938 it provided opportunities for recreation to about 3 million members."

Like Nazi Germany's Kraft Durch Freude organisation, which like so many Nazi institutions and habits appears to have been copied from Fascist Italy, the Dopolavoro organised holidays for its members. Even in their leisure hours Italians were liable to encounter Fascist attempts to control their lives.

IL DUCE AND IL PAPA

The Lateran Treaties with the Catholic Church

Prior to the unification of Italy the Pope had been a temporal as well as a spiritual leader. He was effectively King of those areas called the Papal States. In 1870 the Church's kingdom on earth was reduced to the Vatican. Successive Popes refused to accept this or to recognise the Kingdom of Italy. To millions of loyal Catholic Italians this presented a horrible dilemma. To whom did they owe their loyalty, Church or state? Was it possible to be a patriotic Italian and a good Catholic? After the First World War the Papacy realised that the state of Italy was not a temporary phenomenon. The creation of the Partito Popolare, a political party led by a priest, Don Sturzo, was recognition of this.

Mussolini knew of the Pope's immense influence with Catholic Italians and recognised the dangers of a conflict with the Vatican. Pius XI, who became Pope in 1922, thought the Popolari too left wing and was willing to come to terms with Fascism. Two years of negotiation between Cardinal Gasparri and the Fascists produced three agreements in 1929 of which the best known is the Lateran Treaty. The main points were:

1 The Pope recognised the existence of the Italian state and in return his sovereignty over the Vatican and his country palace of Castel Gondolfo was accepted. The Vatican had the right to send and receive diplomats.
2 The Catholic religion was proclaimed to be 'the sole religion of the state', a largely meaningless phrase.
3 The Papacy received compensation of 30 million Lire for its losses of property at the time of unification.
4 The Pope was to appoint all bishops in Italy but he would clear all appointments with the government in case there were political objections. Priests were not to join any political party. The state would pay priests and bishops.
5 Religious education in schools would be given by people approved by the church.

This agreement turned out to be an immense triumph for Mussolini. It earned him the gratitude of people who, for the first time, could be loyal Catholics and patriotic Italians. It also freed him from the danger of a quarrel with the Pope.

Mussolini did not always agree with the Church in the following years. He suppressed the Catholic Scouts in an attempt to force all young Italians to join the Fascist Youth Movement. Later the Church set up another youth organisation, Catholic Action. While the Pope often objected to Fascist policies, he felt that they were better than communism and so he offered no serious opposition to Mussolini's regime.

BENITO MUSSOLINI

ama molto i bambini.

I bimbi d'Italia amano

molto il Duce.

VIVA IL DUCE!

Saluto al Duce:

A noi!

The 'father figure' image of Mussolini in an elementary school text book

Fascist Youth Policy

Totalitarian regimes invariably make special efforts to win the support of the young, who are seen as representing their country's future. The process of thought control cannot begin too early. Mussolini wanted not just the acquiescence of Italians to Fascist rule but also their enthusiastic participation in the Fascist state.

Education

Mussolini once said that Italians need less education since illiterates had more courage than educated people. He wanted more character and less brain; the creation of a hardened military race hated and feared by others and rejoicing in that hate and fear. Italians must learn to believe, obey and fight. To this end school teachers and university lecturers were required to swear oaths of loyalty to the Duce. In school, all pupils had to take a course in Fascist Culture. School history was rewritten to conform with Mussolini's views on Italy's past and her role in world history. In 1926, 101 history texts were banned and finally, in 1936, a single book became standard. It used the Fascist system of dating in which 1922 (AD) is Anno Primo - the year 0. Ignoring the fact that British troops were rushed from France to Italy after Caporetto, it claimed that Italy saved Britain, France and the USA from defeat at the hands of Germany in the Great War. Much attention was, perhaps understandably, paid to the greatness of Imperial Rome.

A reader for 8-year-olds contained such subtle efforts at indoctrination as "How can we ever forget that Fascist boy who, when near to death, asked that he might put on his uniform and that his savings should go the the Party?"

Fascist policy seems to have made little impact on Italy's real problems. In the 1930 census report, 20% of all adults were shown to be illiterate. In the poorer areas of the south this figure was sometimes as high as 40%. The extent of subsequent progress can probably be deduced from the fact that illiteracy figures did not appear in the 1936 report.

The Fascist Youth

Every Italian boy was expected to join the Party's youth organisations. At the age of only 4 he became a 'Son of the She Wolf' (Romulus, the legendary founder of Rome and his brother, Remus, had been reared and suckled by a she wolf). His sister joined 'The Little Italian Girls'. At 8 the boys moved on to the Balilla and at 14 to the Avanguardisti. Military drill and black-shirted uniforms featured prominently. The girls, on the other hand, wore white shirts since they were not expected to become tough, arrogant empire builders, only the mothers of such wonders.

In Germany Hitler often appeared to copy what Mussolini had done in Italy. The Hitler Youth and the Avanguardisti have much in common although Hitler went much further and banned all other forms of youth organisation while in 1931 the Catholic Church was able to set up its own Youth Organisation, 'Catholic Action' in Italy. Once again Mussolini failed to reach the levels of totalitarian control achieved by the Nazis.

" ... Mussolini was ... obliged to settle for conformity rather than the universal activism necessary to totalitarianism ... Fear of dismissal ensured the quiescence of the rising number of public employees, notably the great mass of school teachers and university professors ... Propaganda, the 'fascistisation' of education, and the conditioning effects of youth organisations, the Dopolavoro, etc., if not creating as many passionate fascists as was intended, did help to secure acquiescence, if they failed to make popular a party widely and rightly considered corrupt, they nevertheless did make a hero of Mussolini. And, of course, for many Italians the regime's achievements, magnified by propaganda, seemed real: social peace and respect abroad were novelties to ... Italians accustomed to social uncertainty and international humiliation. This widespread, if largely passive acceptance of the regime in the early 1930s has inspired a leading Italian historian of fascism, Renzo De Felice, to call these the 'Years of consensus'."
(Martin Blinkhorn *Mussolini and Fascist Italy* p 29)

THE PHILOSOPHY OF FASCISM

Most political creeds have an ideology, a system of ideas and values on which they base their actions when in power. Communism aspires to the equality of all and opposes private ownership and wealth. Liberalism emphasises the need to protect the rights of the individual citizen, an aim which is thought to be best secured by democratic government. What, then, was the philosophy or ideology of Fascism? It will be remembered that

Mussolini had entered political life as a socialist and internationalist and had become a right-wing nationalist for reasons of political convenience.

> "Italian Fascism originated not as doctrine but as method, as a technique of winning power, and as such its principles were unclear even to its own members. Some thought and continued to think it on the left of politics, others on the right, others that it was both left and right simultaneously."
> (Denis Mack Smith *Mussolini* p 159)

Mussolini wanted Fascism to be accepted as an intellectually defensible creed, so in 1921 he gave the party intellectuals the task of defining the creed of Fascism. After two months their quest clearly had led them nowhere. Mussolini defended his creation by saying that Fascism was about action, not words. It was more like a religion than a political dogma. He saw it as

> "an embodiment of beauty and courage, a love of risk, a hatred of 'peacemongers' and above all a burning desire to obey Mussolini's personal authority."
> (quoted by Denis Mack Smith *Mussolini* p 160)

He defended his right to change his opinions and refused to be tied down by an ideology or dogma. However, his craving for intellectual respectability continued and in 1925 he assembled two hundred intellectuals who were required to pronounce that there was no conflict between Fascism and intelligence. They received the same treatment as the Italian Parliament and were not allowed any discussion before making their pronouncement. The situation remained 'as clear as mud'. Since Mussolini experienced difficulty in saying exactly what Fascism stood for, the account which follows should only be regarded as a rough guide.

In *The Doctrine of Fascism* (1932) Mussolini wrote:

> "Being anti-individualistic, the Fascist system of life stresses the importance of the State and recognises the individual only in so far as his interests coincide with those of the state ... It is opposed to liberalism (which) denied the state in the name of the individual. Fascism reasserts the rights of the state as expressing the real essence of the individual. And if liberty is to be the attribute of living men and not that of abstract dummies invented by individualistic liberalism, then Fascism stands for liberty and for the only liberty worth having, the liberty of the state and the individual within the state."

In asserting the rights of the state, Italian Fascism was identical to other totalitarian regimes, notably Communist Russia under Stalin and Nazi Germany. Mussolini would claim that by sacrificing his or her interests in favour of the state, the citizen would benefit. For instance, workers no longer went on strike to press selfish pay claims as this could damage trade and was not in the nation's interest. As a result their companies prospered so that there were more jobs and ultimately higher wages. Opponents saw only company rights increasing while wages stayed the same or fell and courts were used to

punish anyone who dared to criticise the abuse of state power by the Fascist elite.

Italian Fascism was also consistently and openly anti-parliamentary. Eventually all forms of election were eliminated. Instead the Italians were urged to unquestioning obedience of Il Duce, the leader. Mussolini unashamedly presented himself as a superman, the greatest Statesman in the World. Fascist ideas were transmitted to the Italians in a series of simple slogans.

'Mussolini is always right' suggests an infallible superman who should be obeyed. 'Believe! Obey! Fight!' combines the authoritarian emphasis on obedience with the Fascist glorification of war. Despite, or perhaps because of, experience of the Great War Mussolini believed in war. He felt that the Italians had become soft and that, to reawaken the glories of ancient Rome, they would have to be toughened by the experience of combat. His brand of Italian nationalism demanded that other peoples should be conquered and made the subjects of an Italian Empire. Fascist attitudes to war emerge from slogans such as:

- 'He who has steel has bread'
- 'Nothing has been won in history without bloodshed'
- 'A minute on the battlefield is worth a lifetime of Peace'
- 'Better to live one day as a lion than a hundred years as a sheep'
- 'War is to a man what childbearing is to a woman'.

The last slogan gives an interesting insight into Fascist ideas of gender stereotypes and roles. Other slogans reveal other aspects of the Fascist creed.

- 'Live dangerously.' (This may refer to Italian driving!)
- 'Fascism is, above all, the verb *to want*, in the present tense.'
- 'Fascism is the most formidable creation of an individual and national will to power.'
- 'Fascism is an organised, centralised, authoritarian, democracy.'

Does aggressive nationalism combined with the absurd vanity of a single man and a collection of slogans amount to a political ideology? Is it perhaps better to view Fascism as a method for obtaining and holding power, a way to dupe the gullible? Perhaps this is what Ernest Hemingway thought in 1923 when he said 'Mussolini is the biggest bluff in Europe.'

Nationalism

Aggressive nationalism is perhaps the most obvious characteristic of Fascism and is commonly exhibited by right-wing groups labelled 'Fascist'. It was the dominant feature of German Nazism and can clearly be seen in modern British groups such as the British National Party and the National Front. English soccer hooligans and their Dutch counterparts look horribly like blackshirt thugs in their mindless, violent contempt for all things foreign and of the rights of those they see as foreigners.

Whereas the Nationalism of Mazzini was about the rights

of small nations to preserve and assert their identity against foreign domination, Fascism was contemptuous of the rights of small nations and exuded an air of 'my country right or wrong'. This type of nationalism is common among second-rate powers seeking to be first-rate powers, nations with an acute sense of grievance and former great powers in decline. Mussolini aspired to make Italy a first-rate military and economic power. He was not alone among Italians in resenting Italy's treatment by the great powers at Versailles when she did not receive what they saw as her just share of the spoils. Fascist nationalism is therefore the nationalism of the inferiority complex. This is what makes it so violently self-assertive.

Mussolini's treatment of Greece in the Corfu affair is a fine example of Fascist Nationalism at work (see page 43). So too is the treatment of the German-speaking majority in the South Tyrol, transferred from Austria to Italy by the Treaty of St Germain in 1919. Austria had once been the dominant power in Italy so it is perhaps not surprising that the Tyrolese became the victims of a vigorous Italianisation campaign. The region's name was changed to Alto Adige and, despite early assurance that local languages, customs and regional autonomy would be respected, schools were closed. German was not allowed to be spoken in educational establishments, law courts or government offices. Place names were Italianised and individual citizens were sometimes forced to change their names. In the autumn of 1925 a squad ran riot in the Tyrolean town of Bruneck.

> "Nearly all the houses in the town, not excepting the church, had been daubed by the Blackshirts with the tricolours, the badge of the Lictors' fasces, death's-heads and threats. Numbers of townspeople were struck or beaten in the streets and ale-houses for no more than speaking German. 'We are here to mete out thrashings', announced the Fascists."
> (Dr Eduard Reut-Nicolussi *Tyrol under the axe of Fascism* translated by KL Montgomery)

In the thirties the Tyrolese looked to Hitler for help and support but got none. They learned to look after themselves. Today the region has a strong separatist movement and Italian officials and their families in the area often complain of being threatened and terrorised.

While Mussolini's treatment of the Tyrolese may seem shocking it is perhaps as well to bear in mind that this type of attitude was commonplace in the French and British Empires of those times. Indeed, British government power was used by lowland Scots in a protracted campaign to exterminate the Gaelic language. Even after the Second World War, the great war of liberation from Fascism, Highland children were being thrashed with leather belts for the crime of speaking their mother tongue in school.

Anti-semitism only became part of Italian Fascism in 1938. In 1933 Mussolini had made fun of Hitler's ideas on racial purity, while as late as 1938 leading Fascists were still denying any intention of persecuting the Jews. Large numbers of Jews had fled from Germany and taken refuge in Italy, but as Hitler and Mussolini drew closer in inter-national affairs, anti-semitism crept into Fascist doctrine. In September 1938 further Jewish immigration was banned and in November the Fascists passed a race law which included the following provisions:

> "1 Marriage between an Italian citizen of the Aryan race and a person belonging to another race is prohibited.
> 8a A person is of the Jewish race if born of parents both of the Jewish race, even if he belongs to a religion other than Jewish.
> 9 Membership of the Jewish race must be declared and entered on the public registers.
> 10 Italian citizens of the Jewish race must not
> (a) render military service in time of peace or of war
> (d) be proprietors of lands which ... have an appraised valuation of more than 5,000 lire (£50)
> (e) be proprietors of urban buildings which altogether have a value of 20,000 lire (£200)
> 13 The following agencies must not employ persons of the Jewish race (a) the Civil and military administrations of the State (b) the National Fascist Party ..."
> (Clough and Saladino *A History of Modern Italy - Documents, Reading and Commentary*)

This policy was odious to many Italians including the King, the Pope and members of the Fascist Party. Mussolini is said to have answered a protester by saying, "I don't believe in the least in this stupid anti-semitic theory. Whatever I am doing is entirely for political reasons."
(Quoted in Hibbert *Benito Mussolini*)

Mussolini's anti-semitism can be explained not only by Hitler's influence but also by the need to justify Italy's domination of Africans in Abyssinia and Libya. This gave rise to a Nazi-style doctrine of racial superiority. A memorandum in the German Foreign Ministry archives records details of a conversation between Mussolini and von Bulow-Schwante, a foreign ministry official in October 1937 during Mussolini's visit to Berlin.

> "Mussolini inquired in detail about the development of the Jewish question prior to and after the seizure of power, and about its present status. He said that with 70,000 Jews in Italy this question constituted no problem for him. But the racial question of white and black was now coming into the foreground for him. I gave him a detailed account of the Jewish question. Concluding this topic, he told me that after long surveillance of the mail he had fortunately discovered only three cases in Africa in which Italian women had forgotten themselves. He had had them beaten as a deterrent example and then sent them to a concentration camp for 5 years."
> (From *Documents in German Foreign Policy* Series D Vol 1 Doc 2)

This document indicates the general trend of Mussolini's thinking, but how reliable is it in terms of the specific claims made? It should be borne in mind to whom Mussolini was speaking and the image that he would like to cultivate with these people. An old joke about national stereotypes and identities might also help:

"In heaven the police are English, the chefs are French, the lovers are Italian, the engineers are German and everything is organised by the Swiss. In hell the policemen are Germans, the cooking is done by the English, the engineers are French, the lovers are Swiss and everything is organised by the Italians!"

The Scots have not been assigned a role! This image of a chaotic Italy was one that Mussolini was keen to counteract. The document also illustrates something of the Duce's attitude to women. How would Italian men who "forgot themselves" with African women be treated?

Aggressive nationalism was therefore a central feature of both Fascism and Nazism but while the ideas of racial superiority, that the Germans were the master race, and racial purity were central to Nazi dogma, they only crept into Fascism in the last few years of Mussolini's regime.

THE ECONOMY OF FASCIST ITALY

Acute problems in Italy's economy in the early twenties were a major factor in the Fascist rise to power. In 1922 Italy was suffering from serious unemployment in the aftermath of the First World War. She was plagued by chronic industrial unrest, her industry devastated by strikes, lockouts and violence. While the North of the country was relatively well developed, the South was a byword in backwardness. Its peasant agriculture was primitive and there was little or no industry. Italian industry struggled to be competitive against a background of high fuel and energy costs. Italy has no fossil fuels.

Mussolini liked to claim that he was well versed in economics and that this was an aspect of statescraft where Fascism had all the answers to the problems of those times. In reality his knowledge of economic theory appears to have been as superficial as his solutions to economic problems. He ran a series of campaigns, targeted at various problems. Each was described as a battle and presented to the public in terms of simple military imagery. The outcome was a mixture of success, partial success and outright failure.

When the Fascists took power, international trade, and with it the Italian economy, had already begun to pick up. The postwar governments had spent heavily on modernising Italy's railway network. The railways had acquired an international reputation for chaos. The question was generally not whether a train would be late but whether it would come at all. Taking advantage of work started for them by others, the Fascists claimed to have made the trains run on time. This much vaunted Fascist efficiency did not convince everybody.

Elizabeth Wiskemann, who travelled widely in Europe at this time, wrote:

"... I found nothing, not even a trifle, was improved in Germany by the Nazis, (but) the Fascists in Italy did have two trifling things to their credit. I was never taken in by the myth of the punctual trains as I travelled on a number that were late. But I did think it reasonable to impose small fines upon people who put their dirty feet up on seats where others would be sitting on trains. And to keep the people moving in one direction on the narrow pavements of Rome, for instance, was rather sensible ..."
(E Wiskemann *The Europe I Saw* p 174)

It seems that the main-line trains became fairly punctual, with over 5,000 kilometres of line being electrified, while the branch lines retained their distinctive Italian character.

A programme of public works was launched immediately Mussolini took office. Europe's first motorway, connecting Milan to the Lakes of Northern Italy, was begun in 1923. A network of these 'Autostrade' eventually connected the major cities. Sadly, minor roads were neglected as the Fascists appeared to be unable to see beyond the publicity value of major prestige projects.

Mussolini was blessed with a series of able Finance Ministers. Count Volpi, one of the country's top industrialists and financiers, was able to persuade America and Britain to write off much of Italy's war debt. American investment flowed into Italy, much to the regime's advantage.

Italy is seriously handicapped by the total absence of any deposits of coal or oil. To overcome this deficiency, the Fascists built more hydroelectric schemes in the alpine region. These helped to supply industrial towns like Milan and Turin with cheap power.

Outside Rome were the Pontine marshes. The great Emperors of ancient Rome had failed to get these drained and Rome continued to be plagued by malaria and mosquitoes as a result. The draining of those swamps and their conversion to productive farm land was one of Fascism's greatest early triumphs and one whose publicity value was not overlooked.

Later Mussolini encouraged, financially, the construction of ski resorts in the Italian Alps. This provided work, encouraged tourism and provided the Italians with healthy, manly exercise. Il Duce was photographed on skis, stripped to the waist, hairy chest prominently on view.

Similar programmes of public works were later used in Germany by Hitler and in the USA by FD Roosevelt. They provided jobs and the wages paid helped stimulate demand and provide jobs in other industries. The English economist, John Maynard Keynes, called this the multiplier effect. Money spent by the government on wages in a public works project is spent many times over and demand is created by a knock-on effect.

Even a campaign of public works could not counteract the effects of the Great Depression which hit the world and Italy in 1929. In 1933 Italy's unemployment was admitted to exceed one million, in a country whose total population was 42 million. The public works programme did not have any real impact on the grinding poverty of the South. In the impossible international economic climate of those times, this was only to be expected.

Mussolini helping to collect the harvest

The Battle for Grain

Between 1922 and 1930 Italian wheat production increased by 50%. Between 1922 and 1939 it doubled. Wheat imports were reduced by 75% between 1925 and 1935. These were the results of Il Duce's great propaganda campaign, the Battle for Grain, introduced to "free the Italian people from the slavery of foreign bread". Mussolini's photograph appeared in the newspapers showing him driving a tractor, dancing with peasant girls or threshing wheat. Every year gold, silver and bronze stars were awarded to the most successful peasants. The draining of the Pontine Marshes made 60,000 hectares of new land available.

Yet, while Italy needed to import less wheat for bread and pasta, there was a negative side to this achievement. Land more suited to growing rice, in the Po valley, or fruit or olives was switched to wheat production, for which it was less suited. While wheat production rose, Italy grew less rice, less fruit, fewer olives.

The Battle for the Lire

The Wall Street crash in the USA in October 1929 greatly increased the downward pressure on the Italian currency as American loans were recalled. Mussolini was determined that it should not be devalued, a move which he saw as a blow to national prestige and pride. A high value lira would show the world that Italy was economically strong. He had twice revalued the currency in 1922 and then again in 1926 when he had it fixed at a rate of 90 to the £1 sterling. His economic advisers told him that the 'quota 90' was doing untold damage as it was making Italian exports too expensive in the US and other overseas markets. Mussolini refused to say that he was wrong and when faced with the Wall Street crash he began the Battle for the Lire. Workers were forced to accept wage cuts which were designed to cut export prices without having to reduce the currency's value. Eventually, in the thirties, he was forced to reverse this policy and the lire, once a symbol of Fascist strength, was devalued. The press were persuaded to virtually ignore this event.

State Intervention

Due to the effects of the war in Abyssinia and the weakness of Italian banks, the Fascist state increasingly intervened in the industrial economy.

"From 1935 onwards the state's role in industrial financing, raw material allocation, the replacement of imported by home produced materials, and the direct control of major industries increased. By 1939 it controlled four-fifths of Italy's shipbuilding, three-quarters of her pig-iron production and almost half her steel. This level of state intervention greatly exceeded that of Nazi Germany, giving Italy a state sector second only to that of Stalin's Russia."
(Martin Blinkhorn *Mussolini and Fascist Italy* p 26)

The Battle for Natality (Births)

Despite the grinding poverty of the South and high levels of emigration to the USA, Argentina and Brazil, Mussolini decided that Italy needed more people. A larger population would give her more soldiers, more workers for industry, a bigger market for her producers and more settlers for her empire. In 1927 it was announced that the population was to rise from 42 million to 60 million by 1950. Mussolini was of the opinion that a normal woman should aim to have about twelve children. Married men with 6 children were exempt from taxation, while bachelors were subject to punitive taxation and found their careers blighted. The distribution of contraceptives was banned. Il Duce personally handed out prizes to women who had produced spectacularly large families. Since he was notoriously unfaithful to his wife, Rachele, many Italians observed that Mussolini was contributing all he could to the campaign. Despite his heroic efforts the birth rate fell from 27.5 per thousand in 1927 to 23.4 per thousand in 1934. Regardless of this, Italy's population did rise to 43.8 million in 1940, mainly because the USA imposed immigration quotas which cut back heavily on the entry of peoples not of white Anglo-Saxon Protestant origin. 350,000 Italians went to the States in 1920, the last year of unrestricted immigration. Only 4,000 were allowed annually after 1924. It was probably a good thing for Italy that Mussolini's policy failed so dramatically. The country already had enough poverty and unemployment without adding extra mouths to feed.

The Battle for Births gives a clear indication of the Fascist attitude to women and also of how Mussolini's attitudes changed. In his Socialist days he had advocated contraception. In 1924 he introduced punishments for anyone who advocated it publicly. In 1925 he was still calling for more jobs for women but then he changed his mind and called on them to stay at home and breed. He was concerned that 'masculine sports' such as riding, skiing or cycling might cause infertility in women although the ninety three women to whom he presented awards in 1933 for producing 1,300 children must have had very little time to go cycling or skiing! Women were even forbidden to wear trousers.

The Corporate State

"The Italian Economy was reorganised by Mussolini to increase the influence of the state without destroying

capitalism. Since Mussolini had discovered that his support came from those with wealth and property (rather than, as he had originally expected, those without), his economic policy had to satisfy them."
(Robert Wolfson *Years of Change* p 270)

Before the March on Rome the Italian economy had been plagued by violent and destructive strikes. The Fascist answer to this was the Corporate State. Each occupation had to form two syndicates or Unions, one for the workers, the other for the employers. These met separately and together with additional representatives of the Fascist Party and decided on pay and conditions of work. Catholic and socialist trade unions were banned.

In 1925 strikes became illegal. The Fascists tended to side with the employers at meetings of the Corporations. The workers had lost their right to strike and found their wages held down.

"The most obvious beneficiaries ... (were) ... cossetted industrialists, rural landlords and agrarian capitalists, their products protected and their wage bills held down by Fascist labour policies ... The most obvious victim of Fascist policies was ... the urban and rural working class, undefended by genuine unions. Industrial workers suffered official wage cuts in 1927, 1930 and 1934, while agricultural labourers' wages fell during the early 1930s by between 20 and 40%. Although ... prices also fell, between 1925 and 1938 the real value of wages dropped by over 10%."
(Martin Blinkhorn *Mussolini and Fascist Italy* p 27)

On the other hand Italy was no longer plagued by strikes which also damage the prosperity of workers and employers alike.

The corporations aroused much interest throughout Europe. Many saw them as a possible working compromise between the dead hand of communist state control and the free-for-all chaos of unbridled capitalism. Flattered by this attention, Mussolini sought to develop the idea and make it the central feature of the Fascist state. In 1926 he took on the additional role of Minister of Corporations. A National Council of Corporations was established in 1930, again with representation from government, employers and workers. Its task was to plan and regulate economic activity. This body was intended to replace the Chamber of Deputies as the country's law making body but did not do so until 1939 by which time law making in Italy was entirely the result of the Dictator's personal whim and the legislature was merely a hollow sham.

The replacement of free trade unions with state controlled corporations is yet another example of the totalitarian nature of Fascism.

Fascist Foreign Policy
(Italian foreign policy in the thirties is covered in detail in *Appeasement and the Road to War* by Ronald Cameron)
Initially Mussolini wanted to recreate the glories of the Ancient Roman Empire. He intended to dominate the Mediterranean, turning it into Mare Nostrum (our sea). He sought a colonial empire to make good the failings of the Versailles settlement and to give Italy the status she deserved. This would have to be achieved by force of arms. Mussolini glorified war.

The Big Mistake : Italy enter the Second World War
In the thirties economic problems at home drove him into foreign adventures to distract attention from his domestic difficulties. Italy's conquest of Abyssinia in 1935 and her participation in the Spanish Civil War did not solve her economic problems. They further strained her economy and made the situation worse. This was not enough to prevent Mussolini joining Hitler's war, declaring war on France in 1940. The Italians did not share their Duce's enthusiasm for war and at every possible opportunity did the sensible thing and ran away. As an ally they proved a total liability to the Germans. Eugene Dollman, a German interpreter working in Rome, commented:

"Though disunited as only 50 million individualists can be," the ordinary Italian people " were virtually unanimous in their willingness to do anything rather than fight in a war on Germany's side."
(E Dollman *The Interpreter* quoted by C Leeds in *Italy under Mussolini*)

Anybody who is familiar with the achievements of Italian mountaineers such as Bonatti, Gervasutti, Cassin, Comici or Benuzzi will know that it is too simplistic to dismiss the Italians of that era as cowards. They just did not believe in the cause for which they were required to fight.

The Invasion of Italy and the end of an Era.
In July 1943 Italy was invaded from North Africa by the Americans and British. Mussolini was deposed by a revolt in the Fascist Grand Council and by the King. He was imprisoned then rescued by German airborne troops and established as the ruler of a puppet republic in the North. As the allied forces closed in he was captured by Italian Partisans. He and his long-term mistress Clara Petacci were shot and their bodies hung upside down from lamp posts. Before he died, did Mussolini remember the reputed last words of Matteotti - "You can kill me, you will not kill the ideal"? Did anybody think that while this was true of Matteotti's socialism it might also be true of Fascism?

Perhaps the best final epitaph of Mussolini and his fellow dictator has been provided by AJP Taylor:

"Of course both men were lunatics ... All men are mad who devote themselves to the pursuit of power when they could be fishing or painting pictures, or simply sitting in the sun. If men were sane there would be no history ..."
(from *Europe : Grandeur and Decline* p 221-222)

7 The Stirring of National Consciousness in Germany 1815 - 1848

The restoration of peace in Europe was not altogether reflected within Germany. The sentiments unearthed and aroused by the revolutionary wars were not satisfied by the Congress of Vienna and the demands of nationalism and liberalism grew steadily.

There were a number of reasons for the growth of German nationalism - the demand for a united Germany. Firstly, developments in the arts in the eighteenth century encouraged German consciousness. Furthermore, the ease with which Napoleon's armies had dominated the German states demonstrated that individually they were weak and the effort to drive the the French out drew the Germans together. Finally, economic development in the states was hampered by the lack of political unity.

These factors taken together began to generate a pressure for unification. The idea was particularly attractive to two groups. The intellectual middle class was attracted by the ideals of nationalism and liberalism expressed in the universities while the growing class of industrialists felt their development hampered by petty trade restrictions.

Opposing unification were three forces. The rulers of the 39 German states had a vested interest in maintaining the status quo and thus their own prestige and power. Secondly, the other powers in Europe were happy to see Germany divided and relatively weak. Lastly, the German Confederation (Deutscher Bund) or Bund, which had been established after the Congress of Vienna to replace the Holy Roman Empire, actually ensured the preservation of the status quo, though it might have appeared to be a force for unity. For example here are some of the Articles which established it:-

"1 The sovereign princes and free towns of Germany unite in a perpetual union which shall be called the German Confederation.
2 The aim of the same shall be the maintenance of the external and internal safety of Germany and of the

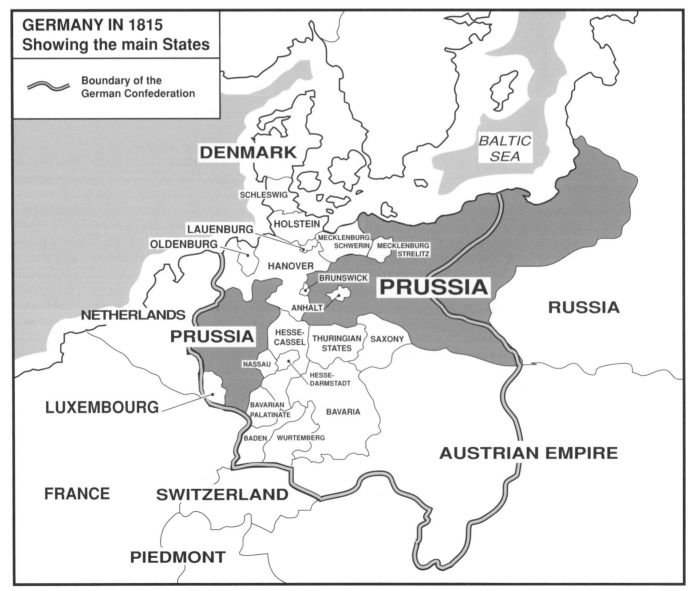

GERMANY IN 1815
Showing the main States

Boundary of the German Confederation

DENMARK
SCHLESWIG
HOLSTEIN
LAUENBURG
OLDENBURG
MECKLENBURG SCHWERIN
MECKLENBURG STRELITZ
HANOVER
BRUNSWICK
ANHALT
PRUSSIA
BALTIC SEA
RUSSIA
NETHERLANDS
PRUSSIA
HESSE-CASSEL
THURINGIAN STATES
SAXONY
NASSAU
HESSE-DARMSTADT
LUXEMBOURG
BAVARIAN PALATINATE
BAVARIA
BADEN
WURTEMBERG
AUSTRIAN EMPIRE
FRANCE
SWITZERLAND
PIEDMONT

independence and inviolability of the individual German states.
3 Austria shall preside in the Diet (parliament) of the Confederation."
(Quoted in Hewison *Bismarck and the Unification of Germany* Arnold)

The Bund had little formal power. Members of the Bund were told how to vote by their own governments and since important decisions had to be unanimous, there was usually a great deal of discussion but few decisions.

Membership of the Bund was a thorny issue. The boundaries were loosely based on the Holy Roman Empire. Parts of Austria and Prussia were not included; Germans in, for example, Schleswig were excluded while Czechs and Poles in Austria were included; states like Luxembourg and Holstein which were ruled by non-German monarchs were also included.

Defining Germany

There was interminable debate among German nationalists as to who should be included in a united Germany. There were two main schools of thought:-

The *Grossdeutsch* (greater Germany) school believed that a united Germany should include Austria and, some even suggested, her Empire. Clearly the Austrians, if they had any enthusiasm at all for a unified Germany, would favour this solution. This was also broadly supported by the south Germans who had always looked towards Austria for protection.

The *Kleindeutsch* (lesser Germany) school wanted a united Germany without Austria or her Empire. This solution suited the Prussians since they, as the largest and most developed area, would tend to dominate. Other north Germans also gave broad support to this idea.

Metternich neatly summed up the position from his point of view,

"I am convinced that Austria alone serves the true interests of Germany ... We have nothing to demand of Germany except her own tranquility. Prussia on the other hand, has an urge to expansion which could only be satisfied to the detriment of the other German states."
(Quoted in Milne *Metternich* ULP p156)

As far as the rulers of the states were concerned, neither solution was very popular. They wanted to retain their independence and power.

Early Nationalists

The first manifestations of nationalist feeling occurred in the universities. Thinkers had started to talk of a 'Germany' towards the end of the eighteenth century. When the settlement of 1815 made few concessions to liberal and nationalist demands, these demands intensified. Some of the pronouncements by patriotic poets were fairly extreme.

Arndt: "The Germans are not bastardised by alien peoples. They have not become mongrels. They have remained more than other peoples in their original purity ..."
(Quoted in RF Leslie *the Age of Transformation* Blandford p243)

Jahn: "Germany needs a war of her own in order to feel her power; she needs a feud with Frenchdom in order to develop her national way of life in all its fullness."
(Quoted in Milne *Metternich* ULP p157)

"Deutschland, Deutschland über alles
Über alles in der Welt"
["Germany, Germany above all,
Above everything in the world"]
(A popular song of the time later to become the German national anthem)
(Quoted in Hewison *Bismarck and the Unification of Germany* Arnold p15)

Others, such as Fichte, the Berlin University lecturer, put the nationalist case more reasonably:

"Whenever a separate language is found there is also a separate nation which has the right to manage its affairs independently and rule itself."
(Quoted in Wood *Europe 1815 - 1945* Longman p52)

In 1817 a liberal and nationalist student society for all Germans was founded. They became involved in some extremist actions which went as far as murder and so became discredited. This also gave Metternich an excuse to act against them. As he said at the time:

"The word freedom has for me never had the character of a point of departure but a goal. The point of departure is order, which alone can produce freedom."
(Quoted in Milne *Metternich* ULP p33)

At a meeting of the Confederation at Carlsbad in 1819 decrees were passed which suppressed the nationalists, causing many university teachers to be dismissed.

There was another flurry of activity in the 1830s. Student societies re-emerged and a festival in Hambach saw the first use of the black, red and gold colours which became the symbol of German liberalism. Metternich again acted through the Bund to suppress them. He commented then:

"The mental superiority that we enjoy over the Prussian government is so decisive that I have yet to see that government fail to go back on what it has only too often advanced with great rapidity and frivolity, once it is sure that our point of view differs from its own."
(Quoted in Milne *Metternich* ULP p159)

Prussia in 1840

Frederick William IV came to the throne in Prussia in 1840. He seemed to sympathise with liberal demands and hinted that a constitution should be developed for Prussia. Prussia attracted some of the university lecturers dismissed from their posts in other German states for their nationalist beliefs. Significant among these were the Grimm brothers who were working on the history of German culture - hence their interest in folk tales.

Economic development was concentrated in Prussia. While

the German population increased by 50% between 1815 and 1855, the Prussian population grew by over 70%. Significantly however, even in Prussia 72% of the population remained in rural occupations in 1846. Industrialisation in Prussia was in its infancy. Coal production, for instance, at 3 million tons annually was less than that of Belgium.

Transport developments concentrated on improving communications in Prussia. Roads were built rapidly after 1815 to link Berlin to the new Prussian territories in the west. By 1850 over 5,000 km of railway track were laid and the beginning of a network was established. The historian, Carr, has stated:-

> "Railways were of great political significance. They helped to break down provincial barriers, brought town and country nearer together and underlined the need for national unification."
> (Carr *A History of Germany* Arnold p32)

The Zollverein

Unquestionably the greatest single economic factor in Germany at that time was the formation of the Zollverein. This was a voluntary customs union among the German states which avoided the restrictions on trade caused by the customs duties imposed by each of the 39 German states.

The Zollverein started when the Prussians established an internal customs union throughout their state. All internal duties were abolished and all import duties were low (on average about 10% of value), thus discouraging smuggling while still providing an income for the government. The Zollverein gave some protection to home industries while making trade easier for them. In the 1820s a number of small neighbouring states joined the union and allowed Prussian officials to administer it.

Two other unions were formed elsewhere in Germany. One, which was located in the South and was eventually supposed to include all South German states, was established between Bavaria and Wurtemberg. It was not a success and joined the Prussian Zollverein in 1834. The other was called the Middle German Commercial Union. It collapsed in 1831 and most of its members also joined the Zollverein.

By 1836 the Zollverein included 25 of the 39 German states and had a free trade area which included 25 million people. A Zollverein Congress was established to decide on policy matters. The Austrian decision not to participate initially left her isolated. As Metternich said:

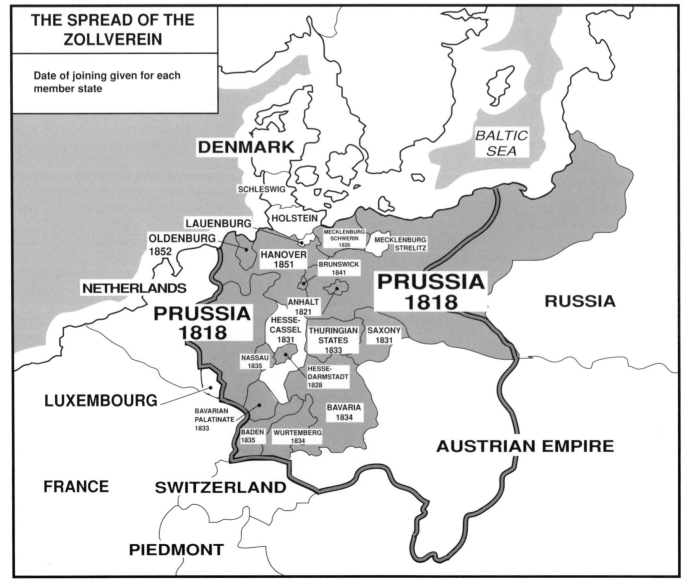

THE SPREAD OF THE ZOLLVEREIN

Date of joining given for each member state

DENMARK

BALTIC SEA

SCHLESWIG

HOLSTEIN

LAUENBURG

OLDENBURG 1852

MECKLENBURG SCHWERIN 1826

MECKLENBURG STRELITZ

HANOVER 1851

BRUNSWICK 1841

NETHERLANDS

PRUSSIA 1818

PRUSSIA 1818

RUSSIA

ANHALT 1821

HESSE-CASSEL 1831

THURINGIAN STATES 1833

SAXONY 1831

NASSAU 1835

HESSE-DARMSTADT 1828

LUXEMBOURG

BAVARIAN PALATINATE 1833

BAVARIA 1834

BADEN 1835

WURTEMBERG 1834

AUSTRIAN EMPIRE

FRANCE

SWITZERLAND

PIEDMONT

"Austria is on the point of seeing herself to a certain extent excluded from the rest of Germany ... and treated as a foreign country."
(Quoted in Milne *Metternich* ULP p160)

The Zollverein drew the German states together and stimulated their economic growth, at the same time firmly establishing Prussia as the economic leader in Germany. Whether the Prussians planned this when it was established is open to question. What is beyond doubt is that by 1840 they could see its potential and exploited it fully.

The historian, Carr, has stated:

"Certainly Prussia was not thinking in terms of political unification when she founded the Customs Union. Nor had the states joined it out of love for Prussia but simply and solely to escape from the financial and economic difficulties which beset them."
(Carr *A History of Germany* Arnold p32)

Another historian, Andrina Stiles, has written

"Many modern Historians support the view that from the 1830s onwards Prussia was using the Zollverein to achieve 'a Prussian solution to a German question'. The argument is that those who found financial advantage in an economic union under Prussian leadership might be expected to take a favourable view of similar arrangements in a political union. The Zollverein was a force for union in the 1840s and therefore a focal point for nationalist sentiments. As a result, Prussia, despite her reactionary political sympathies, came to be regarded by many as the natural leader of a united Germany."
(Stiles *The Unification of Germany 1815 - 1890* Arnold p20)

Germany in the late 1840s
In the German states there was little sign of change on the surface with most remaining proud of their independence, but the Metternich conservatism was under increasing pressure. While the romantic nationalism of the students was being suppressed, the economic nationalists could see their case being proved by the Zollverein. The Bund was seen as little more than a talking shop and had lost the support and respect of the reformers.

Only in Prussia were there significant developments. Leadership of the Zollverein, a new King who had liberal tendencies and a realisation that the unification of Germany could enhance the power and prestige of Prussia meant that she was emerging as the champion of German nationalism.

1848 IN GERMANY

The revolutions in Germany broadly followed the same pattern as the events in the rest of Europe. While most nationalist movements were trying to expel foreigners so that they could establish their own state, the German demand was to unite a series of small states to form one large nation, but there were similarities. The Austrian domination of the Bund and her virtual overlordship of the South German States meant that for Germany to achieve unity she had to counter the influence of an outside power. With the fall of Metternich in Austria in early March 1848, the German liberals and nationalists could advance their cause.

Although there were disturbances throughout Germany at this time, we shall concentrate on events in Prussia. The King, Frederick William IV, who came to the throne in 1840, had shown liberal tendencies: for example he had released political prisoners and abolished censorship. However, his reforms did not satisfy the liberal demands, indeed it can be argued that it stimulated them. There was considerable unease among the conservative Junker land-owners.

The Revolution in Prussia
In 1847 the King called a United Diet - a sort of consultative parliament - for the whole of Prussia. He wanted to raise taxes to build a railway and required the agreement of the Diet to enable him to do this. At the opening of the Diet he declared:

"Never will I allow a written document to come between God in Heaven and this land in the character of a Second Providence, to govern us with its formalities and take the place of ancient loyalty."
(Quoted in Passant *A Short History of Germany* CUP p28)

However the members of the Diet had other ideas. They demanded sweeping reforms, a parliament for the whole of Germany and a written constitution. The King agreed with none of this and dissolved the Diet.

After the fall of Metternich in 1848, there was a series of demonstrations in Berlin. Eventually these became serious enough for troops to be called to disperse them and, inevitably, some demonstrators were killed. King Frederick William, who hated violence and was a little afraid of the events which were going on all over Europe, gave in to the demands of the demonstrators and granted a constitution, agreed to an elected assembly, promised to unite Prussia in Germany and virtually anything else demanded by the demonstrators. He was forced to salute the corpses of those demonstrators who had been killed by an army which was acting on his orders. He even rode through the streets of Berlin wearing the red, black and gold colours of the revolutionaries. The King was not the most stable of characters and it seems likely that he was carried away by the speed of events. He declared:

"I am truly proud that it is my capital, where so powerful an opinion has manifested itself ... From this day forth the name Prussia is fused and dissolved in that of Germany."
(Quoted in Stiles *The Unification of Germany* Arnold p35)

Later he described the period as "the worst time of my life."

Elections were held and an assembly began to debate a Prussian constitution. This was the high point of the revolution. The Junker landowners met in their own assembly and plotted ways to bring about the dissolution

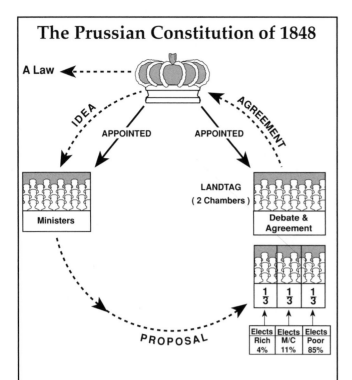

The Prussian Constitution of 1848

A Law ← - - - - -

IDEA

AGREEMENT

APPOINTED   APPOINTED

Ministers

LANDTAG
(2 Chambers)

Debate &
Agreement

1/3	1/3	1/3
Elects Rich 4%	Elects M/C 11%	Elects Poor 85%

PROPOSAL

- All men over 30 were allowed to vote.
- MPs were not paid.
- Parliament given the right to be consulted.
- Parliament given the right to agree the budget.
- Human rights were guaranteed.
- The King chose all the ministers
- The King controlled the Armed Services.
- The King retained the right to rule in an emergency.

The Frankfurt Parliament

In March 1848 representatives from six states, including Prussia, met in Heidelburg and issued a declaration which called for the creation of a single German parliament.

This was quickly followed by the establishment of a *Vorparlement* or pre-parliament. This met in Frankfurt - home of the Bund. 574 delegates from virtually all of the German states debated for four days and at the end had established the ground rules for the election of a National Assembly for the whole of Germany. This assembly was to draw up a constitution for a unified state.

It was decided that the assembly should be elected on the basis of one representative for every 50,000 people. The method of election varied from state to state but generally all 'economically independent' men were allowed to vote. The 596 men elected to the Assembly were probably the best qualified, intellectually, ever to be elected to a parliament. Over 80% had university degrees. In some ways this was to be their undoing. These men were hardly revolutionaries but were so confident of their own ability that there were almost as many solutions to any problem as there were members of the assembly. Discussions and debates were lengthy! AJP Taylor described them in this way:

> "Frankfurt suffered from too much experience rather than too little; too much calculation, too much foresight, too many elaborate combinations, too much statesmanship."
>
> (AJP Taylor *The Course of German History* Methuen p77)

The aim of the assembly was to establish a united Germany, with a constitutional monarchy. The problem was how to achieve this.

They had to decide on the relationship between the individual states and the new Germany. After much discussion they decided that the German parliament was to be paramount. The Bund had tried to draw the states together to agree on things but no individual state was bound by the decisions of the Bund. The new parliament would have this power over the states and they would be bound by its decisions.

They had to decide on a constitution. This took nearly a year. Eventually they decided on a parliament of two houses - one elected by secret ballot by men over 25, the other to be made up of the reigning monarchs. The parliament would control finance and legislation. There would be an Emperor as head of state but he would be a constitutional monarch with power only to delay legislation.

The parliament debated the fundamental rights of German citizens and came up with a list of 50 - but it took them nine months to do so.

Most importantly, they had to decide on what was to be included in a united Germany. It was all very well to argue for a unified German state but if that was taken literally then parts of Prussia and Austria could not be included since they were in no way German. The alternative of including the whole of Austria and Prussia as well as all

of the National Assembly. Frederick William dissolved the National Assembly before it and the Junkers had completed their deliberations and established a constitution of his own.

As you can see from the diagram, the constitution was not very liberal, with the King retaining a great deal of power. However it did allow all men over thirty the right to vote - even though this was heavily weighted towards the rich (likely supporters of the monarch) - and it did establish a two-chamber parliament which had the right to be consulted and, crucially, the power to agree the budget.

In general these proposals were well received in Prussia. The constitution suited the upper and middle classes and this tended to split them from the more extreme demands of others. From then on the King steadily reasserted his own power and most of the early reforms were quietly ended.

Significantly, in Prussia the King remained popular throughout the revolutionary period and the army remained totally loyal to him. Had the King acted a little more forcefully in March 1848, there might never have been a revolution in Prussia at all.

Equally significantly, the Prussian constitution, flawed as it was, remained after 1848 and was to form the basis for government until 1918.

the other states even if they were ruled by foreigners was seen as almost equally ridiculous.

The argument polarised into the two camps - the Grossdeutsch and Kleindeutsch factions (See page56). The parliament debated this endlessly until, in March 1849, they decided on the Kleindeutsch solution by a narrow majority and offered the crown to King Frederick of Prussia. However, by this time the revolutions were fading away and King Frederick declined to accept the crown, stating:

"Every German nobleman is a hundred times too good to accept such a diadem moulded out of the dirt and dregs of revolution, disloyalty and treason."
(Quoted in Stiles *The Unification of Germany 1815-90* p36 Arnold)

In other words he did not want to accept a crown which was offered to him by a parliament - that would devalue his status as Emperor.

The parliament had shot its bolt. The Austrians immediately withdrew their delegates, other monarchs ignored the new constitution and other states began to withdraw their delegates. The assembly gradually disintegrated. Eventually the remaining rump was chased out of Frankfurt by the city authorities.

The great weakness of the Assembly was that it lacked a power base. It could pass any laws it liked, but without an army to enforce its decisions its pronouncements were little more than words. The obvious solution to this was to use the Prussian Army. A Prussian General was made

WHY DID THE 1848 REVOLUTIONS FAIL IN GERMANY?

- 'Revolutions' in Germany were relatively peaceful and did not make sweeping changes.
- The Kings and other Heads of State in Germany were not overthrown.
- Armies remained loyal - particularly in Prussia.
- Reforms which were granted were easily reversed.
- Lack of clarity of purpose among the 'revolutionaries'. Some were republicans; others favoured a constitutional monarchy; others wanted social change; the Grossdeutschland or Kleindeutschland issue was also divisive.
- Lack of lasting support. Revolution fever spread very quickly and just as quickly disappeared.
- The Frankfurt Parliament suffered from a lack of clear, agreed objectives. This made it difficult to take decisions. Factions argued minority views at great length.
- The Parliament lacked a strong leader.
- The Parliament lacked the administration and military force to implement and enforce its decisions.
- Kings and other Heads of State did not see unification as being in their interest.
- After Erfurt, Austria was again dominant in Germany and her policy was to keep Germany divided.

Minister of War but the Prussian Army acted as it and the King of Prussia saw fit and largely ignored the Frankfurt Parliament. (See page65) Even an attempt to secure agreement that the Austrian and Bavarian Armies would join the Prussians in emergencies failed totally.

The historian Eyck has written:

"With the refusal of the Imperial crown by Frederick William the German revolution of 1848 had failed in practice. Nevertheless it had not been in vain. It was a step forward which could never be undone completely. For the first time the Frankfurt parliament had clearly stated the issue, the solution of which was to be decisive for Germany's future, the alternatives of Prussia and Austria, of kleindeutsch and grossdeutsch. Although the first parliament of the whole German people had failed, the organisation of Germany without a German parliament was henceforth out of the question."
(Eyck *Bismarck and the German Empire* Unwin p27)

Erfurt and Olmütz

That was not quite the end of the attempts to gain some form of unity for Germany during 1848 and 1849. The King of Prussia, though he was not interested in the unification of Germany by a parliament, was keen to advance the Prussian position in Germany.

He proposed the creation of a voluntary union of states under Prussian leadership. At first this seemed to be quite promising. A constitution, not as liberal as the one drawn up at Frankfurt, was granted and elections were held following which a parliament met at Erfurt. However at this stage Frederick William lost confidence in his idea and withdrew his active support.

An even more serious threat to the Erfurt Parliament came from the Austrians. They had attended day one of the planning conference, seen what was proposed and had withdrawn. As the fear of revolution in Austria receded they were again able to take an active interest in events in Germany. They proposed that the German Confederation or Bund should be re-established and should include the whole of Austria. In May 1850 the Confederation reconvened in Frankfurt - minus Prussia and the few states who supported her.

The scene seemed set for a confrontation - possibly even a military one. The showdown came in Hesse-Cassel. This state had been a member of the Prussian Union and was clearly a Prussian ally. The parliament in Hesse-Cassel refused to vote taxes for their Elector (monarch). When the other organs of the state government, including the army, sided with the parliament, the Elector fled to Frankfurt and appealed to the Bund to act to put down this rebellion. As the Bund prepared to do so there was a question as to the Prussian reaction. To allow the Bund to restore order in an allied state would be a dreadful humiliation for Prussia and the Erfurt Union. On the other hand the alternative was war and the Prussian Army was not ready for that.

The Austrian Minister Schwarzenberg stated,

> "a union, that in its constitution announces itself to be, or as wishing to become, the German Empire, in other words as about to crowd us out of Germany, such a union we can under no circumstances suffer to exist."
> (Quoted in Hewison *Bismarck and the Unification of Germany* Arnold p16)

In November 1850 the crisis was resolved. Meeting at Olmütz, Prussian and Austrian officials agreed that the Bund should be re-established as it was before 1848, that the Erfurt Union should be dissolved and that the Bund should sort out the problems in Hesse-Cassel. All in all the Olmütz settlement signalled the re-establishment of Austrian power in Germany and a total humiliation for Prussia.

At the end of 1850 it seemed as if nothing had changed in Germany despite the events of the previous three years. In Prussia the rioting which had promised to lead to such dramatic change had disappeared and the King and his army were firmly back in control. The Frankfurt Parliament, disorganised, leaderless and lacking any real power or support from the rulers of the individual states had simply talked away the ripe moments when they could perhaps have effected change. By the time they had made up their collective mind their time had passed.

> "On the other hand, the Revolution in Germany had positive as well as negative aspects. It marked the entry of the German people into the political life of the nation, confirming the trends discernible in the 1840s. True, the men of 1848 did not attempt to build up a mass following. Nevertheless, wider circles of the population began to take an interest in politics.
> ... without the groundswell of public opinion favourable to unification which the revolution had created, the achievements of Bismarck in the 1860s would hardly have been possible.
> ... The Revolution also helped to clarify political attitudes and encouraged the formation of political associations, the forerunners of modern political parties."
> (Carr *A History of Germany* Arnold p65-6)

8 The Unification of Germany

After the dramatic events of 1848 and 1849, the decade of the 1850s was very peaceful in Germany. Economically and socially Prussia prospered but politically she remained very conservative. Manteuffel, King Frederick William's Chancellor, believed that he did not need to consult a parliament to help him govern and no parliament or diet met during his time in power.

King Frederick William IV became more and more unstable mentally and in 1858 he was declared insane. His brother William was appointed Regent and on Frederick William's death in 1861 he became King William I of Prussia.

William was 63 when he became King. First and foremost a soldier, he was straightforward, honest and believed that it was the duty of a King to rule his country. He had strong opinions and was a little inflexible but fair minded. William was influenced by his son who had married a daughter of Queen Victoria and was therefore exposed to liberal ideas. Manteuffel was dismissed and replaced with a more liberal minister. William believed in the unification of Germany and he believed that Prussia should lead it.

He came to power at the same time as events in Italy led to her becoming a united nation. These events stimulated the liberals and nationalists in Germany and in 1859 a Nationalverein or German National Union was formed. This group had as its main aim the formation of a central government for the whole of Germany. In Prussia this movement led to the formation of the Progressive or Liberal Party.

THE CONSTITUTIONAL CRISIS IN PRUSSIA

In 1859 during the war between France and Austria the Prussians mobilised their army to support Austria in accordance with the policy of the Bund. The mobilisation was a shambles.

William took a serious view of this and mindful of the humiliation at Olmutz in 1852, of the Prussian tradition of military greatness and of his own military background he decided that the Prussian Army should be modernised. Therefore, in 1859 he appointed Von Roon as War Minister and Von Moltke as Chief of Staff and together they submitted their reform proposals to the Prussian parliament in 1860. The proposals were:

- an increase from two to three years of full-time army training for all men.
- an increase from three to four years in the reserves.
- the Landwehr (part-time soldiers) to be virtually abolished.
- an extra 49 regiments to be created.
- an extra nine million thalers (about £1.5 million) to be raised each year to cover the increased costs.

- new weapons to be introduced.
- the standing army to be increased from 230,000 to 450,000 men.

The significance of these proposals was much more far-reaching than the King imagined. He saw them as a means of re-establishing Prussian authority on the European stage. Others saw them very differently.

In 1858 the elections to the lower house of the Prussian parliament had produced a huge majority for the Liberals. This was despite the election system developed in 1848 which was designed to favour those who supported the King.

The Liberals saw the army reform proposals as a major threat. They felt that the extended length of service would produce men totally and unthinkingly loyal to the King and government, men who could be used against liberals as had happened in 1848. The reduction in power of the Landwehr would also hit the Liberals since it was largely made up of Liberal supporters, while the power and influence of the Junkers would be reinforced by these changes to the army. Finally they realised that the cost of the reforms would have to be borne by taxation which would have to be paid by themselves - the middle class.

In the Prussian constitution of 1848 the parliament had been given the power to agree the budget - the finances of the state. It was about the only significant power that it did have. If the King could not get agreement for the budget then he could not proceed with the army reforms.

When the budget was presented to parliament in 1860 the Liberals refused to agree to it but they did agree to vote the money provisionally for one year. The budget was, of course, agreed by the upper house of the Prussian parliament whose members had been appointed by the King. The King simply went ahead with the reforms on this basis. In 1861 the budget was presented again and the same thing happened. Even this amount of agreement with the King caused a split among the Liberals. The National Liberals were prepared to follow this policy while the other wing of the Liberals, the Progressives, were not even prepared to grant provisional agreement. Elections were held in 1861 and the Progressive Party made sweeping gains with only 24 supporters of the King being elected. Again the parliament refused to pass the budget, this time by 300 votes to 11. The King dissolved parliament and called fresh elections which were an even bigger disaster for him. Only 12 definite supporters were returned. Again the lower house, the Landtag, refused to pass the budget.

Prussia was in the depths of a constitutional crisis. The King was determined to make the army reforms; the Liberal majority in the Landtag was equally determined that they would not pass them.

The leader of the Progressives, Max Dunker, stated:

> "This is not a fight over a few articles of the Constitution. It is a struggle involving principles; it has become a class struggle, a struggle of the Bourgeoisie against Junkerdom."(Quoted in Mitchell *Bismarck and the Unification of Germany* Holmes McDougall p17)

There was an impasse. The King's advisers suggested that he should abolish parliament and govern by decree. William was not prepared to do this. He considered himself to be such a failure that he contemplated abdication. Bismarck states that he told him:

> "I shall not reign if I cannot do it in such a fashion as I can be answerable for to God, my conscience and my subjects. But I cannot do that if I am to rule according to the will of the present majority in Parliament ... I have therefore resolved to lay down my crown."
> (Quoted in Stiles *The Unification of Germany* Arnold p51)

He was persuaded not to do this since that would signal complete victory for the Liberals. Instead he appointed a new Chancellor to see if he could do anything to resolve the crisis. The new Chancellor was Otto Von Bismarck.

BISMARCK

Bismarck was born in 1815 at the family estate of Schonhausen. His was an old Junker family and he inherited their traditions of love of King, army and country life. In his early life he was rebellious and excelled only at drinking and womanising.

When the King of Prussia called the United Diet in Berlin in 1847, Bismarck, owing to the illness of one of the delegates, was offered the chance to be a delegate himself. He was delighted since he was bored with the life of a country squire. His political career started then and lasted for the next forty years. At the United Diet he spoke up strongly in favour of the King and the rights of the monarchy.

The Prussian government under Manteuffel admired the politics of Bismarck and as a reward for his support he was made Prussian delegate to the Bund. While at the Bund, Bismarck came to resent the power of the Austrians over Germany and he made it his business to challenge them at every opportunity. A good example of this came in the Crimean War. It was in the Austrian interest to become involved in this conflict in Southeast Europe and they wanted other members of the Bund to join them. Bismarck could see quite clearly that this was not in the interests of Prussia or of the other German states and he managed to prevent this happening.

In 1859 when the Prussian Army was mobilised to support Austria during the war with France, Bismarck argued that Prussia should take the opportunity to attack Austria and push her out of Germany once and for all. This was too much for the King and the Prussian con-

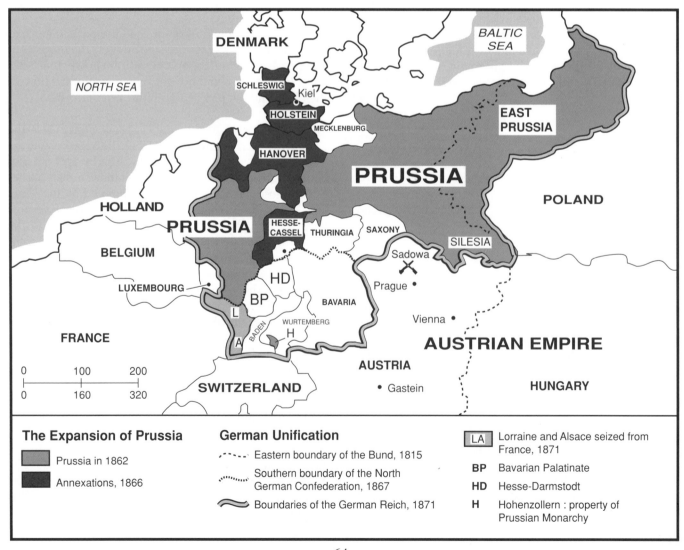

The Expansion of Prussia	German Unification	LA Lorraine and Alsace seized from France, 1871

The Expansion of Prussia

- Prussia in 1862
- Annexations, 1866

German Unification

- ·-·-·- Eastern boundary of the Bund, 1815
- ·········· Southern boundary of the North German Confederation, 1867
- ∼ Boundaries of the German Reich, 1871

LA Lorraine and Alsace seized from France, 1871

BP Bavarian Palatinate

HD Hesse-Darmstodt

H Hohenzollern : property of Prussian Monarchy

servatives. Bismarck was removed from his post at the Bund and sent to St Petersburg, the Russian capital, as Prussian Ambassador in 1859. In 1862 he was transferred to Paris as Prussian Ambassador to France. It was from Paris that he was summoned by Von Roon's brief but effective telegram 'Periculum in mora, Dépêchez-vous' - Delay is dangerous, hurry!

Solution to the Crisis
Bismarck was the last hope for the desperate King. He had a proven record as a monarchist and had little time for Liberals and excessive parliamentary ideals. When the King offered him the post he stated:

> "I will rather perish with the King than forsake your Majesty in the contest with Parliamentary government."
> (Quoted in Stiles *The Unification of Germany* Arnold p51)

Bismarck tried to persuade the parliament to agree the budget. He then resorted to threats. When even these were of no avail he announced that in view of the constitutional crisis owing to parliament's inability to reach agreement (remember it was only the lower house, the Landtag, which refused to pass the budget), the King would have to rule by himself. This was because there was a gap in the Prussian Constitution (Luckentheorie) which meant that there was no provision for a crisis of this kind. No one, least of all Bismarck, really believed that this was exactly the case. However it did give some validity to the fact that the Prussian Government then collected the taxes despite the parliament and ruled without their agreement. Bismarck had got the King off the hook and the King was eternally grateful. From then on the King nearly always accepted Bismarck's advice.

Bismarck realised that he could not govern like this indefinitely. His long-term aim was to unite Germany under Prussian leadership hoping that by doing this he would gain the support of parliament. The Liberal opposition were also ardent nationalists and would find it hard to oppose policies which brought about German unity. He fully appreciated that this was a gamble and was prepared to use any methods he could to make sure that it came off.

Bismarck's methods became known as Realpolitik - in other words doing what is possible not necessarily what is desirable. Many people then and now disagreed with the method but few could deny that it was effective.

> "Germany looks not to Prussia's liberalism but to her power. ... Prussia must gather up her strength and maintain it for the opportune moment, which has already passed several times. ... Not by parliamentary speeches and majority votes are the great questions of the day determined - that was the great mistake of 1848 and 1849 - but by iron and blood."
> (Bismarck, on appointment to office, addressing the Landtag; quoted in Hewison *Bismarck and the Unification of Germany* Arnold p22)

An early example of realpolitik occurred in Bismarck's early foreign policy which can be summed up as a desire to isolate Austria and to have Prussia recognised as the main German state. When the Austrians proposed to reform the Bund in 1862 by strengthening its military,

legal and economic powers, Bismarck quite correctly saw this as a way of undermining his anti-Austrian stance. When the Austrians called a conference of all Bund members to discuss the proposals, Bismarck persuaded the Prussian King to ignore it. Without the Prussians there were no decisions taken and the conference collapsed. In this way Prussian prestige was enhanced and the Austrians were embarrassed.

SCHLESWIG HOLSTEIN AND THE PRUSSO-DANISH WAR

The history of Schleswig and Holstein is long and complicated. Lord Palmerston, a British Prime Minister, stated that:

> "Only three men have ever understood it. One was Prince Albert (husband of Queen Victoria) who is dead. The second was a German professor who went mad. I am the third and I have forgotten all about it!"
> (Quoted in Aronson *The Kaiser* Cassell p56)

Fortunately we do not have to study it in detail, but some background is useful.

Geography: The Duchies were located to the north of Hanover and to the south of Denmark. There was a substantial population of Danes in northern Schleswig but the rest of the area was predominantly German.

Monarchy: Both were governed by Dukes - hence the term Duchies. Since 1780 both had been ruled by the King of Denmark.

Degree of 'Germanity': The Bund included Holstein but not Schleswig as had the Holy Roman Empire. Representing Holstein at the Bund was its Duke - the King of Denmark!

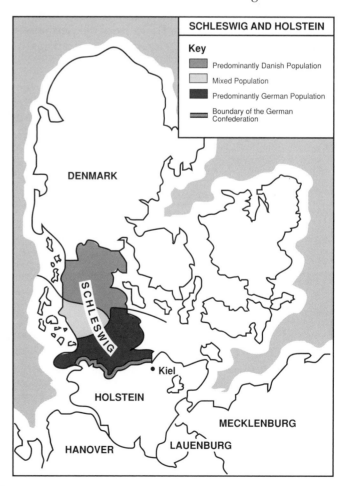

Succession: All these problems pale into insignificance when we consider the complications over the right of succession to the throne. In Denmark the law of primogeniture applied. This meant that the monarch was succeeded by his eldest son. If the monarch had only daughters the eldest of them would succeed to the throne. This is the system of succession which applies in Britain. In the Duchies, however, the Salic law applied. By this law no female, nor any male who traced his descent through a female, could succeed to the throne.

The Problem: Events began to come to a head in the 1840s. It became clear to King Christian VIII of Denmark that his son and heir, Frederick, would have no family and would therefore be the last of his particular line. Who then should succeed him? (A glance at the family tree below should show the problem.) The obvious choice for Denmark was Christian of Glucksburg. He, however, traced his descent through the female line and so was ineligible to rule the Duchies. The rightful successor to the thrones in the Duchies was Christian of Augustenburg but he was hardly a close relative.

The Crisis I

Christian VIII died in 1848 and was succeeded by his son Frederick VII. In line with developments elsewhere in Europe at that time, he announced that he was setting up a parliament for all the areas over which he ruled. It was a shrewd move. One parliament for all the areas ruled over by Frederick would in effect lead to the incorporation of Schleswig and Holstein within Denmark. This would have great significance in any future dispute over the succession.

Liberals and German nationalists in the Duchies objected to this takeover and set up a provisional government of their own at Kiel in Holstein. The cause of the Germans in the Duchies attracted a great deal of attention among the nationalists meeting at the Frankfurt Parliament.

The Duke of Augustenburg also became involved. He appealed to the King of Prussia to help him rid the Duchies of the Danes and to establish him on the throne. This suited the Prussians as it would appeal to the Liberals in their own country and a short victorious war would distract attention from troubles at home. Accordingly the King ordered Prussia to war. The Frankfurt Parliament supported the Prussians but other German monarchs and the European powers generally did not.

The King of Prussia felt uncomfortable as the champion of liberalism and ended the war as soon as he could. The war was inconclusive though it did demonstrate serious deficiencies in the Prussian army.

It is also worth noting here the contempt with which the Frankfurt Parliament was treated. Prussia started the war *then* the Frankfurt Parliament gave its approval; Prussia then ended the war without even consulting it, aptly demonstrating the fundamental weakness of the parliament.

In 1852 the Great Powers (Britain, Russia, Austria, Prussia and France) met in an attempt to solve the crisis. They signed an agreement called the London Protocol. The main terms of the agreement were:

- Christian of Glucksburg was to succeed to the throne of Denmark and the Duchies.
- Christian of Augustenburg was to give up his family claim to the Duchies in return for a cash settlement.
- The Danes were to accept that the Duchies should remain undivided and independent from Denmark.

Crucially, however, the Augustenburg claim was never withdrawn in writing which left an opening for Christian's son to restate it. This settlement suited neither German nor Danish nationalists.

The Crisis II

The problem reappeared in 1863. After King Frederick VII died, King Christian IX pressed on with a proposal to reform the Danish constitution which would in effect join Schleswig to Denmark and draw Holstein closer to her. This again led to a massive outcry from the inhabitants of the Duchies and from German nationalists and troops were sent by the Bund to Holstein to protect it. To further complicate the issue, the new Duke of Augustenburg resurrected his family claim to rule the Duchies. Clearly the Danes were breaching the London Protocol so they did not attract much international support.

Bismarck assessed this situation carefully and decided that it could be exploited for his own ends. He had no real interest in the claims of the Augustenburgs but felt that they could help him discredit Austria and the Bund and at the same time enlarge Prussia. He also wanted to use military force as a way of justifying the army reforms in Prussia, to restore the prestige of the Prussian Army and to show to the Liberals that military force was the way to attain aims.

All that was needed was the war. Bismarck persuaded his

The Royal Family of Denmark, Holstein & Schleswig
The House of Oldenburg

Christian III (1534 - 1559)

Frederick II (1559-1588)

John, Duke of Augustenburg

X

X

X

X

Frederick V (1746-1766)

X

Christian (1776-1808)   Louisa   Frederick

Frederick (1808-1839)   Louisa = Glucksburg   Charlotte   Christian VIII (1839-1848)   Christian Augustenburg

Christian IX = Louisa   Frederick VII   Frederick Augustenburg
1863 - 1906   1848 - 1863

King that the best policy was to try to restore the London Protocol - in other words to have the Danish King ruling the Duchies but both to be kept separate from Denmark. He convinced the King that support for the Augustenburg claim represented support for the revolutionaries which was more than enough to terrify the King. At the same time the reasonableness of the Prussian position encouraged the Austrians to support them.

In late 1863, Austria and Prussia signed a military alliance and committed themselves to the Prussian policy. This was in direct opposition to the wishes of the small states in the Bund. Bismarck stated:

> "The lesser states must learn that if they attempt to subject the European policy of Austria and Prussia to the control of the majority of the Confederation, they will make the continuance of such Confederate relations impossible for these two powers."
> (Quoted in Hewison *Bismarck and the Unification of Germany* Arnold p 24)

The small states supported the Augustenburg claim. Prussia was not very popular with them anyway so she had little to lose but the Austrians by their rather foolish action found that they had lost credibility as a protector of the small German states.

In January 1864 the two presented an ultimatum to the Danes which threatened invasion if the Danes did not withdraw from their proposed annexation. When this was ignored, troops from Prussia and Austria moved through Holstein, already occupied by an army from the Bund, and into Schleswig. On 1 February 1864, the war began. By April it was clear to everyone except the Danes that they were beaten. Pressure from the other Great Powers who had signed the London Protocol led to another conference in London. Bismarck had to move carefully. He did not really want a settlement imposed by other people - this would not have suited his aims. However he could not risk ignoring the peaceful wishes of the Great Powers.

Instead he opted to change tack. He hinted that he would now favour the Augustenburg claim after all. This was too much for the Danes. The conference broke up and the war restarted in June. The Danes who had lost any lingering hope of international support by their refusal to negotiate, suffered even more military defeats and sued for peace in August 1864. By the Treaty of Vienna, signed soon after, Denmark gave up all claim to the Duchies.

Bismarck again changed tack. A group of Prussian lawyers were encouraged to examine the case of the Duchies and to pronounce that they had been Danish all the time! However, as a result of the war, they now belonged to Prussia and Austria by right of conquest.

The Bund troops who were stationed in Holstein were politely told to get out and there was no further talk of the Augustenburg claim. As Bismarck said:

> "I hitched the Duke as an ox to the plough to get it moving, once it was moving I unhitched the ox."
> (Quoted in Wood *Europe 1815 - 1945* Longman. p217)

It was agreed that the Duchies would be administered jointly by Austria and Prussia and there was no suggestion of independent membership of the Bund for them.

The joint administration did not work well. Bismarck had never wanted it to. The Prussians wanted to annexe the territory while the Austrians, too late, argued that the future of the Duchies should be placed in the hands of the Bund. Bismarck could see potential in the Duchies for a future war with Austria but he was not yet ready. Instead he arranged to 'paper over the cracks'. By the convention of Gastein, 1865, it was agreed that Prussia should rule Schleswig while Austria should rule Holstein.

The Convention was another masterstroke on Bismarck's part. The Austrians, now clearly seen as greedy landgrabbers, were utterly discredited in the eyes of the rest of Germany.

> "Austria acted most foolishly of all. She was too conservative to follow the liberal course of liberating the Duchies for Germany; but she would not altogether estrange national sentiment in Germany by following the conservative course of upholding the treaty settlement of 1852. Therefore she followed the worst course of all, and so offended both German nationalism and foreign powers."
> (AJP Taylor *The Course of German History* Methuen p114)

In addition, their only way into Holstein lay through Prussia. Prussia on the other hand controlled the military roads through Holstein to Schleswig. The opportunities to create friction were immense. Austria had been totally outmanoeuvred. Some of the German liberals and nationalists too began to revise their opinions of the Chancellor. A Prussian liberal, Twesten, declared at the start of the war in 1863 that he "would rather suffer the Bismarck ministry for some years longer than allow a German land to be lost to us." (Quoted in Morris *European History 1848-1945* p73)

THE AUSTRO-PRUSSIAN WAR

Historians disagree over whether Bismarck actually used the Schleswig-Holstein crisis to draw the Austrians into a trap. There is absolutely no doubt that he very quickly set his sights on Austria once the crisis had passed over and worked to isolate her from the other European powers.

He turned his attention to France which, as a Roman Catholic power, had closer links with Austria than with Prussia. It was very much in the French interest to keep Germany a collection of smallish states. She could not stand idly by and watch Prussia reshape the map of central Europe without at least gaining something for herself out of it. Bismarck knew Napoleon III, the French Emperor, from his time as Ambassador to Paris and he felt that he was open to temptation.

In October 1865 a secret meeting was held between the two at Biarritz, a French seaside resort. What was discussed was so secret that no written record was kept but Napoleon certainly came away with the impression that Bismarck had promised that if the French stayed neutral in a war between Prussia and Austria, they would be granted territorial compensation "wherever French is spoken", ie. Belgium or even on the west bank of the Rhine. Certainly enough was hinted at to tempt the French.

Bismarck also wanted to gain some allies for Prussia during the war. Italy was not friendly towards the Austrians because they had been such an obstacle to Italian unification. Indeed they still held the province of Venetia which the Italians wanted. If Italy and Prussia fought the Austrians they would be faced with a two front war. Italian participation would make the war more acceptable to the 'liberal' nations like Britain and France. King Victor Emmanuel of Italy did not really trust Bismarck (he at least was wise to him) and he had to be persuaded to sign an alliance with the Prussians. The person who persuaded him was Napoleon III of France. The alliance was signed on 8 April 1866 and it suited the Italians well. It stated that:

• Austria had to declare the war
• Italy would declare war *after* Prussia
• Italy was to get Venetia without question
• The war was to start within three months

In this way the Italians were safe from the risk of being pawns in some great game of Bismarck's. These events are dealt with in more detail in chapter 4.

The day after the alliance with the Italians had been concluded, Bismarck started to turn the screw. He suggested that the Bund should be elected by universal manhood suffrage. This was totally unacceptable to every other German state except Prussia and they, led by Austria, were the ones who had to turn it down. Thus, incredibly, Bismarck was the champion of the liberals while all the others were the reactionaries.

Bismarck now had the problem of getting the Austrians to start the war. He had little difficulty. They too were preparing for war and had also made a secret agreement with Napoleon of France which promised him territorial rewards in return for French neutrality. Napoleon felt that he could not lose no matter who won!

Bismarck deliberately increased tension both in Holstein and with the Austrians travelling to and from it. The Austrians, thanks to their own ineptitude, merely added to their troubles. Their army was so old-fashioned that they had to begin mobilisation long before the Prussians just to be able to compete on level terms. The sight of Austrian troops massing on the Prussian border seemed to leave little doubt about who the aggressor was. Furthermore, Austria was so isolated in Europe that when another international conference was suggested to try to resolve the problem, the Austrians refused to accept it while Bismarck could pose as the one prepared to try to resolve the dispute peacefully.

The Austrians retaliated by breaking off negotiations over Schleswig-Holstein and placed their future in the hands of the Bund. This was a violation of the Convention of Gastein and Bismarck seized on this excuse to invade Holstein. To Bismarck's disgust, the Prussian Commander allowed the Austrian troops to march home - a waste of a potentially good incident.

By this time the Austrians had been provoked enough. On 14 July 1866 they proposed to the Bund that Prussia, by invading Holstein, had violated the rules of the Confederation and that she should be excluded from the Bund. She further suggested that the German States should all begin to mobilise their armies against Prussia.

Bismarck withdrew Prussia from the Bund and invited the other German states to join in a new 'kleindeutsch' federation. The following day ultimatums were delivered to Hanover, Hesse and Saxony demanding that they side with Prussia or be declared enemies. The ultimatum was, of course, rejected and Prussian troops invaded. The Austro-Prussian war had begun. King William proclaimed:

> "It is but a few years since, when there was a question of freeing a German land from foreign domination, I voluntarily ... extended to the Emperor of Austria the hand of friendship. But ... Austria will not forget that its princes once ruled Germany. In the more youthful but powerfully developing Prussia she refuses to perceive a natural ally, but only a hostile rival."
> (Quoted in Hewison *Bismarck and the Unification of Germany* Arnold p28)

The war was a stunning success for the Prussians. It lasted only seven weeks and was fought on three fronts. In the north, Hesse and Saxony rejected the Prussian ultimatum and were occupied, putting up no resistance. The army from Saxony joined the Austrians in Bohemia. By the end of June the Hanoverians had been overwhelmed at the battle of Langensalza, thus securing the northern borders of Prussia.

In the south, the small states all kept their armies at home for defensive purposes, but each was too small to pose any threat and they were therefore irrelevant.

On the Southern Front the Italians suffered heavy defeats. However they did tie down 200,000 Austrian troops and this was invaluable to the Prussian war plan.

The Austrians, with the aid of the 25,000 Saxons, posed the main threat. The decisive battle of the war was fought at Königgratz or Sadowa on 3 July 1866. The battle was a vindication of the Prussian Army Commanders and the army reforms. On the face of it, the two armies were fairly well balanced with 220,000 men each. The commanders were Benedek for Austria and Von Moltke for Prussia, both experienced men. Nevertheless, the differences in the armies were vast.

The Prussians were able to use their extensive rail network both to mobilise and to move their armies and supplies quickly to the front. The Austrians were still equipped with the old-fashioned muzzle loading rifles which soldiers stood to fire and reload. The Prussian army was equipped with modern breech loading rifles which could fire four times as rapidly as the muzzle loaders. Soldiers could lie down to fire them which made shooting more accurate and also presented a much harder target to fire at. The Prussians also used the new telegraph system to communicate with each other and with Berlin.

The Prussian tactics were to attack frontally and from both flanks. Some skilled artillery fire pinned down the Prussian advance and the result of the battle was in doubt until the arrival (late) of the third Prussian army led by Crown Prince Frederick.

The eventual result was an overwhelming victory for Prussia. She had lost about 2,000 men killed and 7,000 wounded. The Austrians had lost about 24,000 killed or wounded with another 13,000 taken prisoner. There was no Austrian Army left between the battlefield and Vienna. The Austrians recognised that they had been defeated and that the war was virtually over.

The Prussians were in a very strong position. The whole of southern Germany was at their mercy and they had the opportunity to inflict a humiliating defeat on the Austrians.

Bismarck, however, started working for peace almost immediately. He recognised that he had achieved his war aim of pushing the Austrians out of Germany. Furthermore, Austria was by no means totally defeated and a long war might result in the Italians being badly beaten or in French intervention. Bismarck also had at the back of his mind the fact that he did not want Austria to be a long-term enemy.

The Austrians were tempted by the offer of generous terms while they were destabilised by nationalist rumblings from the Czechs and Hungarians. There is little doubt that these rumblings were stimulated by Bismarck. The greatest problem was to persuade the King of Prussia and his commanders that they should not carry on for a great victory, the annexation of some Austrian territory and a triumphal march through Vienna. Bismarck wrote to his King:

> "We have to avoid wounding Austria too severely; we have to avoid leaving behind in her unnecessary bitterness of feeling or desire for revenge, we ought to keep the possibility of becoming friends again. "
>
> (Quoted in Hewison *Bismarck and the Unification of Germany* Arnold p30)

The decision was finally taken at a stormy and bitter cabinet meeting on 23 July. Bismarck later commented that he was the only one present not in uniform but he was not intimidated. He was the only one there arguing for peace and it took tears, tantrums, threats of resignation and even the threat of suicide before he got his way. The King stated:

> "Inasmuch as my Minister-President has left me in the lurch in the face of the enemy ... I find myself reluctantly compelled, after such brilliant victories on the part of the army, to bite this sour apple and accept so disgraceful a peace."
>
> (Quoted in Hewison *Bismarck and the Unification of Germany* Arnold p31)

A preliminary peace was agreed at Nikolsburg on 26 July 1866 and the final settlement was agreed at the Treaty of Prague on 23 August 1866.

Briefly the terms of the treaty were as follows:
• Austria handed Venetia to Napoleon of France as had

Bismarck, 'Smith of the German Nation'

been previously agreed by them. Napoleon then handed it to Italy.
• Prussia annexed Schleswig, Holstein, Hesse-Cassel, Frankfurt and Hanover. This was a gain of four million people.
• Austria agreed to take no further part in German affairs.
• The Bund was dissolved.
• The 21 states north of the River Main were to form a North German Confederation under Prussian leadership.
• The South German States were to remain independent but were to pay large indemnities to Prussia.
• The South German States were to form their own Confederation.
• Austria was to pay a small indemnity and was to lose no territory.

The significance of this settlement was enormous. The Austrians, though defeated, were not humiliated and were able, quite quickly, to resume friendly relations with Prussia. The territory which Prussia had acquired made her into a strong, unified state with a North Sea coast and a potential seaport at Kiel. Prussian power and strength had been clearly demonstrated and it was equally clear that the North German Confederation was dominated by them.

Bismarck and his policies had been vindicated. He was now a German hero. The Prussian parliament, with whom he had been at loggerheads, voted him and his Generals a £60,000 reward each. They also passed an indemnity act which gave retrospective official parliamentary permission for the actions taken by Bismarck and his government in the previous four years. Bismarck's great gamble had paid off, but as he was told by one of the generals,

> "Excellency, you are now a great man, but had the Crown Prince arrived later you would now be a great villain."
> (Quoted in Wood *Europe 1815-1945* Longman p221)

THE NORTH GERMAN CONFEDERATION

Following the Austro-Prussian war, the North German Confederation was established. As well as the land annexed by Prussia, all states north of the River Main were members. It appeared to be a voluntary grouping but, in reality, states were given little choice. The two states which tried to avoid joining were quickly occupied by Prussian forces and their leaders deposed.

The North German Confederation was a federal state (Bundesstat) unlike the Bund which had been a federation of states (Statenbund). In other words the confederation was a state in its own right and had control of the Armed Services and Foreign Policy and had the right to make war and peace. The 21 member states, each of which kept its own head of state, had control of their own internal affairs.

The President of the Confederation (in practice the King of Prussia) had the right to appoint the Chancellor and together with him chose the heads of the Armed Services and other departmental heads.

The parliament of the Confederation was made up of two houses. The upper house, the Bundesrat, was made up of representatives appointed by the governments of the member states. The number of representatives allowed to each state was determined by its size. Prussia, for example, had 17 representatives, Saxony 4 and Schleswig 1. The chairman of the Bundesrat was the Federal Chancellor. Delegates voted in accordance with the instructions of their own governments, a simple majority being all that was needed to reach a decision. This was the more important of the two houses. It made its decisions in secret and, since it was chaired by the Chancellor, was open to his influence. The large number of Prussian delegates (appointed by the King and Chancellor) ensured that Bismarck usually got his way.

The lower house, the Reichstag, was elected by universal manhood suffrage using a secret ballot. Despite this democratic system of election the Reichstag did not have much power. It did have to pass the military budget but had no control over how the money was raised. The Chancellor was not responsible to it for his actions.

Passing a law required the agreement of both the Reichstag and the Bundesrat as well as the signatures of the King and the Chancellor

In practice the North German Confederation was dominated by Prussia and in particular Bismarck. He was such a national hero at that time that no one would challenge his position. The first elections to the Reichstag showed this with 125 supporters of Bismarck, 90 opponents and 79 National Liberals who were not committed to either side, but were not prepared to challenge Bismarck's authority.

The Reichstag had no control over the military budget though it did have to agree it. Since this dominated the spending of the Confederation, the Liberals in particular wanted some say in it. A compromise was struck by which they would continue to have no control for the first five years to allow the Confederation to become established but after that date they would be able to vote their approval.

Opinions vary on the North German Confederation. Bismarck speaking during a debate on the North German Constitution said, "Let us put Germany into the saddle, she will know how to ride." (Quoted in Wood, *Europe 1815 - 1945, Longmans p 224*) A modern historian, Granville, has stated, "After the annexations of Hanover, Hesse-Cassel, Nassau, Frankfurt and Schleswig-Holstein without benefit of the consent of their population, Prussia was greatly enlarged. In the north, Prussia had not unified Germany as much as conquered German territories." (Granville, *Europe Reshaped 1848-1878* Fontana)

THE COMING OF THE FRANCO-PRUSSIAN WAR

The North German Confederation did not fulfill the desires of the German nationalists nor indeed the absolute ambition of Bismarck. He fully intended to incorporate the Southern German states but recognised that simply taking them over would cause resentment and undermine the unity of the new state.

Initially Bismarck's tactics were almost exactly the opposite to what might have been expected. The governments of the South German states had expressed a desire for continued independence and that is precisely what they got.

Bismarck knew that these states were very jealous of each other and so were extremely unlikely ever to form their own South German Confederation. The agreed withdrawal of the Austrians from Germany left these states without a natural ally or protector but they were too small to stay in isolation and their only possible ally was the North German Confederation. Bismarck did not try to include them in the North German Zollverein. Instead they were to form their own.

French Compensation
At the conclusion of the Austro-Prussian War, Louis Napoleon of France had tried to intervene to safeguard French interests. He sent his Ambassador to Prussia, Count Benedetti, to see Bismarck to suggest that France should be allowed some land to compensate her for the enormous gains made by the Prussians. This was in line with the promises made at Biarritz. He suggested that France might gain some territory on the Rhine ie. in the South German States! The Prussians rejected this and Bismarck denied that any promises had ever been made to France about territorial compensation. The French Am-

bassador was persuaded to put these demands in writing and these were promptly leaked to the French press.

Napoleon then tried to gain Belgium, an area which was relatively recently independent, had a substantial French population, was not part of Germany and was not allied to any of the Great Powers. All in all, he thought, a less sensitive area. Again Benedetti submitted draft proposals to Bismarck. The suggestion was that Prussia should not oppose a French takeover but Bismarck was confident that he no longer needed to maintain a friendship with France. He therefore rejected the proposal, although he did keep a copy of the document submitted to him. Among other things this document proposed:

"1 His Majesty the French Emperor ... recognises the acquisitions made by Prussia
2 His Majesty the King of Prussia promises to help France to acquire Luxembourg
3 His Majesty will not oppose a federal Union of the Northern Confederation with the southern states of Germany
4 ... His Majesty the King of Prussia, in the event of His Majesty the French Emperor being led ... to deploy his troops in Belgium, will give armed support to France."
(Quoted in Mitchell *Bismarck and the Development of Germany* Holmes McDougall p35)

Finally Napoleon, desperate to demonstrate some success to an increasingly hostile public in France, began to negotiate the purchase of Luxembourg from the King of the Netherlands. Luxembourg was another of the small German States and it was ruled by the King of the Netherlands. Its 700,000 population was French speaking but it was part of the Bund. Since 1815 a Prussian garrison had been stationed there as part of the defences established round the French border. The King of the Netherlands was short of money and would have been happy to sell the land to the French. However, he felt the need to inform the other Great Powers who, by a treaty of 1839, had guaranteed the neutrality of Luxembourg. In this way the proposal came to the notice of the Prussians. Strong nationalist feeling was aroused and, due largely to the Prussians, Luxembourg's continued neutrality was agreed at an international conference.

One effect of all this was that the South German States were drawn closer to the North German Confederation by their fear of French expansionism.

South German States
Even before the Treaty of Prague had been signed and before the scares with the French, secret treaties had been signed with the South German states individually. These promised that in the event of war, not only would the South German States fight with Prussia, but that their armies would be placed under Prussian control.

The South German Zollverein collapsed in 1867 after only one year in operation. Bismarck was happy to allow these states to join the North German Zollverein. He hoped that this step towards economic integration might eventually lead to political union. A Zollparlement was established to discuss economic questions and policy but the South

"TO BE SOLD."

EMPEROR NAPOLEON. "I—A—HAVE MADE AN OFFER TO MY FRIEND HERE, AND——"
THE MAN IN POSSESSION. "NO, HAVE YOU, THOUGH?—I RATHER THINK I WAS THE PARTY TO APPLY TO."
EMPEROR NAPOLEON. "OH, INDEED! AH! THEN IN THAT CASE I'LL—— BUT IT'S OF NO CONSEQUENCE."

Punch highlights the failure of Louis Napoleon to buy Luxembourg from the King of the Netherlands

German representatives on it were very anti-union. It seemed that using economic methods would not be a short cut to union. One South German commentator stated:

"The North German constitution consists of only three articles. Pay up! Be a soldier! Keep your mouth shut!"
(Quoted in Mitchell *Bismarck and the Development of Germany* Holmes McDougall p48)

Bismarck had one other weapon in his arsenal to help persuade the South German States - outright bribery! He was able to lay his hands on money from a number of sources, for example the treasury of Hanover after it had been occupied by the Prussians. This he used to support any factions or parties who supported unification in the South German states. He also lent huge sums of money to the eccentric King of Bavaria who used it to build romantic, mountain top castles at vast expense. Once the debt was large enough, Bismarck was able to bully and blackmail King Ludwig.

All this, however, was a painfully slow process. Bismarck reckoned in 1870 that unification would take another twenty years. Events moved much faster than this, though whether by accident or design is still open to debate.

The Slide to War
Relations between France and Prussia had deteriorated steadily since 1866. The French had tried unsuccessfully to gain allies in an anti-Prussian alliance. The Austrians found it easy to forgive the Prussians for the defeat they

had suffered in the war. The lenient peace imposed on them was particularly helpful here. The Italians tended to support the Prussians in gratitude for their help in securing Venetia. Only Britain seemed to be a possible ally but her policy was to avoid conflicts in mainland Europe.

In a nutshell France had no powerful friends in Europe at this time. Prussia, or the North German Confederation, although she could not count on the active support of other powers, was at least sure that they would not fight against her. In any conflict with France, the strength of the Prussian/German Army, would be enough to ensure victory.

One of the great questions which historians still argue about is deciding when Bismarck decided that a war with France could be used to complete the unification process. Bismarck in later life claimed that this had all been part of his grand plan from early on. He wrote in his memoirs:

> "I did not doubt that a Franco-German war must take place before the construction of a United Germany could be realised."
> (Quoted in Mitchell *Bismarck and the Development of Germany* Holmes McDougall p37)

On the other hand it is possible to find documents which suggest that he was not expecting war even in 1869. He said in a letter in February of that year:

> "I think it is probable that German unification could be promoted by violent events ... that German unification

is at present an unripe fruit seems to me only too obvious."
(Quoted in Hewison *Bismarck and the Unification of Germany* Arnold p 37)

The eventual cause of the war seems petty and trivial and can only be placed in context if we remember what had happened in the previous five years of Franco-German relations.

In 1869 the Spanish parliament was looking for a new constitutional monarch to replace Queen Isabella who had been overthrown. They approached Prince Leopold of Hohenzollern-Sigmaringen. He was suitable as a Roman Catholic, fairly senior in Royal terms and a relative of the Prussian Hohenzollern family. William of Prussia, head of the House of Hohenzollern, was well aware that a Hohenzollern on the Spanish throne would be perceived by the French as a threat. He was against Leopold being a candidate for the throne. Bismarck became involved and argued for the candidacy to go ahead. At the least it would destabilise France, at best it could produce events which he might exploit for his own ends.

In 1870, Bismarck secretly sent three representatives with £50,000 to persuade the Spanish Parliament to make a formal invitation to Leopold to become their King. He also sent these men to the Hohenzollern-Sigmaringens to persuade them to accept. Both missions were successful.

Bismarck went to his country estate so that he would be seen as having nothing to do with the events which were to follow. However, the Spanish parliament, which would

---

Ems Telegram: Original Version

"His Majesty the King writes to me, 'Count Benedetti accosted me on the promenade to demand from me, in an ultimately tiresome manner, authority for him to telegraph immediately that I would pledge myself henceforward never again to give my consent if the Hohenzollerns should renew their candidature. I refused then, finally quite earnestly, as one dare not and cannot for all time enter into such agreements. Of course I told him that I had as yet received no news and, as he had been notified about Paris and Madrid earlier than I, he would certainly see that my government had no hand in the matter.'

Since then His Majesty has received a letter form Karl Anton. His Majesty having told Count Benedetti that he was expecting news from the Prince, with regard to the foregoing demand, has decided, at the suggestion of Count Eulenberg and myself, not to receive Count Benedetti again, but merely to have an adjutant tell him that His Majesty had received confirmation of the news which Benedetti had already had from Paris, and that he had nothing further to say to the ambassador.

His Majesty leaves it to your Excellency whether or not Benedetti's new demand and its refusal should be made known immediately both to our ambassadors and in the press. "

Ems Telegram: Bismarck's version

"After the news of the Prince of Hohenzollern's renunciation had been officially communicated by the royal government of Spain to the imperial government of France, the French ambassador in Ems further demanded that he be authorised to telegraph Paris that His Majesty the King pledged himself henceforward never again to give his consent, should the Hohenzollerns renew their candidature.

His Majesty thereupon declined to receive the French ambassador again, and had the latter informed by an adjutant on duty that His Majesty had nothing further to tell the ambassador."

(Quoted in Hewison *Bismarck and the Unification of Germany* Arnold p 42)

formally choose the King, was not in session at this key time. The secret could not be kept for long and the news leaked out to the French.

The reaction was electric. The French did regard the Hohenzollern candidature as a very real threat. Many, including De Gramont, the French Foreign Minister, regarded it as intolerable. Tension mounted very quickly. The French sent their Ambassador to Prussia, Benedetti, to the spa town of Ems where the Prussian King was taking the waters. He was to tell the King that he should either instruct Leopold to withdraw his claim or face war with France. The King of Prussia did not want a war, least of all over the question of the Spanish Succession. After pressure from the Prussian King, Leopold withdrew from the candidature for the Spanish throne.

Instead of a diplomatic coup for the Prussians, the French had scored a diplomatic triumph. Bismarck was disgusted at the turn of events and openly talked of resignation.

However, the French badly overplayed their hand. Benedetti was instructed to seek assurances from King William that the Hohenzollern candidature would never be renewed. Benedetti approached the King on the promenade while William was taking the air. This informal approach was unusual in diplomatic circles. The King politely told Benedetti that he would make no promises as to future actions.

That should have been the end of the affair. The King despatched a telegram to Berlin telling Bismarck of the events. He then put the matter out of his mind.

Bismarck had returned to Berlin from his country estate after the unexpected turn of events. He was having dinner with his two close allies Von Moltke and Von Roon when the telegram arrived. According to his later recollections he was in a black depression and on the verge of resignation owing to the failure of his plans. When he read the telegram he saw in it potential for action. By shrewd editing, he altered the tone of the telegram to make the meeting at Ems seem like a deliberate snub to the French. (see page 72) He then released the edited text to the press. The result was as Bismarck had hoped. War fever broke out in France. They declared war on 19 July.

The final nail in the French coffin came on 25 July when Bismarck released the text of the earlier French proposal to annexe Belgium. This ended any chance of British help for the French - about the only possible ally they had left.

THE FRANCO-PRUSSIAN WAR

The war followed a similar pattern to the two previous ones. The Prussian Army was aided by soldiers from all the other German States, happy enough to fight to defend 'Germany' from a French attack. The German armies were quickly and efficiently organised, unlike the French. Within eighteen days of the mobilisation order, the Germans had 350,000 men at the battlefront; the French could manage only 200,000. The main battles of the war were all fought in the early stages. On 6 August, the German Armies met

"AU REVOIR!"

GERMANY. "FAREWELL, MADAME, AND IF——"
FRANCE. "HA! WE SHALL MEET AGAIN!"

Punch's prophetic warning of French determination to avenge the humiliating Peace Treaty imposed by the victorious Germans

the French in battle at Worth and Spichern both of which resulted in French defeats and retreat. Thus ended French plans for an invasion of Germany and from then on they were on the defensive. The French Generals argued for a retreat to Paris immediately. This was unthinkable for Louis Napoleon. Instead the French withdrew, under the command of Bazaine, to the fortress town of Metz. Here they were beseiged by the Germans.

As the troops were mobilised, another French Army was organised, commanded by McMahon and Napoleon himself. They met the German Army at Sedan on 1 September. Here again superior German firepower devastated the French Armies.

That night, emissaries from both sides met to discuss terms. Bismarck persuaded the French to surrender to prevent further bloodshed. Next morning 84,000 French soldiers surrendered to the Germans, including the Emperor Napoleon, denied his wish to be killed in battle and thus avoid the humiliation of surrender. Bismarck commented:

"The day before yesterday and yesterday cost France one hundred thousand men and an Emperor. This has been an event of vast historic importance."
(Quoted in Stiles *The Unification of Germany* Arnold p79)

Three days later Napoleon's government was overthrown and a Republic was established in France. Bismarck had

73

hoped that the decisive victories on the battlefield would end the war, but when the new French government heard that the Germans' peace terms included the surrender of the provinces of Alsace and Lorraine, they decided to fight on.

German troops advanced to lay siege to Paris. Despite attempts to raise armies elsewhere in France, the French were never able to mount a serious challenge to the Germans and any pockets of resistance were soon mopped up.

On 27 October 1870, the French Army at Metz was forced to surrender. 173,000 men were taken prisoner. The last, fragile hope for the French was gone and another German Army was released to join the siege of Paris.

Thiers, a minister in the French Republic, toured Europe to try to gain some support for the French, but he found no allies. In January 1871, Paris finally capitulated and the French government negotiated a three week armistice to allow elections to be held. The new government would have the task of negotiating the peace.

The Peace Treaty was signed at Frankfurt on 10 May 1871. It was as harsh as the previous ones had been lenient. The war had gone on for too long and the Germans had lost 28,000 men killed and 88,000 wounded. There was considerable bitterness on both sides. It was therefore impossible for Bismarck to negotiate a lenient peace. German public opinion, the Army and certainly the King would not allow it.

"The enormous sacrifices in blood and treasure which the German people have made in this war, together with all our present victories, would be in vain if the power of the French were not weakened for attack and the defensive strength of Germany were not increased."
(Official German reasons for the Treaty of Frankfurt quoted in Mitchell *Bismarck and the Unification of Germany* Holmes McDougall p47)

Negotiations were between Bismarck and Thiers. In fact, little negotiation took place. Bismarck stated the German demands, the French could either accept them or go back to war. The latter was unthinkable since there was a German Army of occupation in France.

Under the terms of the treaty, the French provinces of Alsace and Lorraine were taken by Germany. In earlier times both had been part of the Holy Roman Empire but had been taken by France in 1648. In 1876 there was still a substantial German-speaking population in the provinces - particularly in Alsace. The Germans, therefore, had some justification for taking the provinces but their main motives were to acquire strong defences on their French border and to gain a tangible reward for victory (something denied them by Bismarck at the end of the Austro-Prussian War).

France also had to pay an indemnity of £200,000,000 within four years. This was a huge sum. A German Army of occupation was to remain in France to ensure that this was paid. France was to lose her fortresses at Metz and Strasbourg which were essential to the defence of France. Bismarck wanted them for the defence of Germany.

After protracted negotiation, France was allowed to keep the fortress of Belfort. In return for this concession, she had to allow a triumphal march by the German Army - with King William at its head - through Paris. This can only be compared, in terms of humiliation, to a triumphal tour of Glasgow by the English football team after a victory at Hampden! Bismarck was forced into this by the vanity of his King and the army.

The Treaty of Frankfurt represented a harsh, victor's peace. It was unlikely that the French would forgive the Germans for being used as a tool to aid their unification. The humiliating aspects of the treaty made this certain. As the French writer Victor Hugo said:

"Henceforth there are in Europe two nations that are formidable - the one because it is vanquished, the other because it is victorious."
(Quoted in Grant and Temperly *Europe in the 19th and 20th Centuries* Longmans p354)

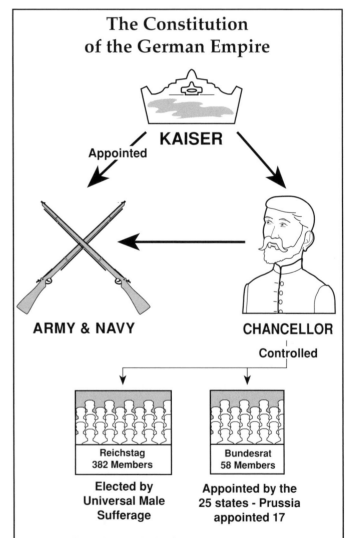

The Constitution of the German Empire

KAISER

Appointed

ARMY & NAVY

CHANCELLOR

Controlled

Reichstag
382 Members

Elected by
Universal Male
Suffrage

Bundesrat
58 Members

Appointed by the
25 states - Prussia
appointed 17

- Prussia had no majority in the Bundesrat.
- All men over 21 were allowed to vote.
- Bavaria held the Chair of the Foreign Affairs Committee.
- The Kaiser could only declare war with the permission of the Bundesrat.
- The Chancellor and the Cabinet Ministers had to attend the meetings of the Reichstag.
- The Chancellor chaired the Bundesrat.
- The Reichstag controlled the budget.

THE CREATION OF THE GERMAN EMPIRE

Almost as soon as the Franco-Prussian War was declared, the South German States declared their support for the Prussians and the North German Confederation. It seemed that complete unification was, at last, about to happen. There were however still two main problems - the South German States and King William.

The South German States

Despite the war fever, there were still a number of people who did not favour unification. This was particularly true in Bavaria. Bismarck was able to call in all his debts and bribes to put pressure on those opposing him. He made it clear that the Kings and Dukes would be able to remain on their respective thrones and also that any head of state who continued to oppose the idea would probably be overthrown by his own subjects since they did favour unification. The possibility of Prussian aid for such action was also discreetly threatened. King Ludwig put the problem in focus:

> "If Bavaria could exist alone, independent of the Confederation, it would not matter, but this would be completely impossible politically because of opposition from the people and the army, as a result of which the crown would lose its status in the country."
>
> (Quoted in Mitchell *Bismarck and the Unification of Germany* Holmes McDougall p45)

The Persuasion of King William

At this advanced stage of events the King began to be a little difficult. He thought that any new title would be too democratic (it had clearly not been given to him by God!) and that therefore he would rather stay as King of Prussia. Secondly, there was the problem of who was to ask him to accept the throne. Once before a Prussian King had refused to accept "a throne out of the gutter". Thirdly there was the complex question of what to call him. He would have liked the impressive 'Emperor of Germany' but this would have implied that he was overlord of all the German States and the other Heads of State would not like that. Much sounder from their point of view would be 'German Emperor'.

Bismarck, skilful as ever, solved the problem by getting King Ludwig of Bavaria to offer him the throne (another debt called in) and he allowed William to retain the title of King of Prussia. The suggested title for his new position was German Emperor or Kaiser.

The Proclamation of the Empire

The German Empire was proclaimed on 18 January 1871 in the Hall of Mirrors at Versailles near Paris. Even at this late stage Bismarck still had problems because, to the end, William insisted on the title Emperor of Germany. In the Treaty of Unification with Bavaria, Bismarck had promised German Emperor. None of the South German Heads

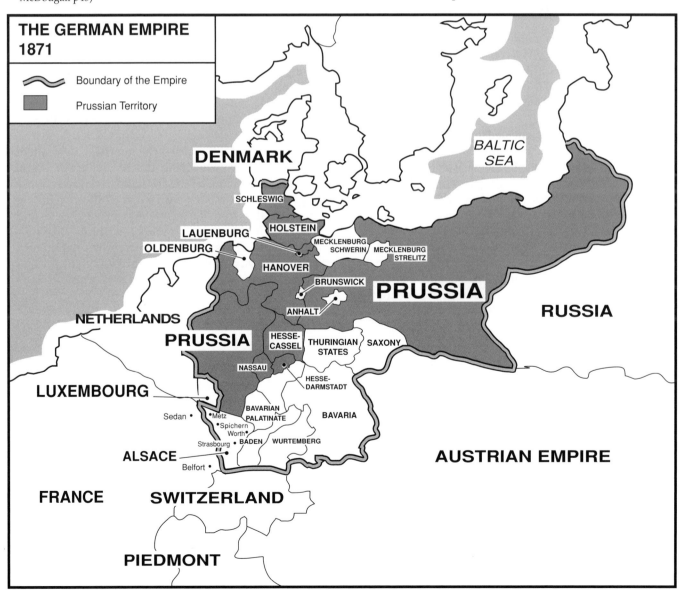

THE GERMAN EMPIRE 1871

Boundary of the Empire

Prussian Territory

DENMARK

BALTIC SEA

SCHLESWIG

LAUENBURG

HOLSTEIN

OLDENBURG

MECKLENBURG SCHWERIN

MECKLENBURG STRELITZ

HANOVER

BRUNSWICK

PRUSSIA

ANHALT

NETHERLANDS

RUSSIA

PRUSSIA

HESSE-CASSEL

THURINGIAN STATES

SAXONY

NASSAU

HESSE-DARMSTADT

LUXEMBOURG

Sedan

Metz

Spichern

Worth

BAVARIAN PALATINATE

BAVARIA

Strasbourg

BADEN

WURTEMBERG

ALSACE

Belfort

AUSTRIAN EMPIRE

FRANCE

SWITZERLAND

PIEDMONT

of State, including King Ludwig of Bavaria, attended the ceremony. This was a considerable slight to William. King Ludwig offered the throne to William by letter!

Bismarck had the honour of reading the proclamation which stated:

> "We, William by the grace of God, King of Prussia ... hereby inform you that we regard it as our duty to the whole fatherland to respond to this summons of the allied princes and free cities and to assume the German Imperial title."
> (Quoted in Stiles *The Unification of Germany* Arnold p85)

Next, however, came the difficult part. Who was to proclaim William and what were they to proclaim him? The solution was to get the Grand Duke of Baden (William's son-in-law and therefore under some pressure to conform) to do the proclamation and for him to proclaim, "Long live his Imperial and Royal Majesty, Kaiser William!"

In this way all problems of honour and title were avoided. Nevertheless, the Kaiser was not pleased. At this moment of triumph he took the huff and stomped off the stage. He didn't even shake the hand offered by Bismarck who commented, "the Kaiser birth has been difficult ... Kings at such times have their odd desires." (Quoted in Granville *Europe Reshaped* Fontana p352)

Thus the most powerful nation in late nineteenth century Europe came into being. The constitution of the German Empire became law on 20 April 1871. As you will see from the diagram on page 74 it was, in essence, an extension of the constitution of the North German Confederation.

In theory the constitution provided for a democratic system of government which guaranteed the freedom of individual states within the framework of a constitution. Prussia, the Kaiser and the Chancellor were not, it seemed, in a position to dominate other states under the Federal System. The Empire controlled the Armed Services and Foreign Policy. Control of virtually all other affairs was left to the governments of the individual states.

In practice, however, Bismarck, Prussia and the Kaiser were very much in control. Prussia comprised 60% of the land area and more than 60% of the population. When a common currency was introduced it was based on the Prussian model, the Prussian Bank became the Reichsbank and the unified legal procedures which were introduced leaned heavily on Prussian methods.

The power of the Reichstag, in which Prussia had a majority, was largely illusory. Its 382 members had the power to question the Chancellor but he was not responsible to it for his actions. Its control of the military budget was seriously undermined after the 'War in Sight Crisis' of 1874 (see chapter 9) when it agreed to vote on this only every seven years.

The Bundesrat was a little more powerful. It initiated legislation and had the power to declare war. The chair of the Foreign Affairs Committee was held by Bavaria. It was made up of representatives of the individual states in proportion to the size of their population. Prussia only appointed 17 out of the 58 members so it seemed that she was hardly in a position to dominate.

However, here too Prussia dominated. Any major change - ie. to the constitution - could be vetoed by 14 votes. Thus Prussia could veto any changes whenever she wished. The Foreign Affairs Committee became no more than a rubber stamp. The Kaiser retained the right, for example, to declare war if Germany was attacked. The fact that Bismarck was Chairman of the Bundesrat enabled him to control it and to manipulate its discussions to his own ends.

Having said all this, the German constitution provided a democratic framework which was ahead of much of Europe at that time. Crucially, however, this system of government did not substantially change until 1918.

> "Bismarck had thus settled the internal Government of Germany by supplying it with an upper house representing states, a pseudo-democratic lower house representing numbers: with a constitution excluding many matters from the competence of both bodies and which could not be amended without Prussia's permission. Prussia through her prestige, her money, her power was emphatically the predominant power."
> (Grant & Temperley *Europe in the 19th and 20th Centuries* Longmans p353)

RESPONSIBILITY FOR GERMAN UNIFICATION

Up until World War Two it was widely accepted that Bismarck alone was responsible for the unification of Germany (see sources 1 and 2). However, today many historians have argued that he would not have been so successful if it had not been for the existence of other forces, such as social and economic, which he undoubtedly used to his advantage (see sources 3 to 8). Indeed, some historians have gone further by stating that the other longer term factors were more important than Bismarck himself (see sources 9 and 10).

Source 1

"The common view of German nationalism is an irresistible current sweeping down the decades to fulfilment in 1870 is a fiction of nationalistic historians, derived from the hopes and aspirations of 'kleindeutsch' leaders, like Sybel and Treitsche, who were their intellectual forebears. Only under the stimulation provided by Bismarck for his own political ends did German nationalism begin to move the masses."
(O Pflanze *Bismarck and the Development of Germany* Vol 1 Princeton UP p13 Quoted in Eyck p vi)

Source 2

Perhaps not written by a historian, but an interesting evaluation nevertheless is this one which states that:

" ... through his inner development (Bismarck) was transformed from a politician into the smith who forged the Reich. Not only so: it was he who created the conditions which rendered possible the creation of Great Germany. In spite of all obstacles he laid the foundation stone for the National Socialist unified State, for he began that conquest over the psychological prejudices and interests of tribes and states which of necessity was bound to continue."
(Adolf Hitler speaking at the launch of the warship, Bismarck in 1939 – Quoted in Baynes *The Speeches of Adolf Hitler* OUP p1579)

Source 3

"The tendency, even among non-Marxist historians, is to concentrate more on the inter-relationship between diplomatic, social and economic factors. Bismarck did not fashion German unity alone. He exploited powerful forces which already existed: the industrial revolution in Germany, the growth of liberalism and nationalism, the disintegration of the 1815 Vienna Settlement during and after the Crimean War, and the increasing determination of Prussia after 1848 to reassert her influence over Germany."
(Williamson *Bismarck and Germany 1862-1890* Longmans p1)

Source 4

"Bismarck's task of unifying Germany was made easier by circumstances. If he played his hand with great skill, it was a good one in the first place."
(Mosse *The European Powers and the German Question* CUP p372 Quoted in Eyck p vi)

Source 5

"To preserve a sense of proportion we must remember that his (Bismarck's) admirers often exaggerate the extent of the obstacles in his path."
(Medlicott *Bismarck and Modern Germany* English Universities Press p188 Quoted in Eyck p vi)

Source 6

"Is it a mistake to begin with Bismarck? So much is written these days, and so insistently, about the primary importance of economic and social forces in history that one runs the risk of being considered old-fashioned if one gives too much prominence to personality. Yet it is certainly unnecessary to apologise for introducing Bismarck's name at the outset. If he had never risen to the top in Prussian politics, the unification of Germany would have taken place anyway, but surely not at the same time or in quite the same way as it did. Whatever may be said about the movement of economic forces, there is no burking the fact that the decision concerning the form unification would take was made, not in the area of economic and commercial policy, but on the battlefield of Koniggratz on 3 July 1866; and it would be idle to deny that when the broken fragments of Benedek's army retreated under the cover of their artillery to the banks of the Elbe on that dark afternoon, they were registering the triumph of Bismarck's policy. It had been he who had possessed the temerity to break with the traditions of Prussian diplomacy and to choose an anti-Austrian policy as a means of dividing the parliamentary opposition that was threatening to paralyse the Prussian Government when he came to power in September 1862; and he had charted the strategy that had jockeyed the Austrian Government into straits in which it felt compelled to assume responsibility for beginning the war despite the fact that its political and military resources made its chances of winning doubtful. Had the Prussian Army not been as good as Bismarck believed it to be, he would have been a dead man before the day of battle was over - at least he told the British Ambassador that this would be so. But he had not been mistaken in this fundamental judgment, and the victory of the army was therefore also his."(Craig *Germany 1866-1945* OUP p1-2)

Source 7

"Contrary to what Bismarck was to claim in later life, the unification of Germany was never one of his original ambitions. Like King Wilhelm, he feared the loss of conservative Prussian identity in a Greater German democracy. His first ambition was to make Prussia the most powerful state in Central Europe. To achieve this, he needed to oust Austria from her position as leader of Germany. What was afterwards to look like a carefully calculated, step-by-step progress to German unification was, on the part of Bismarck, a series of favourable situations, wisely grasped. Despite his celebrated shrewdness, Bismarck was an opportunist. Instead of issuing challenges, he took advantage of them. 'Man cannot create the current of events,' he would later say. 'He can only float with it and steer.' " (Aronson *The Kaisers* Cassell p56)

Source 8

"But he knew as well as anyone that in political life nothing is certain: 'Politics is not in itself an exact and logical science but is the capacity to choose in each fleeting moment of the situation that which is least harmful or most opportune.' And he was the supreme opportunist, taking advantage of French blunders in 1870, for instance, to leave France no way out of declaring war, and thus appearing as the aggressor.

His policies can best be described as flexible. It seems reasonable to assume that he did have general long-term aims, involving Austria and the extension of Prussian power over the other German states. It also seems reasonable to assume that the timing and exact means of achieving these aims were left to short-term decisions based on conditions at the time; for as well as being an opportunist, he was a realist, at least as far as politics were concerned."
(Stiles *The Unification of Germany 1815-1890* Arnold p100)

Source 9

"The main argument has centred round the assumption made by my father that the German liberals would have proved capable of uniting Germany and without the use of many of the unpleasant methods employed by Bismarck which were such a heavy mortgage on Germany's future. My father believed that German unification in the third quarter of the nineteenth century was a natural and desirable development." (Foreward to Frank Eyck *Bismarck and the German Empire* Unwin p v-vi)

Source 10

"There are however historians such as Böhme who take a less Bismarck centred view of German unification. They argue that Bismarck did not make Germany; Germany made Bismarck. They believe that conditions, particularly economic conditions, were such in 1862 that Bismarck was able to build on them and gain the credit for bringing about a unification, which given time would probably have developed naturally. They consider that 'coal and iron' not 'blood and iron' were the Prussian power base. The existing economic ascendancy was the key to political ascendancy. There is some truth in this, and it was a view shared to some extent by Bismarck himself. He appreciated the importance and unifying influence of the Zollverein and Zollparlement in the years before 1870. In the years after that date he initiated the development of new electrical and chemical industries, the exploitation of mineral resources, and the expansion of road and rail networks. By 1890 Germany had been welded into one economic whole." (Stiles *The Unification of Germany 1815-1890* Arnold p101)

9 The Character of the New Nation State of Germany 1871 - 1914

GERMAN DOMESTIC POLITICS 1870 - 1890

It has been said that, having achieved unification Bismarck wanted to prevent further change, but rapid changes in German society and economic affairs ensured that this would be impossible. Economic developments in Germany are dealt with later in this chapter. We shall concentrate here on political changes.

Political parties developed in Germany after unification. While in Britain a predominantly two party system evolved, there were many parties in Germany none of which ever commanded an overall majority. An effective and powerful opposition to Bismarck never really emerged. Table 9.1 shows the Reichstag election results for the German Empire 1870-1890

The main parties can be described briefly as follows:-

The Conservatives: Mainly Protestant Prussian Junkers who were very right-wing and who opposed any form of liberalisation. They were therefore suspicious of some of Bismarck's actions. They were strongest in Prussia.

The Free Conservatives: Drew their support from landowners and industrialists throughout Germany. They were staunch supporters of Bismarck and favoured the creation of the German Empire.

National Liberals: The same grouping who had precipitated the constitutional crisis in Prussia in 1862, they were predoominantly middle class and many were involved in industry. They were strong supporters of the creation of the German Empire and were keen to support the growth of industry. They supported a free trade policy.

Progressives: These emerged from a split in the National Liberals over the issue of an indemnity for Bismarck in 1867. They were similar in policy and support to the National Liberals but were opponents of Bismarck.

Centre: Formed in 1870, its predominant aim was the protection of the Roman Catholic Church. It drew its support from all classes and was most powerful in Roman Catholic South Germany though it had pockets of support in other areas. The Centrists were opponents of Bismarck until 1879 after which they became firm allies.

Social Democrats: A small party in 1870 drawing its support from the lower classes. It was most powerful in centres of industry and was an outright opponent of Bismarck.

National Groups: Representatives from areas like Poland, Schleswig and Alsace were consistently elected on a policy of taking their home area out of the Empire. They were opponents of Bismarck but not large in number.

The Liberal Era

By far the largest and most important party in the 1870s was the National Liberals whose actions in the first decade of the new Empire have come in for a good deal of criticism. Many argued that they betrayed the ideals of liberalism and became merely the tools of Bismarck. In some ways this is a harsh judgement since they were nationalists as well as Liberals and hardly likely to oppose the man who had united Germany. Bismarck for his part, in his usual fashion, exploited the Liberals for his own ends.

The years 1870-1879 were known as the Liberal Era in Germany. At that time there was much to draw the Liberals to Bismarck. He had united Germany and had provided a constitution which tended towards liberal principles. The economic reforms after unification made industrial development easier and moved closer to free trade - ie. little or no customs duty on imports or exports. Many hoped to force Bismarck into still more reform.

The issue of the Army Budget re-emerged when the compromise of 1867 (see page 70) expired in 1874. Bismarck and the Army wanted this fixed permanently but this was seen as an attack on the power of the Reichstag and the Liberals refused to agree to it. Bismarck stirred up the 'War in Sight Crisis' (see page 84) and threatened that he would use similar tactics to those he had used so successfully in 1862-1863. This was enough to make the Liberals afraid of being branded as unpatriotic and a compromise was agreed by which the budget would only be voted on every seven years. Other opponents saw this as a sellout by the Liberals.

By the late 1870s, Bismarck had concluded that the key-

Party	Number of Seats in the Reichstag							
	1871	1874	1877	1878	1881	1884	1887	1890
Conservatives	54	22	40	59	50	78	80	73
Free Conservatives	38	36	38	57	28	28	41	20
National Liberals	150	155	128	99	47	51	99	42
Progressives	47	50	52	39	115	74	32	76
Centre	58	91	93	94	100	99	98	106
Social Democrats	2	9	12	9	12	24	1	35
Nationalists etc.	33	34	34	40	45	43	35	40

Table 9.1

This German cartoon illustrates the conflict between Pope Pius IX and Bismarck during the Kulturkampf

stone of Liberal policy, Free Trade, was no longer suitable for Germany. Although it suited some of the new industries, it was causing great damage to agriculture. Realising that he would lose the support of the Liberals when he began to reintroduce protectionism, Bismarck stated:

> "I am represented as having disowned them, while it was they who turned from me because I could not be as liberal as they were."
> (Quoted in Mitchell *Bismarck and the Unification of Germany* Holmes McDougall p89)

The left wing of the National Liberals remained true to their principles and joined with the Progressive Party to form the Independent Party. The remainder abandoned any real Liberal policies, adopted a realpolitik outlook and continued to support Bismarck.

Throughout the 1880s Bismarck could count on the loyal support of the Conservative Parties who were happy to see him abandon his 'liberal' ways. This, together with the support of the Centre Party, was generally enough for him to get what he wanted.

THE CENTRE PARTY & THE KULTURKAMPF

Northern Germany, including Prussia, was predominantly Lutheran Protestant in religion. The South German States were mainly Roman Catholic as were the captured territories of Alsace, Lorraine and Poland. When Germany was united, there was a fear that the Roman Catholics would be swamped by Protestant interests. For this reason a Roman Catholic party was formed. The Centre Party as it was called, attracted support from other groups - like the Poles - who had no wish to be part of Germany.

The Party was led by Ludwig Windhorst, a North German Catholic from Hanover - another reflection of anti-Empire feeling since Hanover had been forcibly taken over by Prussia. Party policies were right of centre. From the first election for the Reichstag, the Centre Party emerged as the third largest party.

The head of the Roman Catholic Church, Pope Pius IX, was, by the 1860s, extremely conservative. In 1870 the Vatican Council issued a decree of Papal Infallibility. This declared that Papal decisions on matters of faith and morality could not be wrong and therefore must be obeyed by all Roman Catholics.

Some German Catholics refused to accept the new doctrines and were treated quite harshly by the Church. These Altkatholiken (old Catholics) were excommunicated from the Church and sacked from any job under the control of the Church. They appealed for help and protection to Bismarck who was anxious to ensure that national identity was given higher status than religious persuasion.

Bismarck's first tactic clearly demonstrated realpolitik and also proves that his actions were driven solely by a desire to protect Germany and had little to do with a desire to persecute Roman Catholics.

In 1870 when the Italians occupied Rome, the Pope became a virtual prisoner in the Vatican. Bismarck hit on the bold plan of offering him asylum in Germany. The Pope, in return, would instruct German Catholics to support the Empire. To Bismarck's genuine disappointment, the Pope refused the offer.

With this background, the growth of the Centre Party could be seen as a collection of enemies or Reichsfeinden as Bismarck called them. In any future conflict with Roman Catholic Austria or France, for example, who might the German Catholics support? Even worse, who might the Pope instruct them to support? In practice, Germans invariably put their nationality first, but this at least partially explains Bismarck's actions. He said:

"It is essentially a political question. ... It is not as our Catholic citizens are being persuaded, a matter of a struggle of a Protestant dynasty against the Catholic Church ... it is a matter of conflict, which is as old as the human race, between monarchy and priesthood. What is at stake is the defence of the state."

(Quoted in Mitchell *Bismarck and the Unification of Germany* Holmes McDougall p65)

Bismarck was also aware that any campaign against the power of the Roman Catholic Church would be popular with the Liberals in Germany. It was the leader of the Progressive Liberals, Virchow, who coined the term *Kulturkampf* to describe what he saw as a struggle to free the minds of German Catholics.

Many of the actions taken by Bismarck applied only in Prussia since internal affairs were handled by the state governments under the Federal constitution.

The campaign began in 1871 with the abolition of the Catholic section of the Prussian Ministry of Religious Affairs, thus effectively withdrawing all privileges from the Roman Catholic Church in Prussia. Use of the pulpit for political indoctrination was made a crime. This was a direct attack on any attempt to generate support for the Centre Party. Prussian state supervision of all schools was introduced, discriminating against Catholics who preferred to run their own system. In June 1872, Falk, a noted anti-Catholic, was appointed Minister of Religious Affairs. At the same time, members of religious orders, eg. monks, were forbidden to teach. In July 1872 the Jesuits, a strongly Catholic teaching order, were banned from German soil.

In 1872 the German Envoy to the Vatican was withdrawn. In 1874, marriage was made a civil rather than a religious contract and in 1875 all religious orders were abolished in Prussia.

Harshest of all were the infamous May Laws, passed in May 1873, 1874 and 1875. These forbade the public excommunication of Catholics by priests and insisted that potential priests should study for at least three years at a German University and should be examined at the end of their course. (Most priests at this time were trained in Italy.) The state took control of the appointment of priests and all Roman Catholic training colleges were to be inspected by the state. The aim was to undermine the power of the Church and to 'Germanise' it. The Pope declared these actions invalid and most German Catholics ignored them.

Catholics followed a policy of passive resistance which was difficult to counteract. The elections of 1874, 1877 and 1878 actually resulted in gains for the Centre Party. (See Table 9.1) In 1874 a young Catholic, Kullman, tried to assassinate the Kaiser, but this extreme action was exceptional. Priests refused to obey the new orders and by 1876 nine Bishoprics and 1,400 parishes had no priests.

Bismarck entered this campaign to defeat a perceived threat to the Empire. Clearly he was not succeeding - indeed he was achieving almost exactly the opposite result. There were other factors to be considered as well. In 1878, Pope Pius IX died. The new Pope, Leo XIII, was a little more flexible. Secondly, Bismarck was afraid of the threat posed by the 'revanchist' (revenge seeking) government in France after 1875. Thirdly, Bismarck wanted a closer alliance with Austria and the Kulturkampf was a barrier.

Bismarck also made some careful calculations about his political support. Relations with the Liberals were declining. He also noted that a new threat was emerging in Germany in the shape of the socialists. He could not deal with two 'Reishsfeinden' at once and the Roman Catholics certainly represented the lesser of the two evils. Therefore he resolved to end the Kulturkampf.

Falk was blamed for the whole thing and was sacked. The May Laws were repealed, foreign trained priests and most religious orders were allowed back into Germany and the German Envoy returned to the Vatican. Relations improved rapidly. From then until the fall of Bismarck in

---

SOME VIEWS ON THE KULTURKAMPF

"Bismarck had conjured up a quarrel between Church and state in one of the few states where it had hardly existed before, and his undoubted skill and perseverance in settling it on terms which are generally regarded as a compromise on balance favourable to the state should not be allowed to conceal the original miscalculation that made this large-scale diplomatic effort necessary."
(Simon *Germany in the Age of Bismarck* Allen & Unwin p56)

"However much the Chancellor might seek to gloss it over, the damage wrought by the Kulturkampf was great. Much that had been won for the cause of national unity during the war against France had been trifled away during the years in which Germans had been set against Germans on confessional grounds. The heirarchy of the Catholic Church in Germany had been made more ultramontane ... and the great mass of Roman Catholic believers had been imbued with a distrust of their government that was to last for years. ....The Protestant Churches suffered a similar loss ... they were silent in the face of oppression of their fellow Christians and confirmed the already prevalent impression that the Protestant establishment was merely an instrument of the authoritarian state."
(Craig *Germany 1866 - 1945* OUP p77)

1890, the Centre Party, who also favoured protectionism and were anti-socialist, were loyal supporters. By 188, Bismarck could say that the Pope "trusts me ... as may now be seen from the desire expressed by the Pope that the Centre Party should vote for the Army Bill." (Quoted in Mitchell *Bismarck and the Unification of Germany* Holmes McDougall p67)

At the end of the Kulturkampf all that remained was the ban on the Jesuits, the civil contract of marriage and the retention of state inspection of schools. Most catholics supported the Centre Party and they supported the Empire. Certainly they posed no threat to the Empire ... but then had they ever?

THE SOCIALISTS

The roots of socialism can be said to lie in Germany. Karl Marx and Friedrich Engels were both Germans and Marx's famous book *Das Kapital*, was written and published in 1848 in Germany. They were not, however, leading figures in the development of socialism in Germany.

The first socialist party, the German General Workers Association was founded in Prussia in 1863 by Ferdinand Lassalle. Another, the Social Democratic Workers Party was established at Eisenach in 1869. It was led by two men: August Bebel and Wilhelm Liebknecht. Both attracted little support in the years before 1870.

In the first few years of the Empire support for the parties began to grow. In 1874 the two held a joint Congress at Gotha and decided to merge. The party formed was called the German Social Democratic Labour Party. It followed fairly moderate social democratic policies and attracted criticism from Marx and Engels for its moderation.

Although the Lassalleans initially supported the Franco-Prussian War, both socialist groups came to regard it as a war of aggression against France and opposed it. They opposed the annexation of Alsace and Lorraine and warmly applauded the Paris Commune - a socialist regime which organised and ran the defence of Paris for a short time after the fall of Louis Napoleon. From then on Bismarck regarded the socialists as dangerous enemies of the state (Reichsfeinden). He later said:

"It was from the moment when, in the assembled Reichstag, either Bebel or Liebknecht ... held up the French Commune as a model of political institutions ... that I first experienced a full conviction of the danger which threatened us ... from that moment I regarded the Social Democratic factions as an enemy against which the state and society must arm themselves."
(Quoted in Mitchell *Bismarck and the Unification of Germany* Holmes McDougall p73)

This anxiety grew as the popularity of the socialists increased during the 1870s. Bismarck, however, was preoccupied with the Kulturkampf.

After the Social Democratic Party conference in 1875 when they demanded nationalisation of banks and coal mines and the creation of social equality, Bismarck decided that enough was enough. A bill was presented to the Reichstag which would control the press, prevent the publication of socialist propaganda and give the government powers over treasonable organisations. This was not supported by the Liberals who feared that it might one day be used against them, nor by the Centre Party who were at odds with him over the Kulturkampf.

In 1878, Bismarck again saw his chance. An ex-Social Democrat, Max Hodel, attempted to assassinate the Kaiser. Bismarck used this as an excuse to introduce a harsh bill which would have outlawed the socialists and their press. This bill was very badly prepared and the National Liberals refused to support it. Less than one month later there was a second assassination attempt on the Kaiser. This time the would-be assassin, Dr Nobiling, had no connection whatsoever with the socialists. This did not deter Bismarck. He exploited the near hysteria in the nation by dissolving the Reichstag and calling an election. The National Liberals were blamed for their lack of patriotism in allowing the socialist threat to continue to exist. The election resulted in a loss of support for the Liberals, Progressives and Social Democrats and gains for the Conservative parties. (See Table 9.1) Assured also of Centre Party support now that the Kulturkampf was ended (the Centrists were not sympathetic to the anti-clerical socialists either) Bismarck was able to introduce protectionism in trade, repeal the May Laws to end the Kulturkampf, and to pass the anti-socialist law in September 1878. Although the Progressives opposed it the National Liberals did not. Their only concession to liberal principles was to limit its effect to two and a half years. In fact the law was renewed every three years until the fall of Bismarck in 1890.

The anti-socialist law (Socialistengesetz) dealt a severe blow to the socialists. Its main terms were as follows:

"•Associations which aim, by social democratic, socialistic or communistic agitation, at the destruction of the existing order in state or society are forbidden. (The Social Democratic Party itself was not forbidden.)
•Meetings in which social democratic, socialistic or communistic tendencies ... make their appearance are forbidden.
•All printed matter in which social democratic, socialistic or communistic tendencies are directed ... in a manner dangerous to the peace and, in particular, to the harmony between the different classes of the population, is forbidden."
(Quoted in Mitchell *Bismarck and the Unification of Germany* Holmes McDougall p79)

Many socialists were imprisoned and others emigrated but socialism was merely driven underground. Meetings continued to be held, disguised as other organisations, or in venues which it was difficult for the police to find. Printed materials and newspapers were smuggled in from abroad. Support for socialist candidates continued to increase and an increased number were elected to the Reichstag. The policies of the Party became more extreme. Since it seemed that the ruling class would never voluntarily allow socialist policies to be implemented, the only way forward seemed to be through the revolutionary ideals of Marxism.

Bismarck had realised early on that he could not simply suppress the socialists. He recognised that another way of undermining their support was by implementing some of their less extreme policies himself. In this way, he felt, moderate working-class Germans would feel that their interests were being adequately represented. The Kaiser himself said:

"A remedy cannot be sought alone in repression of socialistic excess; there must be simultaneously the positive advancement of the welfare of the working classes."
(Quoted in Mitchell *Bismarck and the Unification of Germany* Holmes McDougall p76)

He embarked on a programme of 'state Socialism'. Despite the fact that Bismarck's motives were determined by questions of realpolitik, the social reforms made in Germany in the 1880s were far in advance of anything done elsewhere in the world and were more than twenty years ahead of similar developments in Britain.

In May 1883 a sickness insurance law was introduced. Employees contributed two-thirds of the cost and the employers the other one-third but the law was not popular with either side as they regarded it as a drain on their wealth. In June 1884 an Accident Insurance Law, funded by employers, was passed which provided cover for nearly all wage earning groups. In May 1889 an Old Age and Invalidity Law was passed which provided state pensions, contributions being made by workers, employers and state. Old age pensions were payable at the age of 70.

These remarkable reforms were attacked by the Liberals for fostering communism and by the socialists as 'crumbs from the rich man's table'. From Bismarck's point of view the exercise was a failure. Working-class voters understood perfectly well why the reforms had been made and support for the Social Democrats continued to increase.

The attempts to deal with the socialist threat were clearly failing, so by his own principles of realpolitik a change of course seemed imperative. This time however, Bismarck was too blinded by his dislike of the socialists and he pressed on to even more extreme proposals.

In 1889 he proposed strengthening the anti-socialist law by allowing the expulsion of known agitators and making the law as a whole permanent. The Reichstag refused to pass this and proposed merely to renew the law as it stood for another three years. Bismarck instructed his supporters to vote against this - thus making the anti-socialist law lapse and therefore socialism legal again. He calculated that this would produce such an upsurge in socialist agitation and violence that it would give him the excuse to use military force to crush the socialists once and for all. The socialists used their renewed legal status to campaign vigorously, but perfectly legally, and successfully in the 1890 election campaign. Overall, Bismarck's anti-socialist policy can be judged a failure. Even though he tried various methods to achieve his aims, he failed ultimately because he allowed his distaste for socialism to cloud his judgement and distort his ideal of realpolitik.

GERMAN FOREIGN POLICY 1870 - 1890.

After 1870 Bismarck became interested in maintaining peaceful relations with the rest of Europe and strove valiantly to find peaceful solutions to any crises which did

---

SOME VIEWS ON THE ANTI-SOCIALIST CAMPAIGN

"The fact that Bismarck's state socialism' ultimately failed in its political purpose should not, however, detract from its intrinsic merits. The system of social security that Bismarck built in the 1880s, including accident, medical, invalid and old age insurance and limited factory inspection, was the first of its kind in Europe."
(Simon *Germany in the Age of Bismarck* Allen & Unwin p71)

"It can be plausibly argued that here, as in the case of the Kulturkampf, Bismarck's political intuition misled him. His attempt to reconcile the workers to the Hohenzollern monarchy by means of social and economic paternalism failed precisely because the problem of integrating the workers was more political and psychological than economic and social."
(Simon *Germany in the Age of Bismarck* Allen & Unwin p70)

"Erich Eyck has written that the fact that Bismarck never mentioned his social insurance legislation in his memoirs proves that it was something in which he had no serious interest and which he had taken up only for the political advantage which he might gain from doing so. ... It would be a mistake to conclude from what is or is not said there that Bismarck was insincere in his repeated assertions that the state had a responsibility for the welfare of its more deprived and handicapped subjects. In his first years as Minister President of Prussia, in 1862 and 1863, he had begun to think of the possibility of state supported insurance plans for the benefit of the working class and his plans for accident, sickness and old age insurance in the 1880s were rooted in the same concern that had motivated the abortive plans of the earlier period. The political was never, of course, far from the centre of Bismarck's thinking, and there can be little doubt that he was aware of the advantage that might be derived from the insurance programme in his campaign against socialism."
(Craig *Germany 1866-1945* OUP p77)

occur. To understand this apparent change of character we need to look again at Bismarck's motives. History has branded Bismarck a warmonger. In the events leading up to 1870, Bismarck used war, where he felt it necessary, to establish Prussian domination in Germany and then to unify Germany. However, he was never interested in prolonging a war once his specified aims had been achieved.

After 1870, with Germany a unified country, Bismarck had no further wish to wage war. His one great fear was that France would start a war of revenge against Germany motivated by the humiliations Bismarck had inflicted on her. Because of this Germany had to be prepared to fight a defensive war.

We can sum up Bismarck's foreign policy in the years after 1870 in this way:

1 Keep France isolated and without allies.
2 Try to stay on friendly terms with the other Great Powers.
3 Try to maintain peace throughout the world since in any crisis the Great Powers would tend to polarise and France could thus gain an ally.
4 To achieve all the above, keep a close eye on world affairs to try to resolve any potential crises.
5 In Bismarck's own words, "Try to be one of three, so long as the world is governed by the unequal equilibrium of five powers." (Quoted in Stiles *The Unification of Germany* Arnold p96)

For the next twenty years Bismarck established an almost bewildering series of secret agreements and alliances, some of which seemed to contradict others, which tied virtually the whole of Europe - with the exception of France - to Germany. It can be visualised as a gigantic web binding Europe together with Bismarck at the centre, the spider spinning the threads. What follows is an overview of the alliances made.

In 1872 the Dreikaiserbund (League of Three Emperors) was established. This was an agreement between the Emperors of Austria-Hungary, Russia and Germany. It was not a formal alliance. They pledged:

"to come to an agreement in the first instance amongst themselves, without seeking or contracting new alliances, in order to agree on the line of conduct they will follow in common."
(Quoted in Mitchell *Bismarck and the Unification of Germany* Holmes McDougall p92)

Bismarck made great play of the fact that this was a joining of the great monarchist nations of Europe against the threat of republicanism. It will be remembered that France after 1870 was a Republic.

In 1875 a new French government under McMahon, a veteran of the Franco-Prussian War, took office in France. This government had a much stronger policy towards Germany and was considered 'revanchist' (seeking revenge). France had recovered remarkably quickly from the war, had paid off her indemnity and the German Army of occupation had gone home. The French began to modernise their army. To Bismarck there could only be one reason for this - a war of revenge. He therefore tried to stir up a crisis in the hope that the other European nations would put pressure on the French to make them back down. He banned the export of horses to France - they were potential cavalry - and he arranged a series of articles in the German press speculating whether war was in sight.

However, the Great Powers had been caught out too often by Bismarck's methods. They suspected that he was planning another war against the French and both Britain and Russia made it very clear that they would not accept another war. Bismarck was then seen to be backing down from a war that he had absolutely no intention of starting! This was one of the few occasions when his plans backfired.

The main effect of this crisis was to demonstrate the fragility of the Dreikaiserbund since the Russians could so easily side with the perceived enemy.

In 1878, Bismarck hosted a European Congress in Berlin in an effort to resolve a crisis which threatened the peace and stability of the whole of Europe. A war had broken out in 1877 between Russia and Turkey. The Russians won easily and imposed a peace treaty which virtually guaranteed Russian domination of the Balkan area by the creation of a large new state, Bulgaria, which would be a Russian puppet. This did not suit the British, French or Austrians. On the other hand, it didn't really affect German interests. Bismarck had declared of the Balkans:

"I can see no interest in it for Germany which would be worth the healthy bones of a single Pomeranian musketeer."
(Quoted in Mitchell *Bismarck and the Unification of Germany* Holmes McDougall p104)

It was suggested that an international conference should be held to discuss the crisis. The Russians could not deny the wishes of three of the Great Powers and so, reluctantly, agreed.

Bismarck had been worried about the events in the Balkans. He could see the dispute between Austria and Russia deteriorating into a war in which Germany would have to take sides, an inevitable consequence of which would be that French isolation would be ended.

This provided his main motive for holding the Congress of Berlin in 1878. Bismarck portrayed himself as the 'Honest Broker' who had no personal axe to grind and who would work to obtain a just settlement for both sides. This was in fact what he tried to do.

The results of the Congress were that Bulgaria was substantially reduced in size, thus reducing Russian dominance in the Balkans. Austria was allowed to keep Bosnia and Herze-Govina (though she didn't formally take it over until 1908). Britain gained Cyprus and France claimed the former Turkish colony of Tunis. Only Germany seemed to gain nothing from the Congress.

The Russians were annoyed that Germany had not supported them more strongly and the Tsar even spoke of "a European coalition against Russia under the leadership of Prince Bismarck." (Morris *European History* UTP p100)

The Austrians were happy with the role played by the Germans and, in recognition, agreed that Germany should be allowed to keep Schleswig without holding the plebiscite (referendum) which had been agreed at the Treaty of Prague in 1866. This only made the Russians even more suspicious of the German actions. Bismarck, despite behaving in a totally honourable fashion, was unable to gain what he wanted from the Congress - continued close friendship with both Austria and Russia.

As a direct result of this, a secret treaty was concluded in 1879 between Austria and Germany called the Dual Alliance. This promised that if either were attacked by Russia, the other would assist in the war. Bismarck wanted this treaty to be aimed against France as well but the Austrians would not accept it. The effect of the Treaty was to tie the Austrians and Germans closer together without giving Bismarck the security he wanted. Bismarck recognised the problems:

> "The ticklish factor in our relations with Russia is of course Austria. We cannot let Austria be overrun and shattered. But just as little must we let ourselves be dragged into war by her."
> (Quoted in Mitchell *Bismarck and the Unification of Germany* Holmes McDougall p99)

Bismarck also tried to extend the alliance by inviting Britain to join it. Although the alliance was anti-Russian it would pull Britain towards Germany and thus ensure that she did not fall into the French camp. The British Prime Minister, Disraeli, saw some attractions in the plan, but when he was replaced by Gladstone after the 1880 Election, the idea was not pursued.

Instead Bismarck reacted with delight when the Russians suggested that the Dreikaiserbund should be renewed. Signed in 1881, the Dreikaiserbundnis was a rather more complex agreement than the original one. The three members now promised that if one were attacked by a fourth power, the other two would remain neutral. At the same time the Balkans were divided into spheres of interest. The Austrians were to dominate the western area, the Russians the east.

In 1882 the Triple Alliance was agreed between the Germans, the Austrians and the Italians. This stated that if any of the countries were attacked by France, the other two would offer support. If any of the countries were attacked by a nation other than France, the other two would remain neutral.

Bismarck's methods here are worthy of note. He knew that the Italians planned to take Tunis, just across the Mediterranean, as a colony. Bismarck actively encouraged the French to take this territory as a way of distracting her attention from her losses in Alsace and Lorraine. He calculated that it would also make her an enemy of the Italians. It worked beautifully. He stated:

THE THREE EMPERORS;

OR, THE VENTRILOQUIST OF VARZIN!

Punch making fun of the Triple Alliance signed by the monarchs of Germany, Austria and Italy

> "I have sent the fiery steed of French ambition caracoling in the sands of Tunis. They will find it heavy going."
> (Quoted in Ayerst *Europe in the Nineteenth Century* CUP p248)

The Italians, however, in common with the rest of Europe, did not know that the Dual Alliance existed.

In 1883 Bismarck ensured greater security for Austria in the Balkans by signing a treaty between Germany, Austria and Rumania which promised that each would help defend the others if attacked. The obvious potential enemy in this alliance was Russia.

In 1887 Bismarck again made efforts to keep good relations with the Russians. Firstly the Russians were told of the existence of the Dual Alliance - even the Austrians were not told that the Russians had been informed! Secondly a Reinsurance Treaty was signed between them. This promised neutrality from one if the other country was at war. Exceptions were if Russia were to attack Austria or Germany were to attack France. This Treaty was to be renewed every three years.

By the late 1880s Bismarck was coming to realise that he was trying to maintain an impossible balance in his foreign policy - particularly with the Russians. Even though they were policical and diplomatic allies with the Germans, the Russians found that the French were much better commercial partners. Bismarck, the typical Junker, realised too late that commercial diplomacy can be just as important as political.

In 1889 Bismarck made another effort to draw Britain into his alliance system. This time he tried to get her to join the Triple Alliance. To gain this friendship, Bismarck was prepared to sacrifice German colonial development and plans to establish a German Navy. He regarded these as a price worth paying for the guarantee of a British alliance against France.

However, previous disputes over colonies as well as the traditional British distaste for involvement in Europe meant that the proposed alliance came to nothing.

What then can we make of Bismarck's Foreign Policy? He was convinced, almost to the extent of irrationality, that France would, given the slightest chance, embark on a war of revenge against Germany. He felt that there was no point in trying to cultivate good relations with France, the only safe thing was to keep her isolated. To do this he devised the system of alliances outlined above.

By the time Bismarck fell from office in 1890 the system was, inevitably, beginning to fall apart. The fact that it had worked for twenty years, and helped to keep the peace in Europe, was a considerable achievement.

GERMAN IMPERIALISM

Prussia regarded herself as a predominantly European power. While Britain, France and even small nations like Belgium and Holland had gained territory overseas, Prussia remained content with expansion in Europe. This is partly explained by her geographical position, by the lack of an adequate seaport and merchant marine and by the fact that she was able to expand fairly consistently into neighbouring states.

Bismarck was not enthusiastic about colonies either. He regarded Germany as a satiated state which had more than enough to do consolidating herself as a nation. He regarded overseas colonies as unnecessary luxuries and recognised that to have them would require a navy and that would, inevitably, cause friction with Great Britain. He was never convinced by the economic arguments for colonies. After the Franco-Prussian War, overtures were made to Bismarck by the French offering either an island off the Indian coast or even territory in Indo-China (modern Vietnam) in return for Alsace and Lorraine. Bismarck was not in the least interested. In 1881 he declared, "as long as I am Chancellor, we shall pursue no colonial policy." (Quoted in Morris *European History* UTP p102)

THE HISTORICAL DEBATE ON BISMARCK'S FOREIGN POLICY 1870-1890

The following views reflect the difference of opinion concerning Bismarck's foreign policy which exists among historians. Source 1 outlines that difference of opinion. Sources 2, 3, and 4 take a balanced view of his foreign policy observing both his finesse and the unfortunate harvest gleaned from such a policy. Source 5 clearly puts the blame on Bismarck for the problems which arose after his departure.

Source 1

"His only object was to maintain the peace of Europe. Those who admire this call it operating the Balance of Power; those who do not, condemn it as dishonest jugglery." (AJP Taylor *Bismarck* Hamish Hamilton p227)

Source 2

"Bismarck has long enjoyed a formidable reputation in the field of foreign affairs. His apologists claim that he was largely responsible for preserving peace in Europe for twenty years; he did not want war himself, so it is argued, and he prevented others going to war by enmeshing the Great Powers in such an intricate diplomatic web that war became too perilous an undertaking. This is to exaggerate his influence. A factor of equal importance was the desire of the powers to avoid a major war in Europe." (Carr *A History of Germany* Arnold p 185)

Source 3

"Since 1879, when he (Bismarck) had turned to Austria, he had moved with assurance and aplomb, taking advantage of the apprehensions of other governments, making the most of the unforeseen opportunities, always retaining the initiative. .... the system that he had elaborated to give Germany security was a very complicated one, and in its complications were the germs of future trouble." (Craig *Germany 1866-1945* OUP p116)

Source 4

"Was he (Bismarck) not condemned, having once upset the European balance of power, to walk a tightrope on which sooner or later he would lose his own balance? Is he rather not to be admired for staying on it so long, for keeping a cool head and for refusing to be distracted by the clowns below?"
(Simon *Germany in the Age of Bismarck* Allen & Unwin p86)

Source 5

"The fact remains however, that Bismarck set the tone for the deteriorating quality of diplomacy, as well as for the growing thicket of international suspicion, during his period in office. Although the chickens did not come home to roost until afterwards, still it was Bismarck who hatched them."
(Simon *Germany in the Age of Bismarck* Allen & Unwin p87)

What happened to change his mind? The period from 1870-1900 has been called the Scramble for Empire during which European nations acquired overseas territory very rapidly. Germans were active overseas as missionaries, traders and explorers and they put pressure on the government to acquire the territories in which they operated.

The greatest pressure, however, came from home. In 1882 a colonial union or Kolonialverband was formed by the Mayor of Frankfurt. This attracted German industrialists and nationalists who felt that colonies were necessary to enhance German prestige and power. Others argued that increasing German emigration (over 200,000 per year by the late 1870s) created a need for German territory overseas.

The first area to attract attention was South West Africa - now called Namibia. This was a fairly barren piece of territory. In 1882 Bismarck promised to support a German merchant, Luderitz, in his attempts to gain a colony there. Treaties were signed with local chiefs and by 1884 the colony had expanded to fill the gap between Portuguese Angola and British South Africa. Togo and Cameroon in West Africa were acquired in much the same way. By 1890 another German explorer/entrepreneur Karl Peters had acquired for Germany the colony of German East Africa - now mainland Tanzania.

In the Pacific, at the same time, some island archipelagos and

Colonial Empires in 1913		
Country	Area (Km²)	Population
Britain	33,000,000	400,000,000
France	11,500,000	56,000,000
Germany	2,950,000	12,000,000
Belgium	2,400,000	15,500,000
Holland	2,000,000	38,000,000
Japan	300,000	17,000,000

Source: quoted in Passant *A Short History of Germany* Cambridge, p115

Table 9.2

a part of New Guinea were acquired. In 1899 the German Empire gained a coaling station at Kiao Chow in China and took sole control of Western Samoa after some years of joint rule with Britain. Lastly, in 1911 she gained some 700,000 sq km of territory in the French Congo in return for recognition of French control in Morocco (see page 96). This land was added to Cameroon. As table 9.2 shows, this was hardly a spectacular collection of colonies.

"Much German colonial territory was not inhabited at all. By 1914 there were less than 24,000 Germans in the colonies and most of these were government officials. The colonies did not attract many German emigrants. Trade with them amounted to less than 1% of the German total. In 1914 they "cost the German taxpayers

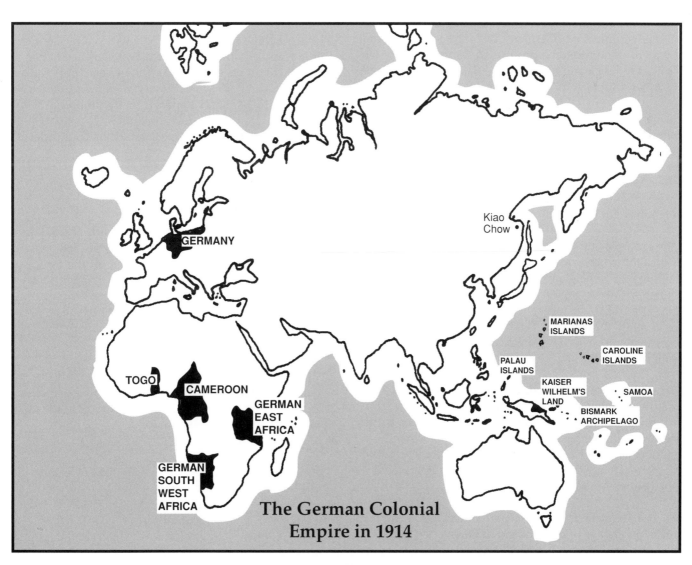

The German Colonial
Empire in 1914

in subsidies six times what the German merchants and investors made out of them in profits."
(AJP Taylor *The Course of German History* UP p151)

What, then, attracted Bismarck and Germany towards colonies? We have already noted the effects of the work of explorers and missionaries, we have observed the desire for power and prestige and we have seen that industrialists were drawn to them because they believed them to be valuable sources of raw materials and potentially lucrative markets. Further to this, there was a genuine fear that if Germany did not get started quickly, particularly in Africa, there would be no land left to acquire.

What though of Bismarck? He is reported to have said in 1888 when pointing at a map of Europe, "Here is Russia and here is France and we are in the middle; that is my map of Africa." (Quoted in Elliott *Bismarck, the Kaiser and Germany* Longmans p75)

He was never keen on colonies but he was prepared to exploit their potential to meet his own ends. AJP Taylor states, "In colonial affairs what mattered to him was the dispute not the reward." (AJP Taylor *The Course of German History* UP p151)

By the 1880s Bismarck had split with the Liberals and had started to reintroduce protectionist policies. He knew that the Crown Prince Frederick wanted to introduce British style government into Germany. Bismarck wanted to find a way to undermine the pro-British leanings of Crown Prince Frederick and to drive a wedge between him and his Liberal supporters in the Reichstag.

Bismarck saw the colonial issue as a way to achieve his aim. The Liberals would not support an imperialist policy, the Crown Prince dare not be seen not to. An imperialist policy was also bound to cause friction with Great Britain. Indeed he further exploited the imperial issue to force a quarrell with Britain in the hope that it would improve relations with France.

One example of this occurred in 1885 when a conference was called in Berlin to discuss colonial issues. Friction was building over Belgian acquisition of land around the Congo in Africa, a move which was opposed by Britain but supported by France. The result of the conference was a victory for the Belgians. This had been engineered by the Germans and at least temporarily improved relations with the French.

On a more positive note the conference agreed that from then on any power which occupied territory in Africa and informed the other powers of its actions could then legitimately claim the land as a colony. Bismarck's hand can again be seen here attempting to ensure that there would be no major crises over colonies which might cause a polarisation of the European powers.

As for the improved relations with France - they did not survive a change of government in Paris.

By 1889 Bismarck again admitted that he was not in favour of an imperial policy. He stated in a speech to the Reichstag in 1889:

"I have never been a colonial man ... only the pressure of public opinion and of the majority view, has made me decide to capitulate."
(Quoted in Mitchell *Bismarck and the Unification of Germany* Holmes McDougall p117)

During this period he had never used any of the colonies for naval or military purposes and had always forced the merchants who established them to meet the costs of running them. This further demonstrates his antipathy towards them.

Relations with Britain improved in the late 1880s and in return for Heligoland - an island in the North Sea strategically important to Germany - Britain gained the East African island of Zanzibar. This was a solution much more satisfactory to both parties.

One of the factors in the downfall of Bismarck was that from then on he offered no support whatsoever for an imperial policy. The new Kaiser, William II, on the other hand, wanted colonies and for Germany to be a world power. He stated in 1895

"We are destined for great things, and I am leading you to marvellous times."
(Quoted in Whittle *The Last Kaiser* Purnell p169)

This lies behind many of the problems faced by Germany in the run up to the First World War. This is covered in more detail on pages 93-96. As will be seen, imperialism was a factor in both Moroccan crises, in the tension over the Berlin to Baghdad Railway, in the building of the German Navy and in the deterioration of relations between Germany and Britain. Perhaps Bismark was right after all.

THE NEW KAISER
& THE FALL OF BISMARCK

During the winter of 1887-1888 the health of the Kaiser began to desert him and he died in March 1888. He was more than ninety years old, had been on the throne of Prussia for thirty years and had been German Emperor for the eighteen years of Germany's existence. Bismarck was distraught at the death of the Kaiser. He had felt secure in his position as long as the old man remained alive. Announcing the death

"Tears choked his voice. He wept not only for a beloved master whom he had always claimed to serve though rarely obeyed. He wept still more for the end of his own mastery in Germany."
(AJP Taylor *Bismarck* Hamish Hamilton p230)

The new Kaiser, Frederick III, was William's 57-year-old son who was terminally ill and reigned for only 99 days. Frederick had married one of the daughters of Queen Victoria and was a great admirer of Great Britain. He wanted Germany to evolve towards a similar politial

DROPPING THE PILOT.

William II and Bismarck part company.

riding. After school he spent a short time at university before serving for two years as an army officer which was the happiest period of his life. One character trait which William had developed was a certain rude boorishness. Much of his behaviour was tactless - though not deliberately so. He was not very popular.

Bismarck regarded the new Kaiser as a young man who would enjoy the trappings of being Emperor but who would leave the job of governing Germany to him. Bismarck said of William in 1888:

> "The Kaiser is like a balloon, if you don't keep fast hold of the string, you never know where he'll be off to."
> (Quoted in Whittle *The Last Kaiser* Purnell Book Services p113)

In the mid-1880s, William and Bismarck were fairly close on policy matters and were united in opposition to the policies and ideas of his father. However, when he became Kaiser he had far clearer ideas of what he wanted to do than Bismarck suspected. Firstly he wanted rid of Bismarck. He said at the time, "I shall let the old man snuffle on for six months then I shall rule myself." (AJP Taylor *Bismarck* Hamish Hamilton p235)

He wanted Germany to become a power on the world stage and to have colonies. Finally, he wanted to be popular with all Germans.

Bismarck, in the meantime, was losing support. Many thought that at the age of 75 he was getting too old to govern while others feared that Bismarck's delegation of work to his son, Herbert, was an attempt to create a dynasty. Bismarck's frequent and lengthy absences from Berlin meant that he began to lose touch with events. A new generation had emerged in Germany which was not overawed by his achievements of twenty or thirty years before.

Bismarck still felt that he was the essential component of the German government and he was quite intolerant when the Kaiser seemed to challenge his authority.

They had two major disagreements. The first concerned policy towards the socialists and the working classes. Bismarck's attitude was that of a paternalistic Junker ie. if workers did what they were told, they would be cared for. William, on the other hand, wanted the working class to become participants in the German State and therefore, he reasoned, committed suporters of it. During a coal strike in 1889 Bismarck sided with the bosses while the Kaiser sided with the miners and ordered their wages raised. When the Kaiser suggested other social reforms, like abolishing child labour, Bismarck avoided the issue by setting up a committee to look into the matter - a well-known delaying tactic. By 1890 Bismarck had resorted to desperate methods to deal with the socialist threat. He presented two bills to the Reichstag in 1890. One was to strengthen the army the other to ban the Socialist Party completely. He hoped that the army bill would induce the Kaiser to support the anti-socialist bill as well. He was even prepared to alter the German constitution to ensure that the bills would be made law. Not surprisingly the Kaiser dismissed these proposals.

system as that in Great Britain. Bismarck, of course, was not happy about this and as early as the mid-1880s had used an imperial policy to drive a wedge between the Crown Prince and his political supporters, the German Liberals.

Further humiliation for Frederick came over the issue of the potential marriage between his daughter Victoria and Prince Alexander of Battenberg, the former King of Bulgaria. Bismarck felt that such a marriage would cause offence to the Russians, with whom he wanted to maintain good relations, and stopped it. There was little doubt about who ran Germany.

Frederick died in June 1888. Bismarck left Berlin shortly after the funeral and did not spend any length of time in the capital and centre of government for nearly eight months. He ran the country using the telegraph system and used his son Herbert as his representative in Berlin.

Kaiser William II was 29 years of age when he came to the throne. He was the son of Kaiser Frederick and Empress Victoria. William's parents were so busy with public life that the young Prince was rather neglected in early childhood. He was not an outstanding scholar but overcame the handicap of a withered left arm to become quite an accomplished sportsman - particularly shooting and horse

The two also disagreed over foreign policy issues. Bismarck believed that he could maintain his delicate balance of alliances and secret agreements. However, the Kaiser, who was not particularly friendly with the Russians, believed that it was no longer possible to maintain a close friendship with Austria and Russia. He did not want to renew the Reinsurance Treaty. Instead he proposed to declare openly that Austria was Germany's closest ally. There was little possibility of compromise on this issue.

Bismarck realised that the Kaiser and certain ministers were working to oust him. He came across a government order dating from 1852 which forbade ministers to approach the King without first consulting the Chancellor. This of course could be made to work both ways and seemed to offer an excellent way of stopping moves to oust him going on behind his back.

The last stages of Bismarck's career were touched with some melodrama. When he heard of plans to oust his old ally, Windhorst, leader of the Centre Party, offered Bismarck his continued support. The Kaiser knew that this could undermine his attempts to get rid of Bismarck and he demanded an interview with the Chancellor. When the Kaiser arrived to see Bismarck - a psychological victory in itself - he found that the old man was not yet dressed. Bismarck kept the Kaiser waiting for three-quarters of an hour. The interview which followed was not pleasant. The Kaiser demanded that the 1852 order be withdrawn, tempers flared and Bismarck threw one of the tantrums for which he was famous. In the course of this documents were scattered. One of these was a letter to Bismarck from the Tsar of Russia which called the Kaiser an 'ill-bred youngster'. After reading this the Kaiser stormed out

defeated and humiliated but it was clear that Bismarck's days were numbered. Senior army figures asked for his resignation. Bismarck was prepared to recognise the inevitable. All he needed was an issue. Foreign policy again came to his rescue. Reports came into the German Foreign Office of Russian troop movements in Poland. Bismarck realised that these were not threatening but not so the Kaiser who demanded that the German Armies should be mobilised and that the Austrians should be informed of the danger. Bismarck's view won the day but he resigned anyway.

> "I hereby request that I be relieved of my offices acknowledging that the experience and ability of a faithful servant are no longer required. Attached as I am to the service of the Royal House and of your Majesty, and accustomed for many years to conditions which I have hitherto regarded as permanent, it is very painful for me to sever my wanted relations with your majesty and to break off my connection with the entire policy of the Reich and of Prussia."
>
> (Bismarck's resignation note 18 March 1890. German Bundestag *Fragen an die deutsche Geschichte* p225; German Bundestag, Publications' Section, Bonn 1984)

The issue was the Kaiser's new policy towards Russia and his interference in foreign affairs. Bismarck hoped that there would be a public outcry which would force his reinstatement, but there was scarcely a whimper.

All that remained for Bismarck was retirement. It took him nine days to pack his wine collection of 13,000 bottles and his papers which he planned to use for his memoirs. Two days before he left Berlin he paid a highly public visit to the grave of the old Emperor at Charlottenburg where he laid three roses on the grave. This gesture was as much

---

Bismarck - Hero or Villain?

"What can the Historian writing in the second half of the twentieth century say of Bismarck? That he was a great man is undeniable. He towered above contemporaries, a veritable giant among pigmies. No other German exerted so profound an influence on German history in the nineteenth century. When he came to power in 1862, Germany was a confederation of independent states fossilised in the mould of 1815; when he left office, Germany was a united nation, a state of great stature, feared and respected by the Great Powers. No doubt unification was inevitable once Germany became an industrial nation. It is also true to say that Bismarck was moulded by the economic and political forces which he struggled to control. This in no way detracts from his historical significance. In his own lifetime and long after his death, Bismarck was idolised by millions of his fellow countrymen who saw in him the embodiment of Germany's will to be a nation. Nor did his services to Germany end in 1871. As Chancellor he helped shape the destinies of the new Empire for two decades, in fact nearly half its lifetime. He undoubtedly committed monumental blunders in his handling of the Church and the working class; but, on the other hand, he helped to promote the modernisation of Germany and was responsible for the social welfare system which, though it disappointed its creator, did in the long run give working people a vested interest and a pride in the Empire."

(Carr *A History of Germany*, Arnold p165-166)

"Bismarck left behind him as his political heritage a nation without any political education, far below the level which, in this respect, it had reached twenty years earlier. Above all, he left behind a nation without any political will, accustomed to allow the great statesman at its head to look after its policy for it. Moreover, as a consequence of his misuse of the monarchy as a cover for his own interests in the struggle of political parties, he left a nation accustomed to submit, under the label of constitutional monarchy, to anything which was decided for it, without criticising the politial qualifications of those who now occupied Bismarck's empty place and who with incredible ingenuousness now took the reins of power into their hands."

(Max Weber quoted in Carr *A History of Germany* Arnold p165-166)

What do you think of Bismarck - villain or hero?

a statement of how Bismarck regarded William II as it was in memory of William I.

"On 29 March Bismarck left Berlin. Crowds lined the streets. A guard of honour, and all the great dignitaries of the Empire - but not the Emperor - were at the station. As the train drew out, the military band struck up a slow march. Bismarck leant back in the carriage and said: 'A state-funeral with full honours'."
(AJP Taylor *Bismarck* Hamish Hamilton p253)

Bismarck never really enjoyed his retirement. He dreamed of being recalled to power. He was elected to the Reichstag as a National Liberal but never took his seat. He was well paid for his autobiography which was published in six volumes. These books, entitled *Reflections and Reminiscences* were a highly personal account of events during his time in office. As works of history they are flawed and inaccurate and attribute to Bismarck greater perception of events than was actually the case.

Gradually Bismarck's health failed. He became bored with life away from the centre of power. In 1898 perhaps the greatest statesman Europe has ever known died - peacefully in his bed. The Kaiser summed him up as, "the great stealer of our people's hearts." (Quoted in Whittle *The Last Kaiser* Purnell Book Services p140)

THE DOMESTIC SCENE 1890-1914

With Bismarck gone there was a power vacuum in Germany. The young Kaiser was determined to play a much greater part in the running of the nation than his predecessors. As a result of this, Bismarck's successors as Chancellor, Caprivi 1890-1894, Hohenlohe-Shellingfurst 1894-1900, Von Bülow 1900-1909 and Bethmann-Hollweg 1909-1917 never held much authority. They did not possess any-

thing like the skill of Bismarck and were quite unable to run Germany as he had done - nor were they able to dominate the Kaiser. Nevertheless Germany continued to develop rapidly in the years before the First World War.

Germany developed into one of the great industrial powers in the world. The benefits of unification - common currency and banking and weights and measures - created a large home market and a common tariff policy was established. The acquisition of Alsace and Lorraine provided large deposits of iron ore which helped supply the industrial centres developing on the Ruhr. By 1914 she was, overall, second only to the USA as the major industrial power. Tables 9.3 - 9.6 give some idea of the pace and scale of change.

The bulk of this increase was concentrated in towns and in industrial areas. The population of the rural areas remained fairly constant.

In the coal and steel industries Germany had either equalled or surpassed Great Britain by 1914.

Only Russia's massive land area had a longer length of track. The merchant fleet by 1914 was second only to the British in size.

In the main, imports were raw materials, particularly food. Exports of finished industrial products increased from 38% of the total in 1873 to 63% in 1913. The bulk of German exports, about 75%, went to the rest of Europe. In 1890 77% of imports came from Europe but by 1913 this figure had declined to 56%.

Germany also pioneered the development of 'new' industries. In the chemical industry, she became the world leader in the production of agricultural fertilisers and

The Growth of the German Economy

Population of 'Germany'

1815	24,800,000
1845	34,300,000
1875	42,500,000
1915	68,000,000

Table 9.3

Coal Production (Tonnes)		Steel Production (Tonnes)	
1871	37,000,000	1881	1,550,000
1891	89,000,000	1890	3,160,000
1913	279,000,000	1910	13,150,000

Table 9.4

Railway Track Length (Km)		Merchant Fleet (Tonnes)	
1871	18,000	1871	982,000
1890	41,000	1900	1,942,000
1913	67,000	1913	3,000,000

Table 9.5

Trade

	Exports	Imports
1870	124.6	173.2
1900	237.6	302.1
1913	504.8	538.5

Table 9.6

PARTY STRENGTH 1890 – 1912						
PARTY	1890	1893	1898	1903	1907	1912
Conservatives & Free Conservatives	93	100	79	75	84	57
National Liberals	42	53	46	51	54	45
Left Liberals	76	48	49	39	49	42
Centre	106	96	102	100	105	91
Social Democrats	35	44	56	81	43	110
Nationalists	38	35	34	32	29	33
Anti-Semites	5	16	13	11	21	13

Table 9.7

produced 75% of the world's chemical dyes. Similarly German expertise led the world in the development of the electrical industry. By 1914 Germany controlled half of the world market. She exported £11 million worth of electrical goods compared with a total of £8 million exported by Britain and the USA together. The work of famous German engineers like Daimler, Deisel and Benz provide good examples of the technological developments taking place.

This progress created a great deal of wealth for German individuals and companies and this prosperity spread right through society. Emigration fell from over 134,000 per annum in the 1880s to about 30,000 per annum between 1900 and 1910 - a figure less than that for Scotland at the same time.

Only in agriculture were there major problems. Imports of American corn easily undercut the home produce and a protectionist policy was necessary to protect German farmers and Junker landowners from ruin.

German industry had two great advantages over its competitors. Firstly there was a close link with the banking system. Some German banks were founded with the express purpose of lending money to encourage industrial development and many bankers were taken on to the boards of large companies to give the benefit of their expertise.

Secondly, German industry formed a series of cartels. There is inevitably, a great deal of risk involved in establishing any industrial enterprise. The fiercer the competition the greater the risks. Industries banded themselves together into associations known as cartels which set the price for the goods produced, agreed wage rates, and, most importantly, established quotas for production. This ensured that each cartel member got a share of the production. The cartels became very powerful and political parties ignored them at their peril. After Germany adopted protectionist policies in the late 1870s they had, virtually, a captive home market where they could fix prices and guarantee sales. With the profits from this they could subsidise expansion overseas and sell goods cheaply. By 1911 the number of cartels had risen to more than six hundred.

A well-developed education system made a significant contribution to econome development. A literate work

force could cope with the complex technological problems posed by industrial development. Furthermore, a career in industry in Germany carried a status which to some extent it still does not have in Britain today.

The Kaiser and Caprivi from 1890 to 1894 followed fairly liberal policies at home through which they aimed to stimulate growth and increase the Kaiser's popularity. Ten year tariff agreements were made with other countries which reduced import and export duties. This reduced food costs to town dwellers though it caused problems for farmers and some industrial cartels.

The ban on the socialists was lifted and social reforms were made, for example hours of work for women and children were limited, factory inspectors were given increased powers and Sunday working was banned. Army service was cut from three years to two. There was a relaxation on the policy of 'Germanising' Alsace-Lorraine and Posen (German Poland). There was considerable opposition to this and William felt obliged to say:

"To those, who increasingly express dissatisfaction with the new course, I reply quietly but with determination 'My course is right and I shall continue to follow it'"
(Quoted in Passant *A Short History of Germany* CUP p119)

So concerned were the Junkers and landed interests by these policies that they formed an organisation to campaign against them. By 1894 the Federation of Agriculturalists (Bund Der Landwrite) was 250,000 strong. Their publication stated in 1892, "the German farmer will now regard the Kaiser as his political enemy." (Quoted in Passant *A Short History of Germany* CUP p119)

The socialists, freed from the repressive laws of Bismarck grew steadily in power and influence. Table 9.7 shows the relative strengths of the parties.

In 1891 the Socialist Party Congress decided to follow Marxist policies which involved a commitment to violent revolution and class warfare. Despite the social reforms made, support for the Party continued to grow which was a factor in the resignation of Caprivi in 1894. William and the new minister Hohenlohe-Schillingfurst followed a much more conservative course. Laws were passed which sought to restrict the power of the socialists and the trade unions. In 1894 William said in a speech:

"Forward into battle for religion, for morality and for order against the parties of revolution."
(Quoted in Elliott *Bismarck the Kaiser and Germany* Longmans p115)

William had realised that it was not possible to be King of the Germans from all classes and all walks of life. From then on he was much more loyal to those who were clearly his supporters.

What developed was a close alliance between the Kaiser and the conservative interests as was shown in the reintroduction of protective tariffs when Caprivi's ten year commercial treaties expired in 1902. This suited the Junkers and industrialists - the alliance of rye and steel. Overall it led to an increase in food prices to the disadvantage of the poorer classes. Policies towards the national minorities also hardened. Bismarck's policy of colonisation of Poland by Germans was reintroduced and in 1909 an act was passed through the Prussian parliament which would allow the confiscation of land from Polish landlords to hand to Germans. The use of the Polish language in education was banned. These actions only resulted in increased demands for Polish independence.

The Kaiser's last two ministers were equally conservative. Von Bülow (1900-1909) and Bethmann-Hollweg (1909-1917) were mostly concerned with foreign affairs while domestic policies remained repressive with little reform. This was particularly noticeable in the field of industrial relations. The development of large trade unions was mirrored by the formation of more employers' associations which established an anti-strike bureau. The scene was thus set for a whole series of industrial disputes and clashes which were usually won by the employers with the support of the Kaiser and his government.

There was a growing desire in Germany for her to become a world power. This found expression in Leagues which acted as pressure groups on the government and also stimulated public opinion. These leagues pressed for Pan-Germanism - unity for all Germans in Europe; colonialism - an overseas Empire; Eastern marches - expansion on the eastern borders of Germany; naval standards - the establishment of a German Navy. The Leagues had their roots in the Bismarck era when such policies were not followed and they attracted support from big businessmen who put money and newspapers which they owned at the disposal of the Leagues. The Navy League, for example, was backed by merchant shipping magnates as well as iron and steel manufacturers. When Germany did build her navy these were the people who made huge profits out of it.

The German Army remained in a position of great influence and also outwith the control of the Reichstag. This was best demonstrated in 1913 during an incident at Zabern in Alsace. An army officer had offended the local population by some insensitive remarks. There were a series of demonstrations which were dispersed by troops and some citizens were arrested. These actions by the army were illegal and the Reichstag publicly censured the government for supporting the army. The Kaiser, in response, decorated the army commander in the area. The Reichstag could do nothing.

In 1914 the Kaiser and his ministers remained in control of Germany with opposition being kept in check by repression. The rise of anti-government parties in the Reichstag would eventually have forced reform on the German system of government. William commented in 1913, "the German parliamentarian becomes daily more of a swine." (Quoted in Whittle *The Last Kaiser* Purnell p146)

By 1910 the socialists and other radical parties were clearly seen as reformers, not revolutionaries and not a threat. When war broke out a Burgfrieden (truce) was declared among the political parties and all reform campaigns were put aside to concentrate on the war effort.

Punch's comment on Germany's search for an Empire

GERMAN FOREIGN POLICY 1890-1914

The Kaiser was keen for Germany to become a major international power and saw his role as that of a major international statesman - something he definitely was not. His attempts at diplomacy were generally tactless and clumsy and very often produced the opposite effect to that which he intended.

The first major foreign policy issue to confront the German government after the fall of Bismarck was the proposal to renew the Reinsurance Treaty with Russia. The benefit of this treaty was that it tied Russia to Germany rather than to France and at the same time assured the Russians about German intentions, particularly since Germany's closest ally, Austria, was Russia's natural enemy.

The Russians were keen to extend the treaty for a further three years but the Germans refused. Caprivi felt that it was impossible to maintain an agreement which seemed to run counter to the key of German foreign policy, the Triple Alliance. The renewal of this alliance in 1891, coupled with improving relations between Great Britain and Germany only served to increase Russian feelings of isolation and, not surprisingly, produced an alliance between Russia and France in 1892. This had been Bismarck's great fear and it came about eventually almost *because* of German diplomatic ineptitude. The Dual Alliance was seen as a great threat by the Germans and planning on ways to counter it began almost immediately.

Some progress was made on improving relations with Great Britain. Caprivi was not a great believer in German colonialism and he was happy to sign a treaty in 1890 which recognised British control over Kenya, Uganda and Zanzibar - areas to which Germany had some claim. In return, Britain recognised German control over Tanganyika and ceded to Germany the island of Heligoland which was just off their coast and had been held by Britain for strategic purposes since 1815. Overall this was a good agreement for Germany but it was opposed by the imperialist faction since it seemed to be giving away potential colonial territory. It was condemned as, "a trouser button for a whole suit of clothes." (Quoted in Whittle *The Last Kaiser* Purnell p167)

That was the one bright spot in relations with Britain and after the dismissal of Caprivi there was a steady deterioration. Much of the blame for this can be laid with the Kaiser whose boorish behaviour on visits to Britain invariably caused offence.

One particularly good example of this can be seen in the affair which became known as the Krüger telegram. Britain was having problems in her South African colonies with the Dutch settlers known as Boers. A badly planned invasion of the Boer homeland, Transvaal, by a British adventurer, Dr Jameson, along with a few hundred supporters caused great embarrassment to the British government. The Kaiser, anxious to exploit the situation for his own ends, sent a telegram to the Boer President, Krüger, congratulating him on keeping the peace "without having to call for help from friendly powers." (Quoted in Morris *European History* UTP p148)

This implied threat caused a storm of outrage in Britain. The aim of the Kaiser's intervention had been to increase Britain's isolation in Europe and draw her into an alliance with Germany but this rather clumsy attempt at Bismarckian diplomacy failed miserably.

One of the main wishes of the Kaiser was to pursue a world role for Germany (Weltpolitik), closely related to which was the decision to build a navy. There was a substantial pressure group of German industrialists urging for this and they had an eager ally in the Kaiser.

"What William I did for the Army, William II wanted to do for the navy."
(Quoted in Elliot *Bismarck, the Kaiser and Germany* Longmans p107)

He was jealous of the power and prestige of the British navy and he felt (as did many others) that a powerful navy would be final proof that Germany was a force on the world stage. The Kaiser said, "The fleet is necessary to show that Germany is as well born as Britain."
(Quoted in Morris *European History* UTP p148)

The reasons for building the navy then had more to do with prestige and glory than any desire to use it to extend the Empire. Almost inevitably, however, the British saw it as a threat and a challenge. With the building of the German navy any lingering hope that Britain and Germany might become friends was effectively finished.

In 1897 Admiral Von Tirpitz became Minister for the Marine and it was he who presented the Naval Bill to the Reichstag in 1898. This envisaged the creation of a fleet of 19 battleships, 12 heavy cruisers and 30 light cruisers, a proposal which was doubled in 1900. The Naval Bill stated:

"Germany must have a battle fleet so strong that even the adversary possessed of the greatest sea power will attack it only with grave risk to herself."
(Quoted in Grant & Temperly *Europe in the Nineteenth & Twentieth Centuries* Longmans p440)

This size of fleet would never have threatened the huge British fleet. At this time Britain operated on the two power standard, ie. the British Navy had to be more powerful than the next two largest navies put together.

In 1906 the Royal Navy took possession of a new battleship, HMS Dreadnought, a ship so fast and powerful that it made all other ships in the navies of the world obsolete. German naval planners, by concentrating on building Dreadnought-type ships, could compete on almost equal terms with the British.

From then until the beginning of the First World War there was a period known as the Naval Arms race when Germany and Britain indulged in fierce competition in naval building, the result of which was a complete souring of relations. To the British a navy was essential for defence, and so to them the Germans could only want a navy for aggressive purposes. Nevertheless, the Kaiser could honestly state that from his point of view "with every new German battleship there was laid down a fresh pledge for peace the golden." (Quoted in Grant & Temperly *Europe in the Nineteenth & Twentieth Centuries* Longmans p441)

The other main thrust of German foreign policy at the turn of the century was in the Near East. In the late 1880s German business interests, particularly the Deutsche Bank, had agreed to finance the building of a railroad from Baghdad to the Persian Gulf. This was an area where both Britain and Russia had interests and they both saw the German action as threatening. Again the motives of the Germans are open to question. Bismarck had stressed that the reasons for involvement were purely financial but the new Kaiser was not so subtle. He boasted, "Let me assure the Sultan (of Turkey) and the three hundred million moslems ... that the German Emperor will ever be their friend." (Quoted in Whittle *The Last Kaiser* Purnell p182) and referred to the railway, now extended to be the Berlin to Baghdad railway as 'my railway'.

Generally these actions drew the Turks, who did not have many friends in Europe because of their appalling record of human rights violations, into friendship with Germany. (Between 1893 and 1898 for example, some 200,000

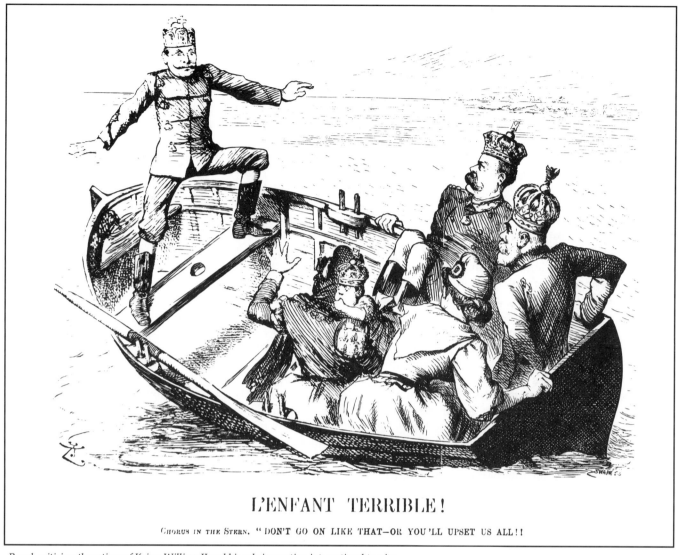

L'ENFANT TERRIBLE!

CHORUS IN THE STERN. "DON'T GO ON LIKE THAT—OR YOU'LL UPSET US ALL!!"

Punch criticises the actions of Kaiser William II and his role in creating international tension

Turkish Armenian Christians had been slaughtered.) The cost of this friendship for Germany, was even further deterioration in relations with Britain and France.

At the turn of the century there were two final attempts on the part of the British to gain a closer understanding with the Germans. Britain was becoming alarmed at her continued isolation in an increasingly competitive world and looked to Germany for a possible alliance. On the face of it they were suitable partners since Britain's rivalries were with France in Africa and with Russia in the Far East. Germany and Britain, however, had made agreements in most areas of potential conflict. The German strategy in 1898 and 1901 when overtures were made was to delay in the hope that the pressure of continued isolation would force Britain into signing an alliance. The Kaiser stated in 1900:

> "We ought to form an Anglo-German Alliance. You to keep the seas while we would be responsible for the land. With such an alliance, not a mouse could stir in Europe without our permission."
> (Quoted in Whittle *The Last Kaiser* Purnell p193)

Had this alliance come about it would have been very unpopular with the Colonial and Naval Leagues in Germany. In the event, the British signed an alliance with

the Japanese in 1902 and the possibility of an Anglo-German alliance faded away. Within three years Britain was quite clearly associated with the Dual Alliance nations of France and Russia.

Much of German foreign policy from then on was aimed, however clumsily, at keeping them apart. A good example of this was seen in the Far East where relations between the Japanese and the Russians had deteriorated for a number of reasons. The Japanese alliance with Britain was defensive in nature but, to the Germans, seemed to offer the potential for a split in the growing friendship between Britain and France. The French were allies of the Russians while the British sided with the Japanese. Any conflict between them would offer the Germans the opportunity to step in and exploit the situation. William actively encouraged the Russians to go to war against the Japanese and offered support during the war by giving supplies to the Russians. He did not foresee the crushing defeat which the Russians would suffer.

William tried one other way of securing Russian friendship. In July 1905 he was cruising in the Baltic and arranged to meet the Tsar at Björkö. He proposed a defensive alliance between Russia and Germany with Britain as the perceived common enemy. Initially the Tsar was enthusiastic and signed the treaty. The Kaiser stated:

"1905 at Björkö has witnessed the turning point in the history of Europe: a great load has been lifted from my dear fatherland which has finally escaped from the terrible Gallo-Russian pincers."
(Quoted in Whittle *The Last Kaiser* Purnell p220)

Ministers in both countries were less enthusiastic and the agreement was not formalised. Russian ministers realised that French economic as well as military aid was too important to pass over. Thus the last attempt at a Russian alliance - a sort of twentieth century Reinsurance Treaty - failed.

At the same time the Kaiser mounted another attack on the growing friendship between Britain and France. As a result of their 'entente' or agreement in 1904 the French recognised British predominance in Egypt in return for similar British recognition of their position in Morocco. By 1905 the French were putting pressure on the Sultan of Morocco. A French takeover of Morocco contravened previous international agreements and the Germans saw this as an opportunity to show the weakness of the friendship between Britain and France by creating a crisis which would embarrass them. The Kaiser visited the Moroccan city of Tangier and made a number of pronouncements which hinted at German recognition of Moroccan independence and questioned the recent agreement between Britain and France over the future of the area. He further demanded that the future of Morocco should be settled by an international conference. The German position seemed strong. The French Foreign Minister, Delcasse, resigned over the issue.

A conference was held at Algeciras in Spain in 1906. Here things began to go wrong for the Kaiser. German diplomatic tactics were blunt and tactless and the end result was that only Austria-Hungary of all the nations present supported the German position. The rest, including even Italy - a German ally - supported the French position. Indeed the British and the French ended the conference as closer friends than before and informal discussions on closer military cooperation were begun.

The Germans felt that the conference proved that they had few real friends in Europe and that they could not expect a fair deal from any conference of powers. Their fears were compounded in 1907 when, as an indirect result of the discussions begun at Algeciras, the British and the Russians reached agreement over their outstanding areas of dispute. This placed Britain firmly in the camp of the Dual Alliance powers, though she was not bound by any treaties. The Germans, on the other hand, were increasingly isolated with only the Austrians as committed allies.

The closeness of this alliance was demonstrated the following year during a crisis which occurred in the Balkans. In 1908, revolution in the Turkish Empire coupled with a more aggressive policy from the Austrian government led to Austria announcing that she was going to annex (take over) the former Turkish provinces of Bosnia and Herze-Govina. She had been given authority to do this by the Congress of Berlin in 1878. Although the Russian Foreign Minister, Isvolsky, had been consulted, the Austrians acted before he had time to clear things with his government.

The result was worldwide condemnation for the Austrian action particularly from Russia and led to a major crisis. The Germans, who had not been consulted by the Austrians at all, were annoyed but felt obliged to stand by the only ally they had left in Europe. Bülow promised, "I shall regard the decision to which you may ultimately come as that demanded by circumstances." (Quoted in Passant *A Short History of Germany 1815-1945* CUP p128)

This became known as the 'blank cheque' given to Austria by Germany. Clear signals were sent out that Germany would back the Austrians - with force if necessary. The Kaiser stated that Austria had "a knight in shining armour at a grave moment." (Quoted in Grant & Temperley *Europe in the Nineteenth and Twentieth Centuries* Longmans p459)

The Russians were forced to back down. On the one hand this was a great diplomatic victory for Austria and Germany but on the other it forced the Russians, aware of their weakness as a single state, towards Britain and France. It also drove the nationalist factions in the Balkans, recently freed from Turkish rule and fearful of Austrian takeover, into extremist actions.

While this crisis was at its height the Kaiser contrived to sour relations with Great Britain still further through an interview he gave to the *Daily Telegraph*. In it he tried to reassure the British that the German Navy was not a threat to them but should be used with the British to control events in the Pacific Ocean - thus offending the Japanese, Americans and Russians. He also talked of the misunderstandings between Germany and Britain and stated:

"You English are like mad bulls - you see red everywhere! What on earth has come over you, that you should heap on us such suspicion as is unworthy of a great nation ... I regard this misapprehension as a personal insult. ... You make it uncommonly difficult for a man to remain friendly to England."
(Quoted in Ayerst *Europe in the Nineteenth Cernury* CUP p347)

Not surprisingly this did little to increase trust and understanding between the two nations.

In 1911 world attention was focussed on Morocco when another crisis caused the great powers to polarise still further. The Sultan, faced with revolution among his subjects appealed to the French for help. They were happy to do so. This was perceived by the Germans, fairly correctly, as a French takeover. They decided to exploit this situation for their own ends and demanded substantial compensation from the French for this takeover - namely the whole of the French Congo. To add some emphasis to this demand a German Gunboat, the Panther, was sent to the Moroccan port of Agadir ostensibly to protect German nationals, in reality to pressurise the French.

The British reaction was not at all what the Germans had expected. They were fearful of the establishment of a German naval base on the Atlantic close to the British base at Gibralter. The Chancellor of the Exchequer in the British government, Lloyd-George, hinted, in a famous speech at the Mansion House, that Britain was prepared to fight if the Germans made any changes without consulting her first. Military preparations for shipping British troops to France were begun and the fleet was made ready for action. Faced with this response, the Kaiser was forced to back down. He recognised French predominance in Morocco and in return Germany gained a strip of the French Congo. The crisis backfired badly on Germany and the Kaiser became convinced that only increased naval strength would give Germany the necessary power to influence events to her satisfaction.

In 1912 one final attempt was made to come to a naval agreement with Britain. The British War Minister, Haldane, visited Berlin in an attempt to put a stop to the naval race. There was inflexibility on both sides but the main stumbling block was a British refusal to guarantee that they would not become involved in disputes on the European mainland. In return for this Germany would promise to restrict the size of her navy. It proved impossible to come to an agreement.

Instead the German Naval Estimates for 1912 were for an increase in spending. The British signed an agreement with the French by which Britain withdrew the bulk of her navy from the Mediterranean and undertook to protect the French Atlantic and North Sea coast. The French for their part promised to look after British interests in the Mediterranean. This concentration of the fleets effectively doubled the naval power facing the Germans and made it virtually impossible for them to compete equally.

The Germans were terrified of having to fight a war on two fronts as threatened by Russia and France and were sure that they would lose such a war. As early as 1905 Count Alfred Von Schlieffen had devised a plan which offered a solution to the problem. This relied on the relative inefficiency of the Russian Army, which took six weeks to mobilise fully and the efficiency of the German Army and transport network in moving their military forces. In short, the plan was to defeat France quickly, ie. in six weeks, then use the whole might of the German Army to attack and defeat Russia.

The plan was to invade neutral Belgium to attack France through her unprotected northern flank. It was assumed that the Belgians, if offered compensation, would grant the German Armies free passage.

Belgian independence had been guaranteed by international treaty in 1839. Signatories had included France, Prussia, Russia, and Britain. It was another essential part of the plan that Britain would not become involved - an assumption that the Germans cherished until the war began. In February 1914 a letter to the German Ambassador in London stated:

> "I think you are inclined to look on the dark side of things, as when you express the view that no matter what happens, in the event of war, England will be on the side of France against us. After all we have not built the fleet in vain."
> (Quoted in Passant *A Short History of Germany 1815-1945* CUP p130)

The plan was daring and brilliant, though in violation of

THE HAUNTED SHIP.
Ghost of the Old Pilot. "I WONDER IF HE WOULD DROP ME *NOW!*"
[April 1st is the hundredth anniversary of BISMARCK's birth.]

Punch again criticises the foreign policy of Kaiser William and compares it unfavourably with that of Bismarck

international agreement, but it was modified before 1914 in ways which weakened the force of the attack through Belgium and this proved to be a fatal weakness.

When the final crisis developed after the assassination of Franz Ferdinand in June 1914, the Germans were in a very difficult position. They were virtually obliged to support the Austrians in whatever actions they chose to take. The Austrians blamed the Serbs for the crime and seized on this as a good chance to crush them for once and for all. The Germans promised support. They felt that they had to support their only ally and that they couldn't be seen to lose out in an international confrontation as had happened after Morocco in 1911.

Austria made a series of harsh demands from Serbia most of which - to the Austrians' surprise - the Serbians accepted. Austria wanted a war. The Germans, as the crisis deepened, tried to convince the other powers that this was a purely local conflict between the two powers. When the Serbs seemed ready to comply with the Austrian demands, the Germans tried to persuade the Austrians to settle for that. They were too late. Austria declared war on Serbia on 29 July 1914.

The Russians, inevitably, were drawn in. Russia saw herself as the natural leader and protector of the Slav peoples of the Balkans. She had backed down in 1908, it was impossible for her to do so again and retain any credibility. The Russians ordered the mobilisation of their army but this was more of a diplomatic statement than a commencement of hostilities.

To the German High Command, thirled to the rigid time-table of the Schlieffen Plan, it was a serious threat. On 31 July 1914, the Germans demanded the cessation of Russian mobilisation. When this was ignored they declared war on Russia on 1 August.

This action of course, activated the Dual Alliance. Germany demanded a declaration of neutrality from France and the surrender of two of her border fortresses as a guarantee of her neutrality. The French, understandably, refused. On 3 August Germany declared war on France and the Schlieffen Plan was put into effect.

The German invasion of Belgium - a violation of her neutrality - was the last straw which shifted British public opinion and enabled her government to join the war on the side of France and Russia. The Kaiser saw events from his very particular point of view and stated:

> "To think that George and Nicky have played me false. If my grandmother had been alive she would never have allowed it."
> (Quoted in Elliott *Bismarck, the Kaiser and Germany* Longmans p107)

In this way the First World War began. There was great excitement in the countries involved - it came as a release of an almost unbearable tension which had been building up for years. Thousands rushed to join the armed forces. Both sides confidently believed that the war would be won quickly and would certainly be 'over by Christmas'.

NATIONALISM AND THE WAR

The First World War, like the French Revolution, was a watershed in the history of Europe. Its component nations, its peoples and societies were changed dramatically as a result of it.

Why did it happen? It is possible to list many reasons for the outbreak of the war - the rivalries over armed strength and colonies, the old enmity between nations exacerbated by events in Europe since 1870, the increasing competition for markets, the complicated events in the Balkans, the militarism of certain states - particularly Germany - the inflexible planning of the military, the excessive power of the military in some countries - particularly Germany - the rush for colonies and the rigidity of the alliance system were all significant factors.

In the Treaty of Versailles signed in 1919 at the end of the war, the Germans were forced to accept sole responsibility for the outbreak of the war. To the Germans this represented a 'victors' peace' and putting the whole blame for the war on Germany was seen as an injustice.

Why did Germany get involved in the war? To answer this question we need to go back to 1870 and Bismarck's assessment of Europe. He recognised that the creation of the German Empire was a huge shift in the balance of power in Europe and that, for a time at least, there was an enhanced danger of war. He was convinced that France

would, someday, embark on a war of revenge. Accordingly, he went to extraordinary lengths to ensure that France was kept isolated and that Germany kept out of areas of conflict with other European powers which goes some way to explaining her desire for alliances. One other German fear was that she would face a joint threat from the nations on either side of her ie. the French and the Russians. When this became a possibility, military plans were developed to deal with it.

Germany, as a young nation state, always felt that she was not treated as an equal by the other powers. This was particularly true in the area of colonies where she joined the race late and never really caught up. In a sense this too explains the German fixation with naval power. Bismarck had no interest in building a navy but by 1890 nationalist pressures more than economic and almost as much as strategic pressures demanded that she should have a navy.

Bearing these fears, insecurities and dangers in mind goes a long way towards explaining why the Germans found themselves at war in 1914.

The final factor which has to be taken into account is the influence of the Kaiser. There is little doubt that his motives were not nearly as bad as has been painted. He took a keen interest in foreign affairs but he was not a diplomat and his tactlessness and blunders only increased German isolation and unpopularity. Chancellor Von Bülow said of him:

> "The Kaiser's motives were not really belligerent. What Wilhelm II most desired was to see himself, at the head of a glorious German fleet, starting out on a peaceful visit to England. The English sovereign, with his fleet would meet the Kaiser in Portsmouth. The two fleets would file past each other, the two monarchs, each wearing the uniform of the other's country ... would then stand on the bridge of their flagships. Then, after they had embraced in the prescribed manner, a gala dinner with lovely speeches would be held in Cowes."
> (Quoted in Aronson *The Kaiser* Cassell p245-6)

Though she was clearly at fault when war broke out (she could have put more pressure on the Austrians, she need not have declared war on Russia) and her national insecurity was a factor in bringing about war, it is still hard to conclude that Germany was solely to blame for the outbreak of the war.

Once the war began, opinions began to harden. Control of the government drifted towards the army and the General Staff. Strangely, the Kaiser did not cope too well with the war. Speaking to a crowd in Berlin when war was declared he said, "I commend you now to God. Go into the churches, kneel down, and pray for help for our soldiers."
(Quoted in Whittle *The Last Kaiser* Purnell p271)

Hardly warlike oratory. He was easily upset and became unstable if he received bad news. From the outset, control of strategy lay with the military and the Kaiser had less and less to do with it as the war progressed.

The September programme in 1914 clearly laid out the German war aims. These were expansionist though couched in terms of seeking secure and permanent borders. Although this was often claimed afterwards, the September programme does not show German reasons for going to war, rather the excited feelings of a nation flushed with the success of the first weeks of fighting.

The war was pursued by the Germans with vigour and considerable originality. The Schlieffen Plan - brilliant though amoral - failed because of the British intervention, Belgian resistance and because the partially mobilised Russian army joined the fighting earlier than expected. However, the Germans themselves fatally weakened the plan by reducing the number of soldiers committed to the attack on France. After defeat at the Battle of the Marne signalled the failure of the Schlieffen Plan, the Crown Prince, in command of the German Fifth Army, stated, "We have lost the war. It will go on for a long time but it is lost already." (Quoted in Whittle *The Last Kaiser* Purnell p277)

After this setback they defended on the Western Front while they inflicted a series of heavy defeats on the Russians and gained a great deal of territory.

In the meantime the allies cleared the seas of German ships and blocked her trade routes. This slow strangulation of the Germans resulted in the submarine campaign designed to starve the British into surrender. This gamble ultimately failed and resulted in the United States joining the allies.

In 1916 the Germans all but exhausted the French army at Verdun. This was a major cause of the mutiny in the French army the following year. In 1917 revolution in Russia, at least partially caused by the war, made the Russians sue for peace. The harsh peace imposed by the Germans at Brest-Litovsk gave her vast tracks of Russian land and, given time, would have replaced the sources of food and raw materials denied by the allied blockade.

However time was not on the side of the Germans. In 1918, weakened by the four harsh years of shortage and rationing, Germany collapsed from within. Her armies were in retreat but were not routed. Her fleet was intact but there was nothing left in the centre.

10 The Weimar Republic : an Experiment in Democracy 1918-1933

Early in 1990, second year pupils in a Highland secondary school were making up questions to be sent by fax to their counterparts in a West German school. The teacher had instructed them to think of questions relating to how the young Germans felt about the steps towards reunification which were under way at that time. With a certain sense of mischief one boy wrote, "Do you think Hitler did a good job for your country?" and was not in the least surprised when his effort was censored on the grounds that it was likely to cause offence. Delete Hitler's name and substitute that of any British Prime Minister you know. Is the question likely to offend anybody? Very unlikely. This shows the magnitude of the Hitler problem. Almost half a century after his death it is still difficult for the Germans to talk to each other about him.

How did the Germans, a nation which in the 19th century had been proud of its civilisation, its poets and thinkers, come to be governed by this legendary beast? It is easy to see why the Germans are ashamed of a man who destroyed liberty in his own country, murdered millions of innocent people and started a war that cost 36 million their lives. Why,though, did they allow such a person to become their leader? Furthermore, if the Germans, with whom we have much in common, could make such a mistake could we make a similar error?

Adolf Hitler was not originally a subject of the German Kaiser. He was born near Linz in Austria in 1889. As a youth he frequently quarrelled with his domineering father who wanted little Adolf to follow in his footsteps and become a customs official or civil servant of the Austrian Hapsburg Empire. Hitler thought that would be dull. He wanted to be an artist, an occupation which implied a life style which Alois Hitler, his father, thought degenerate. He was infuriated by his son's deplorable record at school. Anyone interested in Hitler's formative years can do no better than to refer to Alan Bullock's excellent biography *Hitler, a Study in Tyranny* which includes some fascinating quotations which illuminate the development of a problem personality. For many years this work was the definitive one on Hitler, although in recent years other outstanding publications have appeared.

Hitler once said of his teachers:

"They had no sympathy with youth; their one objective was to stuff our brains and turn us into erudite apes like themselves. If any pupil showed the slightest trace of originality they persecuted him relentlessly, and the only model pupils whom I have ever known have all been failures in later life."
(*Hitler's Table Talk, 1941-44* p698-699)

This may well have been in response to the generally low opinion which his teachers had of him. Dr Eduard Humer said of him in 1923:

"He had a definite talent, though in a narrow field. But he lacked self-discipline, being notoriously cantankerous, wilful, arrogant and bad-tempered. He had obvious difficulty in fitting in at school. Moreover he was lazy ... He reacted with ill-concealed hostility to advice or reproof; at the same time, he demanded of his fellow pupils their unqualified subservience, fancying himself in the role of leader."
(Franz Jetzinger *Hitler's Youth* Quoted by Alan Bullock)

These personality traits are readily recognised in him in later life (Hitler did, however, enjoy his history lessons where he was taught by Dr Leopold Pötsch, an ardent German Nationalist.)

"There we sat, often aflame with enthusiasm, sometimes even moved to tears ... The national fervour which we felt in our small way was used by him as an instrument of our education ... It was because I had such a professor that History became my favourite subject."
(*Mein Kampf* Quoted by Alan Bullock)

Herr Dr Pötsch has a great deal to answer for ! Hitler's father died when he was 13. He left school in 1905, aged 16, without qualifications. He went to Vienna in 1906 and in 1907 and 1908 tried unsuccessfully to enter the Academy of Fine Arts. He rationalised his failure by proclaiming that those who rejected him were such mediocrities that they could not recognise real talent when they met it.

His mother, of whom he was fond, died in 1907. Having failed to gain entry to the Academy of Fine Arts he stayed in Vienna, rather than face the humiliation of returning home. He had enough money to enjoy the standard of living of a junior school teacher. Norman Stone has this to say of his Vienna days:

"Existence was sometimes precarious and Hitler may have done odd jobs from time to time. However, contrary to legends that he later propagated, he was never crushed by poverty, forced to live in a home for tramps, or become a house painter."
(Norman Stone *Hitler* p20)

There seems to be a minor historical debate over exactly how destitute Hitler became.

"By ... 1909 ... his funds had run out; he left his room without paying the rent he owed, and took to sleeping out on park benches, even in doorways. When the colder weather came he stood in line to get a bowl of soup from a convent kitchen and then found a place in ... a shelter for the destitute ... To the defeat and humiliation of his pretensions to become an artist was now added the social humiliation of the spoiled and snobbish young man from a middle-class home

reduced to the status of a tramp ... From this state he was rescued by Reinhold Hanisch, a fellow tramp who had a far better idea than Hitler of how to survive at the bottom of the heap."
(Alan Bullock *Hitler and Stalin. Parallel Lives* p 19)

Hanisch persuaded him that he could make ends meet by going to galleries and making copies of the works of recognised artists onto postcards which Hanisch would then sell to tourists for some small charge.The proceeds were to be split equally between them. For a while the partnership functioned well, but in the end, inevitably, Hitler quarrelled with his agent.

(It was in Vienna that he probably developed his hatred of Jews,)described by Alan Bullock as the only emotion he sincerely felt. Various explanations have been offered for this. There seems to be no satisfactory evidence to support the idea that he contracted VD from a Jewish prostitute. He seems to have had little interest in women. More likely is the suggestion that he was helped and befriended by a Jewish dealer in second-hand clothes. Instead of being grateful for the gift of an old overcoat to keep him warm in the cold Vienna winter, Hitler resented the Jew who had made him feel inferior. In *Hitler, a Study of Personality in Politics*, William Carr mentions the belief that Hitler suffered from monorchism (having only one testicle). This may have led him to feel inadequate and to want to vent his anger on somebody. Carr also mentions the theory of an American, Dr Rudolf Binion. Hitler's mother was treated by a Jewish doctor, Edward Bloch, who used a gas called iodoform during her final illness. In 1918 Hitler was gassed and blinded near Ypres, an experience which he associated with Germany's defeat in the same year. His resentment of the doctor whom he subconsciously blamed for his mother's death led to the gassing of the Jews (the 'final solution') from 1941-45.

In Vienna Hitler displayed many of the character traits which remained features of his personality in later years. He was lazy and unwilling to work regularly. Sometimes he could be excited and enthusiastic, other times he was sullen, moody and morose. Endlessly willing to talk about politics, his ideas consisted mainly of blaming a series of enemies, such as Jews, priests, the Hapsburgs, capitalists and socialists for the ills of society. None of his ideas were in any way original; all were borrowed. Although he abstained from alcohol, coffee, tobacco and meat, he had a passion for cream cakes.

In 1912, faced with conscription to the Austro-Hungarian army, Hitler absconded across the border to the Bavarian capital, Munich. The discipline of army life would not have appealed to him. In *Mein Kampf* (his autobiography written in 1923) he claimed he had left because Vienna had ceased to be a pure German city. The Hapsburg Empire had been instrumental in bringing large numbers of Czechs, Poles, Hungarians, Jews and others, all of whom Hitler saw as inferior, to the city. To some it was vigorous, cosmopolitan and lively. To Hitler it represented the pollution of German culture with inferior influences, compromising the German identity.

"To me the giant city seemed the embodiment of racial desecration ... The longer I lived in this city, the more my hatred grew for the foreign mixture of peoples which had begun to corrode this old site of German culture. The idea that this state could be maintained much longer seemed positively ridiculous."
(Adolf Hitler *Mein Kampf* Trans. R Mannheim p113)

When war broke out in August 1914 Hitler, fired with German patriotism, was granted permission to join the Bavarian Regiment of the Imperial German Army.

Hitler was in action early, taking part in the first Battle of Ypres (November 1914) when the deadly accurate Lee-Enfields of the British Expeditionary Force filled the Kameradengrab (mass grave) at Langemarke with 23,834 young Germans, mostly students fired with Nationalism. Throughout the war Hitler served as a runner, a carrier of messages between the front line and the rear, a dangerous and unpopular job. He was at the front for 4 years, often in the line opposite the British, and fought in most of the really nasty battles such as the Somme and Passchendaele. Although he did not rise above the rank of corporal he won the Iron Cross, First Class, which was normally reserved for officers, in 1918 and the Iron Cross, Second Class, in December 1914. He seems to have been a brave and dedicated soldier.

In his late writings he often stressed that Germany and Britain were natural allies. In October 1918 the British gassed and blinded him temporarily. When the war ended he was recovering in hospital. The news of the Fatherland's defeat seemed utterly incomprehensible, outrageous and unacceptable.

GERMANY 1918–19 DEFEAT & REVOLUTION

Defeat in the First World War threw Germany into turmoil. The impact of this had a lot to do with the coming to power of the strange, perhaps deranged, man, whose personality has been described in the preceding section.

The Communists are dying and the foreign exchange rate goes up, (Gott mit uns), 1920

This cartoon is the work of George Grosz, a supporter of the left who had fought in the Great War. He left Germany when Hitler came to power.

The Germany which emerged at the end of the war was not to his liking.

Military defeat had been accompanied by political change. During the final two years of the war, the Kaiser's autocratic power had been effectively exercised by Germany's two most influential Generals, Ludendorff and Hindenburg.

Revolution from Above

In August 1918 the Allies began to drive Germany back on the Western Front as one by one Germany's allies surrendered. At the end of September, Ludendorff told the Kaiser that defeat was inevitable and that a liberal civilian government would have better prospects of negotiating peace with the western allies. The majority parties in the Reichstag - the Social Democrats, the Catholic Centre Party and the Progressives - were virtually ordered to form a reforming government under Prince Max of Baden and to carry out the new laws, known as the October reforms. These were quickly passed and affected three areas:

- the army came under the control of the civil government rather than the Kaiser,
- the Ministers of the government became responsible to the Reichstag,
- the antiquated and undemocratic voting system in Prussia was reformed.

This phase of change is known as revolution from above because it was instigated by the Prussian Establishment. Power was dumped into the hands of the reformers who were left with the task of bringing the war to an end and were consequently blamed for Germany's defeat in the war and the Peace Treaty that followed. Those who deserved the blame remained national heroes in the eyes of many people.

Revolution from Below

In early November, while the new civilian government was busy negotiating an armistice, the Naval High Command ordered the High Seas fleet to sea for one last desperate battle with the Royal Navy. They hoped that some sort of victory might give Germany a stronger bargaining position. The sailors were unwilling to die for such a lost cause and mutinied. Copying the recent revolution in Russia, they came ashore at Kiel and Hamburg and formed Soviets: workers', soldiers' and sailors' councils. The revolt spread quickly to other towns. In Bavaria, the Communists under Kurt Eisener, a Jew, seized power and proclaimed the Bavarian Republic. Up to this point the Kaiser had been clinging stubbornly to power and thus hindering the peace process, since the Americans in particular were unwilling to make peace with an autocrat. On 9 November Prince Max announced the Kaiser's abdication without the Kaiser's consent and then resigned himself, handing over power to Friedrich Ebert, a Social Democrat.

Divisions among the German Socialists

The First World War had split Germany's socialist party, the Social Democrats (SPD). At first, believing it to be a defensive operation, their Reichstag Deputies had agreed to vote for extra taxes to finance the war. As time went on the more left-wing elements in the Party recognised the war as one of conquest and annexation rather than self-defence. Led by Hugo Haase, Karl Kautsky and Eduard Bernstein, they split with the moderate Majority Socialists to form the Independent Socialists (USPD), opposing the war of annexation and refusing to vote for more war credits. A more radical factor were the proto-communists, the Gruppe Internationale or Spartacus Union led by Karl Liebknecht and Rosa Luxemburg. They had campaigned for organised resistance to the war since the early days and now advocated violent revolution to overthrow the Government.

When Ebert came to power there was a strong surge to republicanism and to prevent the left taking the initiative Philip Scheidemann, Ebert's deputy, ended a speech to the masses in the Reichstag Square with the words:

"Fellow citizens! Workers! Comrades! The monarchical system has collapsed. The Hohenzollerns have abdicated. Long live the Great German Republic ... Long live the free German Republic."

In such a way are important decisions reached in time of crisis.

Two days later Matthias Erzberger, a member of the Catholic Centre Party, signed the armistice on behalf of the German government. Defeat in the war came to be associated with the new regime.

In *The German Revolution*, AJ Ryder has identified the aims of the revolution as:

- Democratisation of the government.
- Demilitarisation of the establishment - reforming the armed forces into a people's army.
- Socialisation - the achievement of a more even spread of wealth throughout society.

The majority socialists were more concerned with the first two aims and felt they had to be completed before the third could be considered. The independents realised that the socialisation might never take place at all if they waited for the other aims to be achieved. They wanted the Soviets (Workers' Councils) to take over and seize control of all business immediately. To their disappointment, a specially convened Congress of all German Workers' Councils agreed by 400 votes to 50 that a proper parliament had to be set up before reforms could proceed. From this many historians have concluded that the German people were more interested in moderate political reforms than in a socialist revolution.

THE WEIMAR REPUBLIC & ITS PROBLEMS

The new regime came to be known as the Weimar Republic because the National Assembly met at the provincial city of Weimar as violent socialist-inspired riots made Berlin an impossible venue for the early meetings. This experimental democracy lasted about fourteen years and died with Hitler's accession to power. The reasons for its failure are as many and varied as they are sad.

The Legend of the Stab in the Back - Dolschstosslegende

When the armistice was signed the German army was in full retreat but no foreign troops had set foot on German soil. German Nationalists, like Hitler, unable to come to terms with reality, claimed that the German Army was never beaten in the field. It was betrayed by the November Criminals, the Socialists, Pacifists and Jews who staged the revolution and stabbed the heroic army in the back. Ebert unwittingly contributed to this myth by allowing the returning soldiers to march through the streets of Berlin with flags, bands and weapons and by greeting them with the words, "I salute you, who return unvanquished from the field of battle." Thus Ebert's government and not the general staff were blamed for defeat and the subsequent hardships. In 1923 Hitler said:

> "Shirkers, Deserters, and Pacifists: these are (the Republic's) founders and their heroic acts consisted in leaving in the lurch the soldiers at the front, in stopping reinforcements, in withholding from them munitions, while at home against old men and half-starved children they carried through a revolutionary coup d'état ... This Revolution has dishonoured the old heroes on whom the whole world had looked with wonder; it allowed the scum of the streets to tear off their decorations and to hurl into the mire all that was sacred to the heroes of the front line."
>
> [N Baynes (Ed.)*The Speeches of Adolf Hitler* p81-82]

The Impact of the Peace Treaty of Versailles

The armistice signed on 11 November 1918 was merely a cease-fire. In theory the war could have restarted if Germany and her conquerors could not agree on the terms of a peace treaty.

The victorious powers met in the old Royal Palace of Versailles, twelve miles from Paris, and in the summer of 1919 handed out peace treaties for the defeated nations to sign. Germany and her allies were not permitted face to face negotiations. Instead they were allowed a limited time to make written submissions, most of which were ignored. When the treaty was produced Scheidemann, the Chancellor and Prime Minister, resigned but after some hesitation a new coalition government accepted it.

Few people in Germany had expected the treaty to be as harsh as it was. Germany had to accept:

1. Responsibility for starting the war - The War Guilt Clause.
2. The obligation to pay reparations for the civil damage inflicted. A sum of £6,600,000 was fixed in 1921.
3. Disarmament - The army was reduced to 100,000 men. Conscription was banned. No tanks, U-boats or military aircraft were allowed - only six small battleships. The Rhineland was demilitarised. No military installations or defences were allowed between the French border and a line drawn 50 km to the east of the Rhine.
4. The loss of all overseas colonies on the grounds that Germans were morally unfit to govern native peoples.
5. Never uniting with Austria. (Anschluss was forbidden.)
6. - Alsace and Lorraine to be returned to France.
   - Eupen and Malmedy to be transferred to Belgium.
   - North Schleswig to go to Denmark.
   - Posen, West Prussia and part of Upper Silesia to go to Poland.
   - The Saar coalfield to be transferred to France for 15 years. Its eventual fate was to be determined by a plebiscite. In all, 13% of Germany's territory and 6 million of her subjects were lost.

Each of these items could be justified on its own, but to the

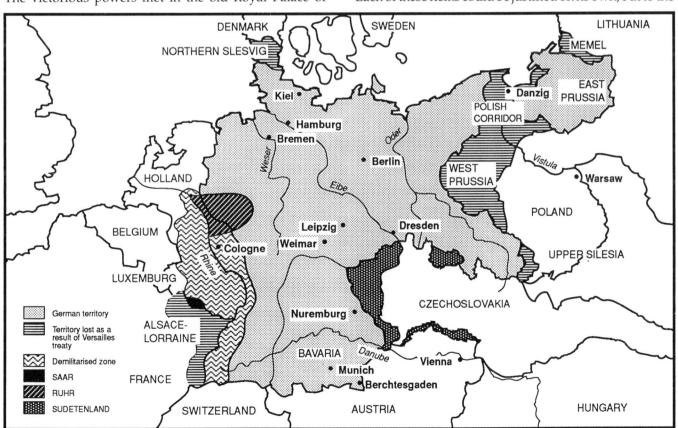

German territorial losses at Versailles

Germans the package as a whole seemed extremely severe. Most still believed that they had been fighting a defensive war.

The territories lost were rich in reserves: Alsace-Lorraine had iron, the Saar and Upper Silesia had coal. Their loss made the payment of reparations seem impossible. There was no guarantee that Germany's neighbours would disarm. She felt that she was left defenceless and surrounded by hostile states. The loss of territory to Poland was especially resented as it left about 3 million Germans under Polish rule and separated East Prussia from the rest of Germany.

Yet it can also be pointed out that Germany's treatment was mild by her own standards as seen in her treatment of France in 1871 and Russia in 1918.

No matter whether it was fair or unfair the Treaty of Versailles was used by right-wing politicians, and particularly by Hitler's Nazis, as a stick with which to beat the Weimar Republic. Again in 1923 Hitler said:

"The Republic, by God! is worthy of its fathers. For hardly was the first deed of shame committed when there followed the second - one dishonour after another ... This November-Republic bore the stamp of the men who made it. The name November-Criminals will cling to these folk throughout the centuries."
[Norman Baynes (Ed) *The Speeches of Adolf Hitler* p80-81]

Not only had the 'November Criminals' stabbed the army in the back, they had also betrayed the country by signing a vindictive and unjust treaty. The repudiation of the Treaty became a central feature of Nationalist and Nazi propaganda. However, the view that Versailles destroyed German democracy and that a more lenient treaty would have saved it has been increasingly called into question. Hans Kohn has written:

"Many Germans blamed the Allies for the weakness of democratic Germany. The truth, however, was that the essential framework of the Treaty of Versailles was not upheld by the Allies. One concession after another was made to the Weimar Republic: The sympathy of the world turned towards Germany; German complaints and the German interpretation of the war were accepted at their face value, especially in Britain and the United States; economic assistance permitted Germany to modernise her industrial structure to a point beyond that of her former enemies. By the end of the twenties Germany impressed every visitor as being much better off than Britain, France or Belgium. Splendid new housing projects, schools, hospitals, parks, monuments, official buildings, and post offices adorned every German city. Amid all this ostentatious wealth the Germans regarded the payment of reparations for the wanton destruction which their armies had done in the war as an unjust imposition. They continued to complain about the disastrous consequences of the peace treaty. This failure on the part of the educated German classes, even more than their unfamiliarity with, or dislike for democracy, wrote the death warrant of the Weimar Republic. The lament of so many decent ... Germans about the burdens and cruelties inflicted by the Allies upon an innocent Germany ... undermined democracy ... and facilitated the rise of Hitler."
(Hans Kohn *The Mind of Germany* p317-318) (NB. Kohn, a native of Prague, became a Professor of History in the USA)

Too Good a Constitution?
The task of drawing up a constitution outlining how the new Republic was to operate was entrusted to Dr Hugo Preuss who produced what many considered as near to perfect a democratic constitution as was possible.

The old kingdoms of Germany - Prussia, Saxony, Bavaria, Thuringia etc. - were given home rule within a Federal framework. Laws were to be made by a two chamber legislature - the Reichstag and the Reichsrat. The Reichstag was directly elected by all Germans. The Reichsrat contained representatives of the individual states. All men and women over twenty years of age could vote.

Elections were by proportional representation. That means that a party which got 10% of the votes would get 10% of the representatives in the Reichstag. (This is different from the British system where in 1983 the Liberal/SDP Alliance got 25% of the votes and 3% of the MPs.)

The Head of State was the President elected directly by the people (not chosen by the Reichstag). He had extensive powers which included the following: *attempt at democracy*

- He was head of the armed forces.
- He appointed the Reich Chancellor.
- He could dissolve the Reichstag and call fresh elections.
- Under Article 48 (sometimes called the suicide clause) he could suspend the constitution and rule directly by decree in time of crisis.

Knocking-off time (Gott mit uns), 1920

Two main problems emerged in the operation of this constitution.

1 Proportional representation encouraged the growth of small parties. It became impossible for any party to gain enough seats in the Reichstag to get an overall majority and give Germany a strong and secure government. Divisions among the parties were so great that it was difficult to construct a lasting coalition of parties. People became tired of an apparently ineffectual system and looked for a stronger form of government.

2 In emergencies the President, especially Hindenburg after 1926, was too willing to resort to direct rule under Article 48. It has been argued that this allowed Germany to drift towards dictatorship. On the other hand it did help to maintain some semblance of elected government in the 1930s when no agreement could be reached among the parties in the Reichstag. Perhaps the constitution was simply too democratic for a people who were unused to running their own affairs and who, in time of difficulty, looked for a strong leader. If the price of democracy is the eternal vigilance of the people, perhaps too few Germans cared enough about it to defend the Weimar Constitution. Peter Gay's phrase "peasants in a palace" aptly describes how unused to democracy the German people were.

A Republic Nobody Wanted

In retrospect it seems that Weimar had far too many implacable enemies and too few supporters who were totally committed to it. In the early 1920s it seemed to stagger from crisis to crisis and was lucky to survive. James Joll in *The Conquest of the Past* reaches the heart of the matter when he asserts that a crucial weakness of the Weimar Republic was "its total rejection by important sections of the German People".

Enemies on the Left - The Spartacist Revolt
The announcement of elections to the Constituent Assembly in January 1919 precipitated an attempted coup by the extreme left-wing Spartacus Union. The task of the Assembly was to draw up a new constitution or rule book for government. Karl Liebknecht saw that Germany was likely to become a middle-class constitutional democracy and believed that this could only be stopped by an armed seizure of power. Rosa Luxemburg disagreed. This gentle, red-haired, green-eyed, sickly Polish woman combined a formidable intellect with a distaste for violence. She saw that the coup would either fail or would end with a regime sustained in power by terror. The German workers were not yet ready for power. Liebknecht ignored her and his supporters seized some key buildings in Berlin and set up machine gun posts on street corners.

The Republic's Minister of Defence, Gustav Noske, was forced to turn to the old Establishment for help. He employed Freikorps (Free Corps), bands of volunteers from the old army, to suppress the rising. Set up by ex-officers and manned by veteran soldiers brutalised by war, the Freikorps were not concerned to save the Republic. Most of them wanted the Kaiser to return. They hated communists and had come to need the discipline, comradeship and violence which the Western Front had given them. The Spartacists, who took this name from the gladiator who led a slave revolt in ancient Rome, never stood a chance. Their revolt was crushed with an orgy of violence. Liebknecht and Luxemburg were captured and killed. The frail, little woman had her skull smashed with a rifle butt and her brains splattered by a single bullet. Her body was recovered months later from a canal. Liebknecht suffered a similar fate.

The Republic seemed to have survived but the revolt had long-term implications.

* The left never forgave the Majority Social Democrats for the way in which the revolt had been crushed. In later years the KPD (Communist Party formed by the Spartacists in December 1918 just before the disastrous revolt) often seemed to work with the Nazis to undermine the Republic. Thus the potential opposition to Hitler was divided.

* The Republic became dependent on its enemies on the right, namely the army, the judges and the civil servants, for its survival.

Enemies on the Right - The Kapp Putsch
In early 1920 the government tried to disband elements of the Freikorps who had outlived their usefulness and who were seen as a violation of the army size limitation imposed at Versailles. A Captain Ehrhardt responded to the order to disband his group by marching on Berlin. The government fled and a new regime was proclaimed under the leadership of an obscure reactionary civil servant, Dr Wolfgang Kapp.

Ebert appealed to the army for help but General Von Seeckt declined saying that the army should not be involved in politics!

> "Troops do not fire on troops. When Reichswehr fires on Reichswehr all comradeship within the officer corps vanishes."
> (Corkery and Stone *Weimar Germany and the Third Reich* p 26)

A general strike broke out in Berlin. Kapp and Ehrhardt faced with the hostility of trade unions, bank workers and even civil servants saw the city come to a standstill before their very eyes. Public transport failed, power was cut off and a new blackout descended. The Freikorps was forced to retreat.

At this stage another problem emerged. The Establishment in Germany had not been changed by the revolution. Civil servants, judges and teachers had all been appointed by the old regime and were loyal to it. Fighting for survival against the left, the SPD depended on the old Establishment for survival and was unable to replace them with people loyal to the new order. Teachers taught children to despise the Republic while judges encouraged terrorism from the right.

In sharp contrast to the Spartacists, the perpetrators of the Kapp Putsch were scarcely punished. The early twenties also saw a wave of assassinations of prominent Weimar

The poor wait for soup from the Salvation Army - Berlin 1930.

supporters including Matthias Erzberger (Catholic Centre Party) who had campaigned for a negotiated peace from 1918 and had signed the armistice, and Walther Rathenau a wealthy industrialist and Weimar minister.

Between 1918 and 1922, twenty two assassinations were attributed to left-wing extremists. Of these ten were sentenced to death and seven others received heavy sentences. In the same period there were 354 murders committed by right-wing terrorists. None of these resulted in a death sentence and only one got a substantial prison sentence. The sentence on a soldier for kicking a Bavarian Communist to death was 5 weeks in prison. The officer who watched was fined 300 RM. On average, left-wing terrorists got 15 years, right-wing terrorists got 4 weeks. The Kaiser's judges did not see it as their job to protect Weimar leaders.

After the army had refused to suppress the Kapp Putsch, a Communist revolt broke out in Saxony and Thuringia. Here the army became involved in politics with enthusiasm and with help from Freikorps units tortured and murdered communist prisoners.

Economic Difficulties

Weimar enjoyed a brief period of prosperity in the mid to late twenties. Before and after this period, however, the economic climate was less satisfactory.

In April 1922 the Foreign Minister, Walther Rathenau, who was Jewish, signed a Treaty of Friendship and Economic Cooperation with Soviet Russia, an act which apparently did not endear him to the German right, who murdered him two months later. The treaty, signed at Rapallo, contained secret clauses designed to enable Germany to evade some of the disarmament clauses of the Versailles Treaty. For example, German soldiers would train on tanks in Russia. French intelligence soon got wind of this. N.B (center of wealth)

Franco-Belgian Invasion of the Ruhr and the Great Inflation
By early 1923 Germany had fallen behind with her reparations to the tune of 140,000 telegraph poles and a few train loads of coal. French and Belgian troops invaded Germany's richest industrial area, the Ruhr, easily accessible from the occupied Rhineland. Rapallo was the reason, reparations the pretext for this action. Britain, who was not consulted, later protested but took no action against France and Belgium.

The German government regarded this as a violation of the covenant of the League of Nations, a view also held by neutral nations like Sweden. It called on German workers and officials in the area to refuse to cooperate. An untidy strike broke out. The French brought in their own officials and began intimidation and imprisonment of strikers.

Since the Ruhr provided 85% of Germany's coal, the invasion had a devastating effect on the country's economy. Unemployment rose everywhere. Despite falling tax revenues the government persisted with the economic support of the Ruhr strikers. Money was being printed and paid out but there was little in the shops to buy. The First World War and its aftermath had caused inflation in all

106

Index of German Wholesale Prices	
December 1913	100
December 1918	245
December 1919	800
December 1920	1,400
December 1921	3,500
December 1922	147,500
December 1923	126,000,000,000,000

Table 10.1 (Source : W Arthur Lewis *Economic Survey. 1919-1939*)

participating countries. Germany was no exception, but at this stage it got completely out of hand as table 10.1 shows.

Germany became an economic madhouse. People collected their pay in suitcases and wheel barrows. Bank notes and postage stamps were overprinted time and again with higher values.

In cafes it was wise to pay for your coffee when you ordered it. The price would rise while you drank it. Men insisted on being paid twice daily and in having a break from work while they spent their wages. A kohlrabi (a type of cabbage with edible stock) cost 50 million marks. A postage stamp cost as much as a Berlin villa had in 1890.

Some inhabitants of mental hospitals became very confused. Asked, "How old are you?" a man might reply, "58 million years"; "How many children do you have?" "3 thousand million". *Ha Ha Ha*

In many ways inflation suited the government. It could pay back its internal debts at a tiny fraction of their original value. Some businessmen also benefited. By carefully manipulating credit, Hugo Stinnes took over businesses in Hungary and Rumania. He also acquired 150 newspapers and periodicals and a large share in 69 building companies, 66 chemical, paper and sugar works, 59 mines, 49 lignite mines, 57 banks and insurance companies etc. Sadly for Stinnes he died the following year.

Debtors and cunning speculators gained from the great inflation. Wage earners generally survived. Anybody with savings was ruined. Pensioners and people on fixed incomes were the worst affected. People who had sacrificed for a lifetime, denying themselves to save for their retirement, could no longer buy a box of matches with what had been a big nest egg.

Middle-class longing for the good old days and a strong leader to restore them was intensified. Democracy appeared not to be working for Germany.

Hitler Again
What was Corporal Hitler doing at this time? At the end of the war, having recovered his sight, he stayed in the army as a political instructor, his job being to sort out recruits who came into the service with left-wing ideas. In September 1919 he was sent to investigate an obscure group in Munich called the German Workers Party led by a locksmith, Anton Drexler. He discovered that the party did not represent a strain of Bolshevism but that it was volkisch (nationalist tinged with ideas of German racial superiority) and set out to appeal to the working class.

Hitler launched a vigorous verbal attack on a speaker whose ideas he disliked. Drexler was impressed and asked him to join. He became the seventh member of the committee and rapidly began to dominate the Party.

In February 1920 the Party took a new name - Nationalsozialistische Deutsche Arbeiter Partei (National Socialist German Workers Party) known as the NSDAP or Nazi Party. At the same time a 25 point programme drawn up by Hitler, Drexler and others was put forward. It contained 3 main elements

Nationalism
1 All Germans including those in Austria, Czechoslovakia and Poland to be united in one Gross Deutschland.
2 Treaties of Versailles and St Germain (signed by Austria at the end of the war) to be renounced.

Anti-Semitism
Jews to be denied citizenship, excluded from public office and in some cases deported from Germany.

Socialism
Various measures were to be employed against industrialists, big landowners and financiers. All were designed to favour small traders, peasant farmers and workers. Drexler believed in the socialist part. Hitler almost certainly saw it as a way to get the votes of different sections of the community from the dissatisfied nationalist lower middle class to peasants and factory workers.

In the early days of the Party Hitler emerged as a developing demagogue or mob orator, a rabble rouser, and an effective propagandist. He used simple, direct and often violent language. Words like smash and crush featured prominently in his vocabulary. Always he told the same story:

- Germany had been betrayed in 1918/1919 by the November Criminals.
- Germany had not been defeated in the war. Her army had been stabbed in the back.
- Germany's economic woes were due to both economic exploitation by the bank Jews and the Treaty of Versailles.

scapegoats!

In the summer of 1920 another of the Party's distinctive institutions began to emerge. Known first as the Gymnastic and Sports Division and later as the Sturmabteilung (SA and Storm Troopers) it provided the Party with the muscle it needed to break up rivals' meetings and to protect its own. Every political party in Germany had a unit like this. The SA recruited many old Freikorps men and veterans from the war who longed for the old days of comradeship and whose lives reacquired some meaning when they put on their brown shirts and breeches and went out to brawl with the Reds or to parade through the streets under their Hakenkreuz or Swastika banner. Ernst Röhm a tough, homosexual ex-officer who had joined the

Party before Hitler, was the most important of the SA's early leaders.

The Beer Hall Putsch *Munich 1923*

In the early days many of Hitler's associates aimed to achieve power by violent overthrow of the state. To this end they formed alliances and groupings with other similar parties, of which there were several. Hitler disliked this since it denied him the absolute authority which his personality craved. In 1923 it landed him in jail and taught him important lessons.

The story of the attempted Putsch or coup is immensely complicated. The basic plot was for the Nazis, in collaboration with various establishment figures, including General Ludendorff, to seize control of the government of Bavaria and then march on Berlin, capitalising on the chaos and unrest engendered by the French occupation of the Ruhr and the great inflation. The previous year Mussolini had taken power in Italy following his 'March on Rome'. Hitler was clearly influenced by this and was trying to emulate the Fascists. Much of what Hitler did was modelled on Mussolini's example. In 1930 he said, "Germany could take as its model the Fascist State."(Baynes p 112)

The attempt began with Hitler firing shots from a revolver into the ceiling of the Burgerbraukeller (a beer hall) and announcing to a packed meeting there that the governments of Bavaria and Germany had been overthrown. With difficulty the senior officers of the army kept their men under control. The next day Hitler and Ludendorff led a march on the old Bavarian War Ministry. The police opened fire. The man with whom Hitler was linking arms dropped dead, pulling Hitler down and dislocating his shoulder. The march broke up. Ludendorff marched angrily through the police line. Hitler was arrested. He was tried for treason and given the minimum sentence - five years. He was released after serving nine months in the comfort of Landsberg Castle.

Among those who visited him in Landsberg was Karl Ludecke:

" 'From now on,' he said 'we must follow a new line of action. It is best to attempt no large reorganisation until I am freed, which may be a matter of months rather than years.' I must have looked at him somewhat incredulously. 'Oh yes,' he continued. 'I am not going to stay here much longer. When I begin active work it will be necessary to pursue a new policy. Instead of working to achieve power by an armed coup, we shall have to hold our noses and enter the Reichstag against the Catholic and Marxist deputies. If outvoting them takes longer than outshooting them, at least the results will be guaranteed by their own Constitution! Any lawful process is slow. But already, as you know, we have thirty two Reichstag deputies under this new programme, and are the second largest party in the Bavarian Landtag-diet. Sooner or later we shall have a majority - and after that, Germany. I am convinced this is our best line of action, now that conditions in the country have changed so radically.' I was not a little surprised to hear the Führer talking this way. Only a few weeks earlier he had voiced .... his violent

opposition to any participation in the May elections, and had raged when Party members had entered despite his ban ... The unexpected success in the elections had undoubtedly swayed him."
(Karl Ludecke, *I knew Hitler* p217-218)

From the failure of the Munich Putsch Hitler had drawn three lessons.

1 He could not seize power by force. He would have to acquire power by legal and constitutional means. The Germans are a law-abiding people.
2 He would have to get power on his own. Pacts and conspiracies with others were doomed to failure. He could trust nobody.
3 In 1935 Hitler told Mr G Ward Price, a British journalist:

"I was following Mussolini's example too closely. I had meant the Munich Putsch to be the beginning of a 'March on Berlin' which should carry us straight to power. From its failure I learned the lesson that each country must evolve its own type and methods of national regeneration."
(Norman Baynes (Ed.) *The Speeches of Adolf Hitler* p159-60)

Hitler's Ideas

In Landsberg he wrote his autobiographical work *Mein Kampf* - My Struggle.

Mein Kampf - The World According to Adolf Hitler

After the Nazi takeover in 1933 Hitler's book achieved an almost bible-like status in Germany. Every family had one even if few were ever read. It has been described as a strange, rambling, pompous, barely readable book in either the original German or in translation. Published in 1926, 18,000 copies had been sold by 1928. After Hitler had been in power for 7 years it had sold 6 million copies. He wrote a second book, mainly on foreign policy, in 1928 which his publisher 'sat on'. The *Zweites Buch* (Secret Book) was finally published in 1961. From these books, and from his speeches, a summary of Hitler's political philosophy can be synthesised. None of his ideas were in any way original. All had appeared in one guise or another before.

Social Darwinism: He borrowed from Houston Stewart Chamberlain, an Englishman who had lived in Germany before the Great War, the adaptation of Darwin's 'Survival of the Fittest' concept to human society. Most biologists and scientists regard this as absurd, as, most probably, Darwin would.

All life is a struggle. The best and fittest came out on top. The Germans and other Nordic Races in the Aryans represented the greatest advance of human evolution. The Germans, the Aryans, the Herrenvolk were the master race, physically and intellectually superior to all others, and recognisable by certain physical features - big, blond, etc.

Other races could be graded according to their state of evolution. The lowest forms of human life were the Untermenschen (sub-humans) - the Jews, negroes and the Slavs. In 1930 he said of the Indian Freedom Movement:

"... it is clear that this is a rebellion of the lower Indian race against the superior English-Nordic race. The Nordic race has a right to rule the world and we must take this racial right as the guiding star of our foreign policy."

[Norman Baynes (Ed.) *The Speeches of Adolf Hitler* p 989]

Civilisation had placed restraints on human instincts which had frustrated and perverted the process of evolution. Societies which sought to protect the weak, the sick and the old did so at the expense of the strong. Thus the whole balance of nature was upset. Hitler intended to foster the growth of the strong and healthy parts of society.

Racial purity and racial hygiene: To preserve the superiority of the Aryan race interbreeding with the Untermenschen must be prevented. Jews must not be allowed to pollute German blood. The Jews were seen as the source of most of Germany's problems. They could not create a nation of their own. They hated the Germans and sought to bring them down to their own level by an endless succession of fiendishly cunning conspiracies. Consequently Jews must be eliminated from German society. No Jew should have German citizenship.

Lebensraum: If mankind was to progress the master race must have room to expand. It was the Aryans' duty to mankind to take living space from the Untermenschen - the Slavs of Russia. Thus Lebensraum has to be taken by war - a natural struggle which would sort out the races. The superior races would prosper. The Untermenschen would wither away.

> "Land and soil is the goal of our foreign policy ..."(p593)
> "State boundaries are made by man and changed by man ..." (p596)
> "If we speak of soil in Europe today, we can primarily have in mind only Russia and her vassal border states..." (p598)
> (A Hitler *Mein Kampf* translated by R Mannheim)

Within the new Germany the old differences of class, religion and wealth would disappear. All Germans would learn to think of the needs of the state before their own needs. A new Nazi class system would emerge. Its layers would be as follows:

- The New High Aristocracy : The most worthy and responsible Nazi leaders.
- The Herren Class: The new Nazi middle class. Soldiers, Party members, important wealth producers.
- The Masses: German but voteless and powerless. A mixture of people from all the old classes, workers, traders, professional people, landowners etc.
- The new slave class made up of lesser races working for the master race.

Democracy was seen as a form of weakness. Germany needed a strong leader (Führer) to provide a natural sense of direction.

Communism was a Jewish conspiracy to make all races

Stresemann

equal and deny the Aryans their rights as the master race. Communism also had to be destroyed.

Of this chilling ideology William Carr has written:

> "If traditional moral values counted for nothing then the door was open, logically, to the sterilisation of the unfit, euthanasia of the old and the physical extermination of any element deemed by the rulers to be 'socially undesirable'."

> "Pity was out of place in a world governed by the inexorable operation of biological laws beyond human control. To feel concern for concentration camp inmates, the old and sick being put to sleep in euthanasia centres, subject peoples suffering under the heel of the oppressor, or enemy soldiers dying on the battlefield was sheer sentimentalism, the corrupting legacy of a Christian-humanitarian past. The Nazi was expected to be hard and ruthless in obeying the dictates of the higher law of nature for the sake of his own people."
> (William Carr *Hitler. A Study of Personality in Politics* p113-114)

1924 - 1929 — HITLER'S LEAN YEARS

When Hitler emerged from Landsberg Castle his party was in a state of disarray. While the Führer was comfortably locked up and writing his book the leading Nazis who remained at liberty quarrelled among themselves. The public lost interest in them.

Prosperity slowly returned to Germany. The government was dominated by Gustav Stresemann, a National Liberal once loyal to the Kaiser but who had accepted the new order. For a short while in 1923 he was Chancellor but from 1924 until his death in 1929 he was Foreign Minister. His achievements were immense.

1   He persuaded the French to leave the Ruhr by agreeing to pay reparations again.
2   He was able to restore the value of the German mark by replacing the old mark with the new Rentenmark.
3   He persuaded the allies to reduce the reparations burden. The Dawes Plan (called after the American General who chaired the commission) laid down an easier schedule of payments. This measure, backed by foreign loans, allowed a measure of prosperity to return and unemployment to fall. By 1928 Germany appeared more prosperous than Britain or France.
4   He achieved something of a rapprochement with France. In the Locarno Pact of 1925 Germany accepted the permanence of her frontier with France (although not of her Polish frontier). He was able to secure Germany's admission to the League of Nations in 1926. Germany was becoming accepted as a member of the community of civilised nations again.

When people are desperate and miserable they tend to turn to extreme parties offering extreme solutions of the kill or cure variety. Both the Nazis and the Communists were parties who thrived on suffering. Stresemann and his times denied the Nazi fire the oxygen of misery and it was all but extinguished. Still able to muster 6.6% of the vote in the Reichstag elections of 1924 their share had fallen to 2.6% by 1928.

Nevertheless, these were not completely wasted years. Hitler and his associates worked hard to improve the efficiency of the Party, especially the effectiveness of the organisation and propaganda machine. Hitler was able to assert his leadership over the Party and to impose his authority on it. It became exclusively the Hitler Party. Suspicious of Röhm and the hold he had over the SA, he created his own personal bodyguard the Schutzstaffeln (Protection Squad) or SS. This black-uniformed paramilitary elite swore an oath of allegiance directly to Hitler. The SS was led by Heinrich Himmler and represented the Nazi ideal in its purest form. To join, a man had to be big, strong, fit, highly intelligent yet willing to give unquestioning obedience to the leader.

The republic's prosperity and stability were both fragile and illusory. It still had too many enemies and far too few committed adherents. The prosperity that held it together came to an end in 1929 when the collapse of the New York Stock Exchange plunged the world economy into recession. Stresemann died that year. Had he lived, there would have been little he could have done.

The Great Depression
In economic terms no man is an island - no country is independent. The developed nations buy each other's products and are mutually dependent. The problems of one country affect all others.

During the Stresemann era German prosperity had been heavily dependent on American loans. These dried up

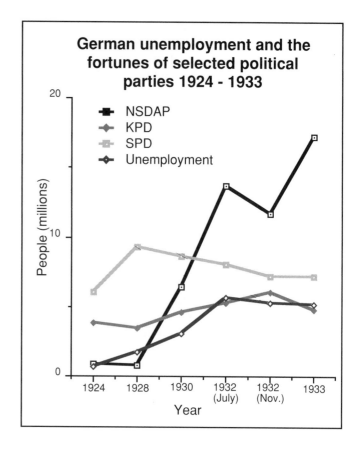

when share prices in the New York Stock Exchange plummeted in the Wall Street Crash of October 1929. Bankruptcy, bank failures and business collapses followed. American unemployment reached 12 million by 1932. The loss of American business affected everybody. Soon there were 3 million unemployed in Britain and 6 million in Germany. The Nazis were back in business. Misery had returned.

The Death of Weimar 1929 - 1933
In response to the Great Depression, reparations were again rescheduled under the Young Plan of 1929. (Owen Young was an American banker.) The Nazis protested vociferously about reparations being paid at all. The allies finally abandoned the whole idea of reparations in 1932 when Germany's economic situation was so desperate that further payments were obviously impossible.

Heinrich Brüning of the Catholic Centre Party became Chancellor in March 1930. He could not command a majority in the Reichstag but nor could anybody else. He was only able to govern by the liberal use of the President's emergency powers to rule by decree. This set a precedent which the Nazis later exploited to establish a totalitarian state.

Rising unemployment meant falling tax revenue and Brüning felt forced to cut back on government spending to avoid printing money and causing inflation. He cut unemployment benefit. Desperate people began to break the law to get into prison where they would be fed. The starvation which Germany had known during the war and during the great inflation of 1923 had returned. In desperation people looked to the extreme parties - the Nazis and the Communists, each of whom offered drastic cures for the troubles. These parties were, of course, the sworn enemies of parliamentary democracy and, despite

GERMAN ELECTION RESULTS 1919-33

Date	19.1.19	6.6.20	4.5.24	7.12.24	20.5.28	14.9.30	31.7.32	6.11.32	5.3.33
Electorate (millions)	36.766	35.949	38.375	38.987	41.224	42.957	44.226	44.374	44.685
Votes cast (millions)	30.524	28.463	29.709	30.704	31.165	35.225	37.162	35.758	39.654
% Poll	83	79.2	77.4	78.8	75.6	82	84	80.6	88.8
Number of seats	423	459	472	493	491	577	608	584	647
DNVP	3.1 10.3% (44)	4.2 15.1% (71)	5.7 19.5% (95)	6.2 20.5% (103)	4.4 14.2% (73)	2.5 7% (41)	2.2 5.9% (37)	3.0 8.3% (52)	3.1 8% (52)
NSDAP	- - -	- - -	1.9 6.5% (32)	0.9 3.0% (14)	0.8 2.6% (12)	6.4 18.3% (107)	13.7 37.3% (230)	11.7 33.1% (196)	17.2 43.9% (288)
DVP	1.3 4.4% (19)	3.9 13.9% (65)	2.7 9.2% (45)	3.1 10.1% (51)	2.7 8.7% (45)	1.6 4.5% (30)	0.4 1.2% (7)	0.7 1.9% (11)	0.4 1% (2)
ZENTRUM (Centre)	6.0 19.7% (91)	3.8 13.6% (64)	3.9 13.4% (65)	4.1 13.6% (69)	3.7 12.1% (62)	4.1 11.8% (68)	4.6 12.5% (75)	4.2 11.9% (70)	4.4 11.2% (74)
DDP	5.6 18.5% (75)	2.3 8.3% (39)	1.7 5.7% (28)	1.9 6.3% (32)	1.5 4.9% (25)	1.3 3.8% (20)	0.4 1% (4)	0.3 1% (2)	0.3 0.9% (5)
SPD	11.5 37.9% (165)	6.1 21.7% (102)	6.0 20.5% (100)	7.9 26% (131)	9.2 29.8% (153)	8.6 24.5% (143)	8.0 21.6% (133)	7.2 20.4% (121)	7.2 18.3% (120)
USPD	2.3 7.6% (22)	5.0 17.9% (84)	0.2 0.8% (nil)	0.1 0.3% (nil)	0.02 0.1% (nil)	- - -	- - -	- - -	- - -
KPD	- - (4)	0.6 2.1% (62)	3.7 12.6% (45)	2.7 9% (54)	3.3 10.6% (54)	4.6 13.1% (77)	5.3 14.3% (89)	6.0 16.9% (81)	4.8 12.3%
Others	0.5 1.6% (7)	2.0 3.4% (30)	3.4 11.8% (45)	3.5 11.5% (48)	5.2 17.8% (67)	5.8 16.9% (69)	2.3 6.3% (33)	2.3 6.4% (32)	1.7 4.3% (25)

Figures against each party show, firstly votes polled, in millions correct to nearest hundred thousand, secondly percentage of poll achieved, thirdly, in brackets, the number of seats won in the Reichstag. Elections of 19.1.19 were for the National Assembly. All the others were Reichstag elections.
(Based on E Kolb *The Weimar Republic*)

POLITICAL PARTIES OF THE WEIMAR REPUBLIC 1919-32

Parties of the 'Weimar Coalition' - Supporters of the Republic.

The SPD (Sozialdemokratische Partei Deutschlands) — Moderate Socialist. Main founding party of the Republic. Still a major force in German politics.

Centre Party (Zentrum) — Catholic Party. Supported parliamentary governments. Often in coalition governments but moved to the right after 1922.

The DDP (DeutschDemokratische Partei) — Middle-class, non-Catholic, liberals. Committed to Parliamentary government. Saw need for social change. Offshoot of old National Liberal Party.

The DVP [Deutsche Volkspartei (German People's Party)] — Members of the old National Liberal Party who had accepted annexationist aims during the Great War. Unenthusiastic about the Republic. Party of big business. Led by Gustav Stresemann.

Right-Wing Enemies of the Republic

The DNVP [Deutschnational Volkspartei (German National People's Party)] — Conservatives. Very right-wing and totally opposed to the Republic. Patriotic with racial tendencies. Party of the landowners. Led by Hugenburg in 1932.

The NSDAP [Nationalsozialistische Deutsche Arbeiter Partei (National Socialist German Workers' Party)] — The Nazi Party. Openly hostile to Parliamentary democracy and the Republic. Authoritarian, 'patriotic', racist.

Left-Wing Opponents of the Republic

The USPD [Unabhangige Sozialdemokratische Partei Deutschlands (Independent Socialists)] — Splinter of old SPD favouring a more radical revolution in 1918-19. Right wing of party eventually re-joined SPD. Left wing joined Communists.

The KPD (Kommunistische Partie Deutschlands) — Marxist/communist. Emerged from the Luxemburg-Liebknecht 'Gruppe Internationale'. Hated Republic which it never forgave for the suppression of the Spartacist revolt.

their mutual loathing of each other, often collaborated in the Reichstag to paralyse its proceedings. In the streets their paramilitaries - the SA and the Communist Rotfrontkampferbund (Red Front Fighters) - fought pitched battles. Germany, once the most orderly of countries, was disintegrating. In 1932 Brüning was replaced by Franz von Papen and then by General Kurt von Schleicher. Neither had anything new to offer or any real solution to the problems. Both continued to rule by decree. By 1932 the Nazis had become a force to be reckoned with. Hitler contested the Presidential elections in April 1932. The decisive result in the second ballot was:

- Field Marshall Paul von
  Benechendorff Hindenburg   19.4 million
- Adolf Hitler   13.4 million
- Ernst Thalmann (KPD)   3.7 million

Hitler had done very well against one of Germany's national heroes.

In the Reichstag elections of July, the Nazis got more votes than any other party. The 37.3% was the largest vote they ever polled in a comparatively open, fair and free election. It was obvious that, as the largest party in the Reichstag, no government could run without their cooperation. Schleicher and Papen offered Hitler the position of Vice Chancellor in a coalition government, an offer which he declined demanding much greater power and many more cabinet positions for Nazis. He stood his ground despite a lecture on duty from Hindenburg. Since no viable government could be formed new elections had to be called.

The November poll saw the Nazi vote drop to 33.1% - unemployment had also been falling. Some felt that Nazi support had peaked but they were still by far the biggest party. Attempts to run a government without them failed. Again Papen was obliged to talk to Hitler who, by this time, was worried about losing more votes. A deal was struck. Hitler was to become Chancellor, and Papen Vice Chancellor, with only two other Nazis in the cabinet.

Papen felt that he would be able to manipulate the ex-corporal who, for all his skills as a rabble rouser, had no experience of running a government. The Nazis would also have to share the blame for the mess Germany found herself in and would inevitably lose votes. It did not turn out like that!

"To his friends, von Papen boasted that he had succeeded where Schleicher and Brüning had failed, in securing the leader of the largest party in Germany to provide the mass support which the conservatives and Nationalists could never win for themselves. And he had done this, von Papen added, without giving away anything that mattered: Hitler might be Chancellor, but it was he as Vice Chancellor who had the confidence of the President, and the conservatives and Nationalists who had the majority in the cabinet. To those who questioned whether there were not dangers ahead, he replied: 'No danger at all. We've hired him for our act.' "

(Alan Bullock *Hitler and Stalin. Parallel Lives* p 283)

The Source of Nazi Votes					
Parties	1924	1928	1930	1932 (July)	1932 (Nov.)
Working-class parties (SPD & KPD)	10.5	12.3	13.0	13.1	13.1
Middle-class parties (Protestant)	13.2	12.9	10.3	4.0	5.3
Centre Party (Catholic)	4.1	3.7	4.1	4.5	4.2
NSDAP (NAZIS)	0.9	0.8	6.4	13.7	11.7

Table 10.2 (Source: G Barraclough *Factors in German History* Reproduced in JCG Rohl *From Bismarck to Hitler*)

Hitler, the Nazi, was sworn in by President Hindenburg and assumed power that he did not relinquish until his death twelve years later.

Explaining Nazi Electoral Success
Why had the Nazis been so successful in attracting votes? A study of their methods is a revealing exercise.

Widespread Appeal
Unlike other parties the Nazis did not restrict their appeal to one social class.

- To the workers they promised jobs and a fairer share of national wealth. This represented the socialist side of National Socialism which was largely forgotten when Hitler came to power.

- To German farmers faced with bankruptcy and the loss of their land, they promised to get the bank Jews off their backs and also to pay them fair prices for their produce. The Nazis did well in rural parts of North Germany in the 1932 elections.

- To the army they promised to overturn Versailles and begin rearmament.

- To businessmen they promised to destroy communism and to curb trade union power. This won Hitler the support of Alfred Hugenburg and the financial help of a group of right-wing politicians and wealthy men known as the Harzburg Front. Money began to pour into the Party. Hugenburg, an ex-director of the Krupp steel company, owned several newspapers and a chain of cinemas. He was able to guarantee Hitler very favourable news exposure. His influence did not end here as he was also the leader of the DNVP, the Conservative Nationalists.

- To the middle classes, who had suffered from the inflation of 1923 and the Great Depression he offered a scapegoat in the bank Jews whose destruction, he claimed, would restore prosperity to Germany's Mittelstand - the middle class. Many small shopkeepers had been losing business to new department stores. These he castigated as Jewish monopolies, guilty of unfair trading. The difficulties experienced by Jewish small-scale traders were conveniently ignored.

Many civil servants, teachers and middle-class professional

people voted Nazi. They saw themselves as the Mittelstand, the middle of society and its healthy core. They saw themselves as upholding true German values against communism and anarchy emanating from the workers, and decadence and moral corruption from the very rich and the aristocracy. They were attracted to the Nazis' promise to create a society in which distinctions based on birth and wealth would be replaced by those based only on merit.

As in Britain in the late 1980s and early 90s, unemployment in Germany had hit hard at the young and school leavers. To young people who had never had a job, the Nazis offered hope in place of despair. Those who had never been employed had not experienced trade union influence and consequently rejected the socialist loyalties of their parents and voted Nazi.

These factions often had conflicting interests, but failed to realise that the Nazis could not satisfy the demands of all the groups they promised to help.

> "Civil servants - for instance - wanted high salaries, whereas farmers and craftsmen resented the high taxes needed to pay for them ... farmers wanted agricultural protection to ensure high food prices, whereas self-employed artisans in the towns wanted low food prices."
> (J Noakes *Nazi Voters* in *History Today* August 1980)

While the Nazis promised to cure the ills of most sections of society they were, of necessity, vague about the details of how they would achieve their miracles. Table 10.2 gives some idea of where the Nazis were most effective in gaining votes.

Effective Propaganda

The Nazis delivered their message with impressive skill. Although a skilled propagandist himself, Hitler delegated responsibility for propaganda to Dr Josef Goebbels, the Party's Berlin boss. Goebbels, a cripple, was highly intelligent and a clever speaker. He has been described as the most loyal of all the Nazis to Hitler. It was Goebbels who said, "If you tell a lie, tell a big lie and tell it often. People will believe you." This became the essence of Nazi propaganda and won the votes of many social groups with widely conflicting interests.

Effective Electioneering

Hitler was convinced of the persuasive powers of the spoken word. In his view the masses were less likely to be swayed by carefully argued books and newspaper articles. His ability to work a crowd, his sense of timing, his feel for their mood cannot be doubted. He was the Nazi Party's greatest electoral asset and during the crucial elections of 1932 he seized the opportunities offered by a new mode of travel, air transport, to appear at election meetings all over the country. The aircraft was paid for by his wealthy supporters in big business. The Nazi appeal, as always, was to people's prejudices and emotions and not to their reason. Military-style brass bands were always a big feature of Nazi meetings and mass rallies. Music has a well-known power to arouse the emotions. At the start of an open air meeting the band would be there pumping out stirring patriotic music. The SA would parade, their uniforms giving an impression of glamour, order and power. Hitler would be late deliberately. Expectation and tension would build and then the Führer would appear and euphoria would take over. Some of those who heard him speak later recalled that after a meeting they felt elated and aroused but could not remember what he had said. For the next week the edited highlights would be shown in cinema newsreels around Germany, courtesy of Alfred Hugenburg. Since there was no television in the thirties most families went to the cinema at least once a week. The Nazis were among the first to realise the tremendous persuasive powers of this medium.

Effective Paramilitary Organisation

The elections of 1932 were very violent affairs, with the death toll running into hundreds. In Hamburg, communists fired from the rooftops into Nazi marchers. Nineteen died and about three hundred were injured. The SA, however, was more than able to hold its own and the Nazis were the outright winners in the competition to disrupt the meetings of rivals and intimidate, maim or kill their supporters.

Weakness of the Weimar Republic

Finally, the political and economic weakness of the Weimar Republic made Hitler's success possible.

11 The Nazi Dictatorship in Germany under Hitler

When Hitler took office as Chancellor on 30 January 1933, he was merely the head of another shaky coalition, albeit the first to command a majority in the Reichstag since 1930. Of the twelve cabinet members only two ministers and the Chancellor were Nazis. At this stage he still needed the support of the Reichstag and could be dismissed by the President if he failed in his task. Democratic government was not quite dead in January 1933. In the months that followed, Hitler worked hard to achieve 'Machtergreifung' - the seizure of power - and to achieve absolute personal dictatorship. The regime which he established was not the rule of a government or a party but the personal rule of one man. Once in power Hitler acted quickly and decisively to strengthen his personal authority and establish a totalitarian dictatorship. (A totalitarian regime is one in which the government has total power and attempts to control all aspects of the people's lives.)

STEPS TO DICTATORSHIP

Step 1 - The Reichstag Eliminated

Hitler had no intention of sharing power with anyone else, least of all with an elected Reichstag which he despised. He knew, however, that German respect for law and procedure was such that he had to get rid of it in a way which appeared legal, and that he would need a two-thirds majority in the Reichstag to change the constitution. Another election was called for March.

This election would be different. Although a semblance of legality would be preserved, the rules would be drastically bent to favour the Nazis and crucial agencies of the state would intervene on their behalf.

Hermann Göring, ex-air ace of the Great War and one of the Party's first members, was one of only three Nazis in a cabinet of thirteen. He was Minister without Portfolio. He had no department but he did have another job, Minister of the Interior of the State of Prussia. That gave him control of a police force that covered two-thirds of Germany. Any illusions that he would be controlled by the Minister President of Prussia, Vice Chancellor Papen, were soon dispelled. Göring issued his orders:

"The police have at all costs to avoid anything suggesting hostility to the SA or SS."

Hitler and Hindenburg

"It is the business of the police to abet every form of National Propaganda."

"The police are to show no mercy to the activities of organisations hostile to the state." (ie. communists or socialists)

"Police officers who use fire-arms in the execution of their duty will benefit from my protection. Those who fail in their duty will be punished ..."
(Heiden *History of National Socialism* p 216 Quoted in Alan Bullock *Hitler, a Study in Tyranny*)

The SA and SS were then given the status of an 'auxiliary police force' and the full power of the state turned against the anti-Nazi parties whose supporters were liable to be beaten into a pulp or arrested. Not surprisingly, little was heard of their viewpoint during the election. It was at this time that Göring established the notorious Gestapo, the Prussian State Secret Police. Later they were amalgamated with Himmler's SD, the SS Security Service.

The Reichstag Fire

On 27 February 1933 the Reichstag building mysteriously burned down. A young Dutch Communist of questionable sanity, Marinus van der Lubbe, got the blame and was executed for it. There are those who believe that the SA set fire to the place and that van der Lubbe was effectively framed. The fire certainly played into Hitler's hands. Many Germans accepted his claims of a Communist conspiracy against the state. President Hindenburg certainly did and signed the most significant of all the emergency decrees - the one which gave the most widespread powers. Marxist newspapers were closed down and anti-Nazis, especially Communists, were locked up. This 'Decree for the Protection of the People and the State' remained in force throughout the period of Hitler's Reich. It gave power to

- arrest "enemies of the state."
- suspend the rights of free speech and assembly.
- censor newspapers.
- take over the powers of the Länder (states) in an emergency.

The Election, March 1933

Klaus Hildebrand has written:

"the last 'semi-free' elections in Germany took place in this climate of legalised insecurity and open terrorism, exercised in the first instance against the Communist Party (KPD). The two parties of the left, the communists and the social democrats (SPD), were already prevented from taking part on a regular footing. Yet even in these elections, which were illegal by the standards of European parliamentary democracy, the Nazis only gained 43.9% of votes. Thus the Party was never returned to power by a majority of the German people."
(K Hildebrand *The Third Reich* p 5)

The Nazis were dependent on their allies like the DNVP (Nationalists) for a Reichstag majority. However, when the emergency decree was used to ban the Communist Party and arrest their 81 deputies, the situation was very much more favourable.

The Enabling Act. (Law for Removing the Distress of the People and the Reich)

Hitler then proposed that he should be allowed to govern for four years without further reference to the Reichstag. "You gave the other parties 13 years, now give me 4." As the deputies arrived at the Kroll Opera House for the special session, the route to the entrance was lined by the black uniformed SS. Despite this obvious threat to anyone who voted 'No' the SPD held out, but with 26 of their members 'missing' they no longer had the votes to hold back the Nazi tide. The Catholic Centre Party voted 'yes', perhaps intimidated into acquiescence or perhaps merely following their custom of cooperation. They had participated in most Weimar coalitions. Of this grim period in German History, Göring said at his trial as a war criminal in 1946:

"It was understood by all of us that as soon as we had come into power we must hold that power under all circumstances. We did not want power ... for its own sake, but we needed ... (it) to make Germany free and great. We did not want to leave this any more to chance, elections and parliamentary majorities, but we wanted to carry out the task to which we considered ourselves called."

Does this illustrate any fundamental differences between Nazism and a democratic ideology ?

Step 2 - The Elimination of All Remaining Political Opposition

A One-Party State.

Hitler banned not only the KPD but also the SPD. Other parties gave up and dissolved themselves. A law issued in July 1933 declared the NSDAP to be the only party in the Reich.

Trade Unions

Totalitarian by nature, the Nazi Party would allow no organisation to exist independently of itself to contest its authority. In May 1933 all Trade Unions were banned. The Nazis claimed their regime to be a truly National Government, so "divisive organisations, setting Germans against Germans," were no longer acceptable. All workers and employers now belonged to the Nazi Labour Front under Robert Ley. strikes were outlawed, contrary to national interests, and the Labour Front was empowered to fix wage levels. Union officials who objected were sent off to concentration camps. Most people got the message and were silent.

One of post war Germany's most distinguished historians has written:

"What united both ... Hitler and the old elites ... was their commitment to the national power-state at home and abroad ... In the organised subordination of the people to the holders of political power, and in bellicose assertiveness and expansion, there was a harking back to the traditions of Imperial Germany ... With the destruction of the parties and trade unions and the creation of a totalitarian state-directed union in the 'German Labour Front', objectives were attained that

The arrest of communists, Berlin 1933

Bismarck had striven in vain to realise ... Unquestionably, those business magnates who supported National Socialism before 1933 did so precisely for the sake of the goals realised immediately following the change of government - elimination of the trade unions and the political labour movement, abolition of the parliamentary system of government, rearmament - all of which were intended to bring ... their businesses onto the profit side of the ledger, at the cost of a muzzled working class."

(Fritz Fischer *From Kaiserreich to Third Reich* p82-83)

Step 3 - Elimination of Opposition within the Party

The Night of the Long Knives
Within the Nazi Party there were those who did not see it purely as the personal tool of Adolf Hitler. Many of them expected the socialist aspect of National Socialism to be implemented, a hope which was especially strong in the SA. The storm troopers expected their services on the streets to be rewarded with good jobs in government and industry but

"now they grumbled, the Nazis had gone respectable, and many who had secured a Party card only the day before were allowed to keep their old jobs, while deserving Alte Kämpfer (old warriors) were left in the streets. With characteristically elegant language the SA began to talk of clearing out the pigsty, and driving a few of the greedy swine from the trough."

(Alan Bullock *Hitler, A Study in Tyranny* p 284)

This embarrassed Hitler as he still needed the support of

wealthy industrialists with no use for SA thugs. Röhm also wanted the army and SA united under his leadership. Again this was awkward as Hitler needed the support of the army for his foreign policy. The generals did not want Röhm as their commander. The solution was simple and revealed much about Hitler's personality.

On the night of 30 June 1934, the SS rounded up and shot perhaps as many as 400 people. 77 deaths were later admitted. Röhm was the most prominent Nazi victim. In the late twenties he had left Germany and helped train the Bolivian army. When Nazi fortunes revived, Hitler had asked him to return to lead the SA. On the night of the long knives he got his reward from a man who had only recently thanked him for his loyalty and service. Among the other victims were:

- General von Schleicher who had been Chancellor in 1932.
- Gregor Strasser, a left-wing Nazi who had fallen out with Hitler in 1926.
- A group of Silesian Jews; shot to amuse the local SS.
- Catholic political and youth leaders.
- Dr Willi Schmidt, music critic, a case of mistaken identity. They were looking for an SA man of the same name. When her husband's body was returned, with the apologies of the SS, Frau Schmidt was warned not to open the coffin !

The meaning of the slogan 'Ein Volk, ein Reich, ein Führer' (one people, one government, one leader) became clear that night. The authority of Adolf Hitler was to be absolute. All must obey. Hitler *was* the Nazi Party and oppo-

The SS State

In *The Constitutional Law of the Greater German Reich* by Ernst Rudolf Huber, it was stated:

"The Führer combines in his own person the entire supreme authority of the Reich; all public authority both in the State and the Movement stems from the Führer. The correct term for political authority in the people's Reich is therefore not 'the authority of the State' but 'the authority of the Führer' ... The authority of the Führer is total, ... it covers every facet of the life of the people ... The Führer's authority is subject to no checks or controls."
(quoted in Krausnick, Buckheim, Broszat and Jacobsen *Anatomy of the SS State*)

Would you like any individual to have so much authority over you? The means of imposing this authority was the SS , the Schutzstaffeln.

The SS was started in 1925 as an elite bodyguard for Party leaders and for Hitler in particular. At that stage he was uncertain of the loyalty of the SA. In 1929 Heinrich Himmler, a Bavarian, was appointed its leader. He was fanatically loyal to Hitler and shared all of his major prejudices.

Main Functions of the SS in the Third Reich
- To act as bodyguards to Hitler and other members of the Nazi elite.

- To provide the Nazi state's internal security service. Himmler assumed control of the Gestapo (Geheime Staatspolizei), the Prussian State Secret Police founded by Göring. He ran it in conjunction with the SD (Sicherheitsdienst), the SS security police. These sinister, black-uniformed agencies arrested, interrogated and often tortured and murdered suspected opponents of the regime.

- To guard concentration camps. This was the task of the Deaths-Head units. (Totenkopfverbande)

- To provide politically motivated elite troops to fight alongside the Wehrmacht or regular army. By the end of the war the Waffen-SS had grown to over 700,000 men, many of whom were 'Auslanders' (Germans from outside the prewar borders of the Reich) and non-Germans, especially Latvians, Lithuanians, Estonians and Ukrainians. During the fighting that led to the fall of France in 1940, the Waffen-SS habitually shot French and British prisoners. A Wehrmacht area commander told the Head of an SS Division, "You are a butcher and no soldier."

- To provide special task force groups, Einsatzgruppen, to control occupied areas in wartime and to eliminate opposition and resistance groups.

- To take charge of the programme of genocide directed against the Jews after the Wannsee Conference in 1942.

- To set an example of 'racial purity' and provide Germany with a ruling Aryan elite. An SS man wanting to get married had to get a certificate to say that his intended bride was of suitable Nordic stock.

Hitler gave the SS the motto 'SS Man. Your honour is loyalty'. They had to swear this oath:

"We swear to you, Adolf Hitler, as Führer and Chancellor of Germany, to be loyal and brave. We vow to you and the superiors appointed by you obedience unto death. So help us God."

Candidates for the SS required to be not only fit and strong but also intelligent. The danger that such a body of men might develop their own independent outlook never materialised. They stayed loyal to Hitler to the bitter end. The SS diversified its operations and became a highly profitable organisation. Its influence became so widespread and it was a law unto itself to such an extent that the Third Reich has been called the SS State.

"... there were tens of thousands of office employees who belonged to the General SS and there were hundreds of high-placed officials who belonged to the Honorary SS... Among the activities of the SS there were offices whose concern was Germanic Archaeology and ancestral research, other offices devoted to forging foreign bank notes, collecting information on alchemy and astrology, institutes for the cultivation of medicinal herbs and wild rubber roots. The SS also controlled a mineral water and a porcelain factory, numerous nightclubs in foreign capitals and a publishing firm
(Gerald Reitlinger *The SS : Alibi of a Nation* . Quoted by GS Graber in *History of the SS*)

The 'final solution' also presented business opportunities. After Jews had been gassed in the extermination camps, their bodies were stripped of valuables.

"The gold fillings from the teeth were melted down and shipped with the other valuables, such as wedding rings and watches, taken from the Jews to the Reichsbank. Under a secret agreement between Himmler and the Nazi president of the Reichsbank, Funk, the loot was deposited to the credit of the SS in an account with the cover name of Max Heiliger."
(Alan Bullock *Hitler, a Study in Tyranny* p701-702)

Concentration camps were usually beside quarries where the inmates slaved to provide the stone needed to build the Autobahnen. After the collapse of Germany, leading members of the SS were able to finance their escapes to South America with the help of funds built up by such enterprises.

sition from within would be treated just as ruthlessly as opposition from outwith the party.

Step 4 - Gleichschaltung (Coordination; literally 'putting into the same gear')

This process began after the night of the long knives. It simply meant that all organs of state were to be integrated into the Nazi Party.

President and Chancellor to Führer
Hindenburg died in August 1934. Hitler declined to take on his role as President, claiming that this would always be associated with the Great War hero Hindenburg. In-stead, he would be known as Führer (leader). In this way he escaped having any limitations placed on his power by a constitution.

The Civil Service
As early as 1933, Hitler had begun to dismiss from the Civil Service Jews and officials felt to be anti-Nazi.

The States
Hitler distrusted local democracy as much as democracy at a national level. State governments could become the focus of opposition to the regime, so they were placed under the control of Nazi Reich governors who also had to watch for signs of insubordination among local Nazis.

Heinrich Himmler : SS Chief

Heinrich Himmler, head of the SS, Minister of the Interior, head of the German Police, accumulated such enormous power that he could easily have deposed Hitler. However,

"It would be utterly foreign to Himmler's nature to stab in the back the man whose creed sanctioned his own ways and turned him, the insignificant, ugly, little man, into the paragon of the race."
(Norman Stone, *Hitler* p 83)

Himmler was so loyal that he stood to attention when speaking to his Führer on the telephone.

"There is nothing in Himmler's background to explain why he should have developed into a monster."
(GS Graber *History of the SS* p 2)

His father was a private tutor who taught Prince Heinrich of Wittelsbach, a member of the Bavarian Royal Family. He seems to have been a decent enough person. His mother was a devout Catholic and thoroughly domesticated. His elder brother was perfectly normal.

Heinrich would have liked to have fought in the Great War but he was a little too young. As a young man

"He abhorred Jews, he could not abide Freemasons, he conveyed a profound hatred of capitalism, almost matched by his intense aversion to Bolshevism. What he was *for* was not so easy to discern."
(GS Graber *History of the SS* p 1)

After the war he trained in agriculture, married a divorcee eight years his senior and wasted her money when he failed as a chicken farmer. Encouraged by Röhm, he joined the Nazis and played a minor part in the unsuccessful beerhall Putsch of 1923. He was destined for greater things.

"The SS was a paradox and in this it reflected the character of its leader. Himmler was a bizarre combination of naive crank, pedantic schoolmaster, and coldly efficient bureaucrat ..."
(J Noakes and G Pridham *Nazism. 1919-1945*. Vol 2 p 490)

Thus, as head of the SS, Himmler ordered the murder of millions of innocent people, yet on the only occasion he witnessed an execution he fainted. He was not a sadist. He simply believed that he was furthering the cause of Germany and humanity by having people killed. Sometimes he ordered the execution of SS men for corruption or unauthorised brutality. He took a close personal interest in his SS men. He once ordered a man with heart problems to stop smoking for two years and issued orders on how porridge was to be eaten in women's homes. Norman Stone wrote:

"The most frightening thing about him, as with other Nazi leaders, including Hitler, was that he never grew up. His whole life was simply the same note repeated over and over again, with increasing shrillness."
(Norman Stone *Hitler* p 83)

Heinrich Himmler committed suicide after his arrest by the British Army on 23 May 1945.

The Churches

A head-on clash with the churches was inevitable since Christian beliefs are the antithesis of Nazism. Hitler was not a religious man. He may even have seen God as a rival for the loyalty of the people. At first he tried to stay on good terms with the various denominations and actually signed a concordat with the Pope in 1933. The churches, however, found that they could not Christianise Nazism and could not help being offended by its violence and paganism. The Catholic Church had its youth organisation closed down and many priests were arrested. Catholic schools became Nazi schools and religious teaching was banned.

An attempt was made in 1933 to coordinate the Protestants into a Reich church under a Nazi bishop. Many pastors joined, but others became increasingly outspoken and ended up in concentration camps. Among these was ex-U-boat skipper, Martin Niemoller, who founded the non-Nazi Confessional Church. Neimoller survived the camps. Many others did not. Some, like Dietrich Bonhoffer, a member of an underground conspiracy to depose Hitler, were murdered by the SS in the closing stages of the Second World War, just as liberation seemed at hand.

The Courts

In democratic states, judges, once appointed, are free from political interference. This independence of the judiciary prevents the government from using the courts to persecute its opponents. It took some time for this freedom to die in Nazi Germany.

- 1933-4 Anti-Nazi and Jewish judges sacked.

- 1934 'Treason' cases were transferred to 'Peoples Courts' under reliable Nazi judges. In these, opponents of the regime could be dealt with, without reference to real law.

- 1935 People could be tried for committing 'Acts Hostile to the National Community' even if they had not violated any existing law. This catch-all measure enabled the Nazis to punish anybody they did not like in an apparently legal and quasi-judicial fashion. It was a direct violation of one of the most important principles of the Rule of Law. Namely, that nobody must be punished unless shown to be guilty of breaking a known law, in a fair trial, before a regular court of the land.

Eventually, judges who were considered to have been too lenient or who had misconducted trials (ie. acquitted the accused) were reprimanded. Hitler sometimes 'corrected' sentences. From 1942 onwards judges whose verdicts did not reflect Nazi ideology could be sacked.

Other Aspects of the Nazi Regime

Youth Policy

Since the Third Reich aspired to total control of all aspects of society, its Youth Policy was regarded as critical. The Nazis knew that they would never win the hearts and minds of many of the older generation. Although they might not admit it publicly, they would remain loyal to the KPD, the SPD or to a church. The young, on the other hand, were the future and could be brought up to be loyal Nazis. Only the Nazi Youth Organisations were permitted. All others, such as the scouts, were either abolished or coordinated.

Hitler greets the Hitler Youth, circa 1935

Boys aged 14-18 were expected to attend the Hitler youth where indoctrination was mixed with entertainment and military training. Total loyalty and obedience to the Führer's will was stressed. The superiority of the master race was taught alongside sport and rifle training. War was glorified and a fiercely competitive ethos reigned. Addressing the Youth of Germany Hitler said:

" ... we ask of you to be hard, German youth, and to make yourselves hard! We cannot use a generation of 'mother's boys', of spoiled children. What we need is boys and girls who can one day become brave men and women. We ask for a hard youth ..."

(N Baynes (Ed.)*The Speeches of Adolf Hitler* p 547)

Older girls could join the League of German Maidens. Like, perhaps, most men at that time, Hitler regarded women as physically and mentally inferior to men. They had, however, an important role as homemakers and mothers, the mothers of the soldiers of Hitler's Reich. Consequently, the League not only pedalled Nazi ideas, but it also ran a programme of physical activities so that the girls would be fit for childbearing. There was also the Hitler equivalent of the Cubs (Jungvolk) and Brownies (Jungmadel) for younger children.

Schools.
Jewish and anti-Nazi teachers were sacked. The rest had to join the Nazi Teachers League. Each school day began with pupils and teachers raising their right arms in the Nazi salute and intoning "Heil Hitler". ('heil' means good health. The other Nazi cry was "Seig! Heil!" 'Seig' means Victory.)

The curriculum was also changed. Nobody dared to record how the teachers felt about the extra work this involved. There was a great deal of PE in preparation for childbearing or war. The History course reflected the Führer's views of the Great War, Versailles and Weimar. Biology, the Nazi science, was used to illustrate the evolution of the Aryan master race. Geography prepared children psychologically for another defensive war against brutal, encircling enemies, France and Russia.

THE NAZI ECONOMY

One of the most pervasive myths about Nazi Germany was that it was a huge economic success. Certainly, under Hitler, unemployment fell rapidly.

How, then, did the Nazi economy function and how can the success which it did enjoy be explained? It should be remembered that the great depression reached its trough, worldwide, in 1932. When Hitler came to power unemployment had already started to fall, and with it the Nazi vote. It would have continued to fall without the Third Reich.

The Nazi economy was directed by Dr Hjalmar Schacht, a sharp-minded banker and financial wizard. He pursued a policy of government spending on public works of the type advocated in Britain by the economist JM Keynes and followed by Mussolini in Italy, Roosevelt in the USA and, to a lesser extent, Britain's National Government.

Economic Performance under Hitler

German Unemployment (000)

	January	July		January	July
1932	6.042	5.392	**1936**	2.520	1.170
1933	6.014	4.464	**1937**	1.853	0.563
1934	3.773	2.426	**1938**	1.052	0.218
1935	2.974	1.754	**1939**	0.302	0.038

Table 11.1

Consumption in German Working-Class Families (1927 & 1937)

	1927	1937	% change
Rye bread (kg)	262.9	316.1	+20.2
Wheat bread (kg)	55.2	30.8	-44.2
Meat and meat products (kg)	133.7	109.2	-18.3
Bacon (kg)	9.5	8.5	-10.5
Milk (litres)	427.8	367.2	-14.2
Cheese (kg)	13.0	14.5	+11.5
Eggs (number)	404	237	-41.3
Fish (kg)	21.8	20.4	-6.4
Vegetables (kg)	117.2	109.6	-6.5
Potatoes (kg)	499.5	519.8	+4.1
Sugar (kg)	47.2	45.0	-4.7
Tropical fruit (kg)	9.7	6.1	-37.1
Beer (litres)	76.5	31.6	-58.7

(Includes family budgets of low-paid civil servants and salaried workers)

Table 11.2

Real Wages in Germany (1928-1938)

	Real wages*	Money wages*	Real earnings#	Wages as % of NI	Private Consumption as % of NI
1928	110	168	106	62	71
1930	122	180	114	-	-
1931	125	171	106	-	-
1932	120	144	91	64	83
1933	119	140	87	63	81
1934	116	140	88	62	76
1935	114	140	91	61	71
1936	112	140	93	59	64
1937	112	140	96	58	62
1938	112	141	101	57	59

Table 11.3

* base year 1913/14 = 100   # base year 1925/6 = 100
Real wages are wages corrected to allow for inflation.
Money wages are calculated on the actual wages paid.
Real earnings include wages, salaries, pensions and interest on savings etc.
NI = National Incomes , the sum of all incomes in Germany

Comparative Economic Performance 1913-1938 (1913 = 100)

	Industrial Output	Output per man hour	Real Wages	Annual growth rate (%)
USA	164	208	153	2.9
Sweden	231	143	150	2.2
Italy	196	165	na	1.3
UK	139	167	133	1.7
Germany	144	137	109	1.2
France	119	178	128	0.7

Table 11.4

Source: Tables 11.2, 11.3, 11.4 RJ Overy *The Nazi Economic Recovery*

A gymnastics class organised by the KdF in Berlin, 1937

Hitler was excited by the possibilities of motor transport. He did not drive himself, but he liked to be driven fast in his supercharged Mercedes. Large sums were spent creating a network of Autobahnen (motorways) almost thirty years before the M1 opened in England. Speaking in 1938 Hitler claimed:

"... 1500 miles are under construction. The system of Autobahnen is the largest building undertaking in the world and already, with a displacement of 240 million cubic metres of earth, by far exceeds the building achievement of the Panama Canal." ... "Between 1934 and 1937 approximately 6,000 miles of highway were widened" ... "Approximately 3,400 bridges were built in connection with the Autobahnen."
(N Baynes (Ed.)*The Speeches of Adolf Hitler* p 961)

Money also went into railways and workers' housing. In the same speech Hitler claimed:

"In 1937 340,000 dwellings were constructed, this being more than double the figure for 1932." "Altogether since the National Socialist assumption of power over 1,400,000 dwellings have been made available on the housing market."

The money which was needed but could not be borrowed was simply printed. The resulting inflation never really got out of control since wages were not allowed to rise. The Nazi Labour Front saw to this. More people were employed, but most working-class families found their living standards falling slightly. Under Hitler German workers drank less beer, but not for reasons of health.

As German rearmament got under way more and more men were employed in shipyards, aircraft factories and engineering works. This was inflationary and caused imports to rise sharply since the industries involved were paying men but producing nothing which wage earners might buy. Schacht was concerned that the economy was overheating. He protested and was dismissed.

Nazi economic policy was neither as original nor as successful as its admirers claimed. But for the outbreak of war they would have been forced to come to terms with rising inflation and a trade deficit. Wartime emergency measures and restrictions enabled them to duck these issues.

Kraft durch Freude (KdF) Strength through Joy.

To compensate for the stagnation of living standards, the KdF organisation was created to enhance the quality of life. Loyal workers could take their families to Nazi Holiday Camps, which were totally different from those reserved for Jews and dissidents. Perhaps they even could go on a cruise on a luxury ship to the Norwegian fjords or the Mediterranean at very heavily subsidised prices. KdF also subsidised theatres and sports facilities. Finally, when the Führer decided that the masses should share his pleasure in motoring, Dr Ferdinand Porche was ordered to design a people's car. The strange little vehicle which emerged, with its characteristic flat four, horizontally opposed, air cooled engine has entered motoring legend as the VolksWagen beetle. The prototype appeared in 1935 and the first production models in 1938, but they were never made in large enough numbers to do more than help sustain the belief that Nazism was working for ordinary people. During the war they were used as staff cars and some were disguised as tanks and used with great imagination by Rommel in the Western Desert to persuade the British to retreat. However, according to reports compiled by SPD contacts inside Germany, the people's car did have a number of useful effects

"For a large number of Germans the announcement of the People's Car came as a pleasant surprise ... For a long time the KdF Car was a big talking point among all classes ... The leadership of the Third Reich has killed several birds with one stone. In the first place, it removes for a period of several years money from the German consumer which he would otherwise spend on goods which cannot be supplied. Secondly ... they have achieved a clever diversionary tactic in the sphere of domestic politics. This car psychosis, which has been cleverly introduced by the Propaganda Ministry, keeps the masses from becoming preoccupied with a depressing situation. Hitler has acquired domestic political credit with the car savers until the delivery of the car. For ... while they are saving up for a particular commodity, people are willing to make quite a lot of sacrifices."
(J Noakes and G Pridham (Ed.)*Nazism 1919-1945* vol 2 doc 240)

GERMAN OPPOSITION TO HITLER

Hans Rothfels was badly wounded fighting in the Kaiser's army in the Great War. During the Weimar Republic he became a Professor of History but had to leave Germany in the thirties because of his opposition to the Nazis. He worked at Oxford University and in the USA before going home on Hitler's death. In his book, *The German Opposition to Hitler*, he wrote of:

"... the thesis that prevailed throughout the war and at its conclusion, at least in former enemy countries, to the effect that no opposition to Hitler worth speaking of existed. The conviction existed that as a political nation the Germans differed from other peoples, for they had, it was believed, voluntarily associated themselves with or submitted out of cowardice to the tyrannical rule of criminals, either through innate wickedness, or from the acquired habit of blind obedience, or under the influence of some baneful philosophy ... Opposition only began, it was believed, when, confronted with defeat, the 'Prussian Generals' attempted to save their own lives and preserve the General Staff for a third world war."

Rothfels clearly did not share this view. He pointed out that the Nazis never polled more than 37% of the vote in a fair and free election (July 1932) and that in the election of March 1933 they still only managed 44% despite massive intimidation and the hysteria whipped up in the wake of the Reichstag fire. Clearly, at this stage, most Germans opposed Hitler even though the opposition was so hopelessly divided as to be completely ineffective. Did they later come to love their Führer? One view is that:

"Although the regime deployed a formidable apparatus of terror, it is clear that it was also based on a large measure of consent from broad sections of the population."
(J Noakes and G Pridham *Nazism 1919-1945*, Vol 2 p 570)

It is however a little difficult to quantify the extent to which Germans accepted or supported the regime after November 1932.

"... in trying to understand what Germans really felt during these years the historian is faced with serious problems. Not only were there no opinion polls but it was impossible for people to express their views in public with any freedom: the results of elections and plebiscites were rigged; the media were strictly controlled ... In short, an independent public opinion did not exist in the Third Reich."
(J Noakes and G Pridham *Nazism 1919-1945*, Vol 2 p 568)

The Nazis, of course, accepted no political opposition. With the exceptions of the SPD and the KPD all the parties went into voluntary liquidation soon after the Enabling Act was passed. The SPD and the KPD went underground. The SPD organisation in exile received regular reports from its agents in Germany. A contact man in Westphalia reported in 1936:

"We have no idea what is going on in the world ... A large section of the population no longer reads a newspaper. Basically, the population is indifferent to what is in the papers. It is not always the same but, in people's opinion, it is often untrue. The Nazi papers are no longer read because in the long run one cannot force people and because ... the people lack the means to subscribe to a paper. Finally 80% have no inward connection with the National Socialists."
(J Noakes and G Pridham *Nazism 1919-1945*, Vol 2 p 576)

Rothfels divided Germans into four categories; Nazis, nominal Nazis, non-Nazis and anti-Nazis. He pointed out that:
"When the American Military Government checked over one million applicants for employment in the US zone (after the war), it was found that in 50% of cases there was 'no evidence of Nazi activity' "

It was not easy being an opponent of Hitler's regime. In 1943 the Gestapo had a strength of 40,000 men. The SD had 3,000 full-time officials and 50,000 part-time agents, mainly spies in factories and public places. Everywhere there were paid informers ready to denounce any expression of hostility to the government. They seem to have been busy since it is estimated that between 750,000 and 1,200,000 Germans passed through the concentration camps and there were 12,000 political executions.

"The German opposition to Hitler was not only numerically broader than has often been conceded, but was much more widespread than could have been expected in conditions of terror."
(Hans Rothfels *The German Opposition to Hitler* p 153)

Sadly those who paid the penalties for opposing the Nazis often received scant sympathy abroad, where they were later criticised for being ineffective.

"When the 'Brown Book of the Hitler Terror' which sought to draw attention to these misdeeds, was published by Alfred Knopf in New York, it was

Nazis parade at a Nuremburg Rally

reviewed in the New York Times by ... the former American Ambassador to Berlin, James W Gerard. Confronted with the revelations contained in the book he thought it proper to write: 'Hitler is doing much for Germany, his unification of the Germans, his destruction of Communism, his training of the young, his creation of a Spartan State animated by patriotism, his curbing of parliamentary government, so unsuited to the German character, his protection of the rights of private property are all good.' "
(Hans Rothfels *The German Opposition to Hitler* p 18)

Emigration

Many anti-Nazis fled the country one step ahead of arrest by the Gestapo. Willy Brandt was one of these. An SPD man, he continued to organise resistance in exile. He returned to West Germany after the war and was elected Mayor of West Berlin and later Chancellor of the Federal Republic. Clearly he was not regarded as a traitor for his anti-Nazi past. Edward Heath collaborated with him to produce the Brandt Report on how the problems of global poverty should be tackled. Bertolt Brecht, the Bavarian communist playwright, was another émigré. After working in the USA he returned to found the Berliner Ensemble Theatre Company.

Types of Resistance

Opposition could, of course, take many forms. Resistance by political and religious groups have already been mentioned in this book. The following tale of defiance comes from *The Past is Myself* by Christabel Bielenberg, an English girl who married a young, liberal, German lawyer.

" ... it happened a full year after Hitler had decreed that all the Jews still living in Germany must wear the star of David ... sewn on the lapel of their coats ... 'Submarines' they were called, those Jews who at the time removed their stars and went underground, surfacing here, there or anywhere, where they might hope to find refuge. They had no ration cards and, every week, Ilse Liedke went round her friends collecting spare food coupons, which were becoming more and more difficult to provide. She had a blonde with her that morning; rather extra blonde who ... seemed unwilling to come into the house. Ilse, too, seemed satisfied that her companion should stay outside and, after glancing at our telephone to see that it was not plugged in, she explained why. The woman was a Jewess."

Frau Dr Bielenberg took the risk of providing the Jewess and her husband with a few days sanctuary before they were moved to a safer place. Ilse, Christabel and their families could all have been sent to concentration camps for these actions. There were many Ilses and many Christabels.

On 20 July 1944 Colonel Klaus von Stauffenberg entered the Führer's bunker in Berlin. He placed his briefcase under the heavy oak table near where Hitler would stand and then left the room. At 12.42 there was a massive blast. Four men died. Hitler's hair was set on fire, one arm was temporarily paralysed and his ear drums damaged. His right trouser leg was ripped off and his leg badly burned. He survived. This attempt on his life was the final achievement of a resistance group called *The Kreisau Circle*.

The Kreisau Circle

This, the most famous of all the opposition groups, centred on Graf Helmuth von Moltke, a member of one of Prussia's most distinguished families. It contained people from widely different backgrounds and outlooks and often met at Moltke's home at Kreisau in Silesia. It contained military men like Stauffenberg who, for some time, had been convinced that Hitler was leading Germany to military ruin and who was also troubled by the human rights issue in Nazi Germany. There were lawyers such as Adam von Trott zu Soll, Carl Langbehn and Peter Bielenberg, who were outraged by the Nazi brutality and their contempt for the rule of law. Trott worked in the German Foreign Office and went to Britain in 1939 and to the USA in the early stages of the war to try to enlist foreign help and support. There were socialists, trade unionists, Christians and a hard core of liberal aristocrats, such as von Moltke himself.

Stauffenberg provided a link with a more conservative opposition group which included General Ludwig Beck, Carl Goerdeler, the Mayor of Leipzig, and Ulrich von Hassell, a senior diplomat. Beck was involved in many conspiracies to get rid of Hitler between 1938 and 1944. Goerdeler was to have become Chancellor if the plot to kill Hitler had succeeded. This group favoured a return to the sort of autocratic Germany of the Bismarck era, but with toleration of minorities and the rule of law. They saw the assassination of Hitler as a necessary first step. As the war progressed, they established stronger links with the Kreisau Circle.

The members of the Kreisau Circle spent much time discussing the type of Germany they wanted in place of Nazism because they were worried about the dangers of overthrowing the regime without having a clear idea of what should replace it. They seem to have favoured a sort of Christian-socialist democratic state and even looked beyond that to some form of European Union. Rothfels quotes a letter by Moltke to a friend:

"We can only expect to persuade our people to overthrow this regime of terror and frightfulness if we are able to point to a goal beyond the paralysing and hopeless immediate future ... For us, Europe after the war is less a problem of frontiers and soldiers, of top-heavy organisations and grandiose planning. The real question which will face postwar Europe is how the picture of man can be restored in the hearts of his fellow citizens. But this is a question of religion and education, of the organic connection between occupation and family, of the proper relationship between responsibility and rights."

The Gestapo had already arrested Langbehn and Moltke when Stauffenberg made his attempt on Hitler's life. He knew that time was running out. Stauffenberg has been criticised as

"A super-Prussian, a soldier through and through to whom the salvation of the Fatherland and the salvation of the Wehrmacht were synonymous."
(Hans Bernd Gisevius *To the Bitter End* paraphrased in Rothfels, p123)

Rothfels rejects this idea claiming that

"... like the other men in the Kreisau Circle, Stauffenberg lived rather in a universal than a military or nationalistic perspective. His thoughts and plans were directed to the liberation of all peoples living under a tryrannical regime ..."

Evidence remains that Stauffenberg had presented the British with peace proposals to be implemented after Hitler's removal. He expected the restoration of Germany's 1914 frontiers in the East, effectively killing Poland. He also wanted to retain Austria and the Sudetenland, and to acquire the South Tyrol. Alsace-Lorraine would become autonomous. To some this seems outrageous, to others it is merely the belated implementation of Woodrow Wilson's sacred doctrine of self-determination. Stauffenberg was not a socialist. He wrote:

"We desire a new order that makes all Germans the bearer of the state and guarantees them law and justice; but we despise the lie of equality and bow before the ranks created by nature... We desire leaders ... drawn from all ranks of the people ..."
(Quoted by FL Carsten and included in JCG Rohl *From Bismarck to Hitler* p165)

It is easy for those who did not run the risks to criticise the German resistance to Hitler for not having acted sooner, or more effectively or for different motives. The critics did not have to face the Gestapo. Unlike Adam von Trott they were not going to end up hanging by piano wire from a meat hook, nor were they going to be shot like Stauffenberg.

MASTER RACE AND UNTERMENSCHEN

The chance to demonstrate the superiority of the Herrenvolk and to deal with the Jews were two of the most appealing prospects which power offered Hitler.

Persecution of the Jews was not a new phenomenon in Europe - even here Hitler was far from original. It was official government policy in early twentieth century Russia to force one-third of Russia's Jewry into exile and to murder another third. Anti-semitism had died down in Germany in the 19th and early 20th centuries. It was, however, central to the Nazi ideology, although some might protest that ideology is too grand a title for Hitler's 'weltanschauung' (world philosophy), preferring to view it as a sordid catalogue of prejudices and grievances.

In 1933 all Jews were expelled from the civil service, sacked as teachers and driven out of the news media. Boycotts of Jewish shops and businesses were organised. Anti-semitism was taught in schools, where Jewish children were humiliated in front of their classmates. Richard Grünberger has pointed out that economic persecution was patchy:

"... the weeding-out of Jews from different sectors of the economy proceeded at a markedly disparate pace. Jewish academics, civil servants, lawyers and intellectuals were eliminated within weeks of the

seizure of power, whereas doctors, economic journalists and technicians enjoyed a period of grace. Jewish entrepreneurs, on the other hand, were, on occasions, actually prevented from liquidating their businesses since this might harm the government's drive to full employment, while Jewish employees... suffered harassment and instant dismissal. Despite boycotts, many Jewish shopkeepers managed to stay in business until 1938, a year in which some of them were actually beginning to experience boom conditions."
(Richard Grünberger *A Social History of the Third Reich* p575)

The 1935 Nuremberg Laws (Law for the Protection of German Blood and Honour) denied German citizenship to Jews and made it illegal for them to marry aryans. Couples taking their marriage vows were asked, "Are you both of Aryan blood?" This question is said to have annoyed the Führer when he married his girlfriend, Eva Braun, on the last full day of their lives. Jewish doctors were not to treat Aryans and young German women were not to work for Jews as domestic servants in case they were seduced !

According to Grünberger:

"Jews living in small towns and villages were subject to window smashing and physical assault, sometimes culminating in murder. This made them seek the anonymity (of) large centres like Frankfurt and Berlin ... Country areas tended to be more anti-semitic than urban ones ... Berlin and Hamburg, Germany's only towns with populations exceeding 1 million, were also the least anti-semitic ... They were less turned in on themselves than smaller centres which did not have comparable segments of Western-minded bourgeois and Marxist influenced workers ... Catholic areas were marginally less prone to anti-semitism than Protestant ones." (Catholic Austria and the Sudetenland were important exceptions to this.)
(Richard Grünberger *A Social History of the Third Reich* p575-576)

On the night of 9 to 10 November 1938 Goebbels set the SA loose to burn synagogues and Jewish houses, wreck shops and murder ninety people. This event is known as *Kristallnacht*, the night of broken glass. A Polish Jew had shot a German diplomat in Paris. Much worse was to come.

The Final Solution to the Jewish Problem
The decision to exterminate the entire Jewish population of Germany and Europe was not taken until the Third Reich had been in existence for over eight years. Initially the aim was different. A Nazi propaganda book for schools, published in 1940, records:

"Order 10 of the State Citizenship Laws; all Jewish organisations are incorporated into 'Reichs-vereinigungen der Juden Deutschland' (Union of all German Jewish Organisations). The reason for its existence is the furtherance of Jewish emigration from Germany. ... This organisation is also entrusted to see that facilities exist for Jews to attend all types of school ... which would help in the furtherance of emigration..."
(Max Eichler *Reichsburger-Handbuch* pub. Berlin 1940)

After the fall of France in 1940 it was decided that Jews should emigrate to Madagascar, a French-controlled is-

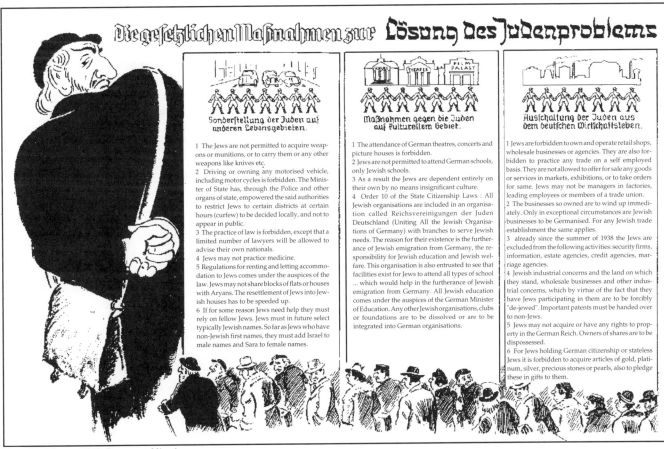

Translated from a 1940 German publication

125

land off the East coast of Africa, where they could establish their own colony.

Concentration camps appeared in Germany as soon as Hitler took power. Even here the Nazis were not original, the idea being borrowed from the British who had used them to break Afrikaaner resistance during the Boer War in South Africa (1899-1902). Göring's SS Police set up the first in Germany. In 1937 there were four, Dachau, Sachsenhausen, Buchenwald and a women's camp at Lichtenberg - names that will remain for ever a byword of evil. To these dreadful places were sent the perceived enemies of the regime - trade unionists, Quakers whose religion bans participation in war, socialists, gypsies, homosexuals and Jews. The camps were run by the SS Death's-Head units (Totenkopfverbande), presided over by the deranged chicken farmer, Heinrich Himmler. Inmates were regarded as an economic resource, suitable to be worked to death, often quarrying rock for the autobahns. Alan Bullock also describes the gruesome and usually pointless medical experiments carried out by SS doctors.

"Among the ordeals to which they were subjected were intense air pressure or intense cold until the patient's lungs burst or he froze to death, the infliction of gas gangrene wounds; injection with typhus and jaundice; experiments with bone grafting; and a large number of investigations of sterilisation (for racial hygiene) including castration and abortion ... The results of these experiments were usually death, permanent crippling and mental derangement."

All these 'experiments' were conducted without anaesthetic! During the Second World War persecution intensified. It included

"... the prohibition of Jews from keeping budgerigars in Berlin, on the grounds that the birds would use up birdseed that should be kept for Aryan birds."
(Norman Stone *Hitler* p160)

Surely this has to be the final *reducio ad absurdum* of the Nazi Weltanschauung ? It was almost certainly not a joke, nor was the decision to wipe out the entire Jewish population of Europe which Hitler took at the notorious Wannsee Conference after America's entry into the war in

December 1941. Special Extermination Camps were set up. These had only one purpose - genocide, the systematic murder of an entire race organised on a factory mass production basis. After experimenting with shooting, and gassing with vehicle fumes piped back into a bus in which the victims were travelling, the diseased Nazi mind came up with 'The Final Solution'. The first attempts had been too slow. Real productivity would be achieved by mass gassing.

Rudolf Höss, Commandant at Auschwitz, admitted:

"I visited Treblinka to find out how they carried out the experiments. The Commandant told me that he had liquidated 80,000 in the course of one half year ... He used monoxide gas and I do not think his methods were very efficient. So at Auschwitz I used cyclon B, (crystallised prussic acid dropped into water in the death chamber). It took from three to fifteen minutes to kill the people ... We knew when they were dead because the screaming stopped ... Another improvement we made over Treblinka was that we built our gas chambers to accommodate two thousand people at a time."
(Nuremberg Documents 3,868-PS. Quoted by Alan Bullock in *Hitler A Study in Tyranny*)

Höss might have added that they frequently had to replace the concrete linings of the death chamber as their victims ripped it off with their finger nails and bones in their death agony.

The insane, the mentally ill and the physically handicapped also featured in what the Jews now call the holocaust. The final solution is the ultimate reality of Nazism. That is what it is really about. It is a barren collection of prejudices scavenged from the rubbish tips of human thought; a curse rather than an ideology. The achievement in which it gloried most was the murder of innocents; old people, mothers, fathers, babies and teenagers like Anne Frank. It created nothing in which decent people could take pride or pleasure. Half a century later it remains an embarrassment, even to those who were totally innocent of any involvement with it. Sadly, we cannot afford to forget. Henry Ford is often quoted as saying, "History is bunk." A rival proverb runs "Those who forget the past are condemned to relive it."

Index

Bibliography

This bibliography is intended as a guide for further reading by students. It should not be seen as an exhaustive list of sources referred to in the writing of this book. Sources used for this purpose are acknowledged in the text and the acknowledgements.

Italy

Bayne Jardine CC *Mussolini and Italy* Longmans (1966)
Blinkhorn, Martin *Mussolini and Fascist Italy* Routledge
Clough, Shepard B & Saladino, Salvatore *A History of Modern Italy* Columbia University Press
Hearder D & Waley DP *A Short History of Italy* Cambridge University Press (1963)
Hibbert C *Garibaldi and his Enemies* Penguin Books (1987) (Longman 1965)
Kedward, HR *Fascism in Western Europe 1900-45* Blackie (1969)
Kirkpatrick, Sir Ivone *Mussolini : Study of a Demagogue* Odhams Press
di Lampedusa, G*The Leopard* Collins and Hartwell Press (1961)
Leeds, Christopher *Italy under Mussolini* Wayland Publishers
Mack Smith, Denis *Mussolini* George Wiedenfield & Nicholson (1981)
Mack Smith, Denis *Italy - A Modern History* University of MIchigan Press (1969)
Morrogh, Michael*The Unification of Italy - Documents and Debates* Macmillan Education LImited (1991)
Procacci G *History of the Italian People* Pelican Books (1973) (Weidenfield & Nicolson 1970)
Stiles, Andrina *he Unification of Italy 1815-70* Hodder and Stoughton (1986)
Thomson D *Europe Since Napoleon* Pelican Books 1966 (Longmans 1957)
Trevelyan GM *Garibaldi and the Thousand* London 1909
Trevelyan GM *Garibaldi and theMaking of Italy* London 1911
Viotti A *Garibaldi - the Revolutionary and his Men* Blandford Press (1979)
Wolfson, Robert *Years of Change - European HIstory 1890-1945* Edward Arnold (1978)

Germany

Aronson, T *The Kaisers* Cassell (1971)
Bielenberg, Christabel *The Past is Myself*Chatto & Windus (1968)
Bullock, Alan *Hitler : a Study in Tyranny* Odhams (1952)
Bullock, Alan *Hitler & Stalin, Parallel Lives* Harper Collins (1991)
Carr, W *A History of Germany 1815-1945* Edward Arnold (1969)
Craig, Gordon A *Germany 1866-1945* OUP (1981)
Elliot, BJ *Hitler and Germany* Longmans
Grenville, JAS *Europe REshaped 1848-1878* Fontana (1976)
Grunberger, Richard *A Social History of the Third Reich* George Wiedenfield & Nicholson (1971)
Hiden, JW *The Weimar Republic* Longmans (1974)
Hildebrand, Klaus *The Third Reich* Allen & Unwin (1984)
Kolb, Eberhard *The Weimar Republic* Unwin Hyman (1988)
Mitchell I *Bismarck* Holmes McDougall (1980)
Noakes,J and Pridham, G *Nazism 1919-1945* 3 volumes of documents and commentary, Exeter University Press (1984)
Rothfels, Hans *The German Opposition to Hitler* Oswald Wolff Books
Stone, Norman *Hitler* Hodder & Stoughton (1980)
Taylor, AJP *Bismarck*Hamish Hamilton (1955)
Waller, Bruce *Bismarck* Blackwell (1985)
Whittle, T *The Last Kaiser* Heinemann (1977)
Williamson, DG *The Third Reich* Longmans (1982)